STRENGTH
for the
JOURNEY

ALSO BY PETER J. GOMES:

The Good Book: Reading the Bible with Mind and Heart

The Good Life: Truths That Last in Times of Need

Sermons: Biblical Wisdom for Daily Living

STRENGTH
for the
JOURNEY

BIBLICAL WISDOM FOR DAILY LIVING
A New Collection of Sermons

PETER J. GOMES

HarperSanFrancisco
A Division of HarperCollinsPublishers

HarperCollins books may be purchased for educational, business, or sales promotional use. For information please write: Special Markets Department, HarperCollins Publishers, Inc., 10 East 53rd Street, New York, NY 10022.

HarperCollins Web site: http://www.harpercollins.com

HarperCollins®, ⛪ ®, and HarperSanFrancisco™ are trademarks of HarperCollins Publishers, Inc.

FIRST HARPERCOLLINS PAPERBACK EDITION PUBLISHED IN 2004.

Designed by Kris Tobiassen

Library of Congress Cataloging-in-Publication Data has been ordered and is available upon request.

ISBN 0–06–000078–3 (pbk.)

04   05   06   07   08   ❖/RRD(H)   10   9   8   7   6   5   4   3   2   1

To

MILTON L. AND JANE AULT LINDHOLM

with whom has been shared the best that
Bates College has to offer:

in testimony of a friendship

Contents

Acknowledgements

As in all of my books of sermons, I must first acknowledge with thanks and appreciation those who first heard them preached. A preacher's dream is a listening congregation, those who listen both with mind and heart, and for over thirty years I have been blessed with such a congregation. I thank them here.

Cynthia Wight Rossano has prepared all of my books, including this one, for the press. She and her skills, subtle, pertinent, and persistent, are as essential to this process as air is to flame. For these and all her many kindnesses I record grateful thanks.

Finally, to John Taylor "Ike" Williams, my resourceful agent, and to Stephen W. Hanselman and all of the good people at Harper San Francisco, I tender thanks for making the tasks of a publishing preacher more delightful than I could ever have imagined.

Peter J. Gomes

Sparks House
Cambridge, Massachusetts
November 2002

A Servant of the Word

When I think of a sermon, I certainly do not think first of one of my own; rather, my mind goes back along the corridors of time—a rather sermonic phrase—to recall sermons that I have heard. At least at first, I think I became a preacher of sermons not because of what I wanted to say but because of what I had once heard. The sermon was always an attractive art form to me, for I loved the sound of words, the magic of language, and the capacity of an efficient sermon to compel my imagination. When I was a boy I looked forward to the sermon on Sunday mornings, unlike my more restless and perhaps impatient friends. It was an adrenaline rush not unlike that of watching the acrobats at the circus: would they yet again "fly through the air with the greatest of ease," or would there be a disaster this time? My morbid curiosity led me to want to do what this or that preacher could do, and although not yet theologically literate, from a very early age I wanted to make the word become flesh.

To this moment I can recall the sermons and preachers of another day. Every Sunday we listened to the *Old-Fashioned Revival Hour* on the radio, broadcast from the municipal auditorium of Long Beach, California, and I heard old Dr. Charles E. Fuller send forth his gospel. I remember our old pastor, Norris Elwyn Woodbury, weeping in the pulpit as he preached about his years as a Baptist missionary in Burma before the Second World War, and I remember the passion of his sermon on the folly of the space race, when Russia launched Sputnik, scaring us all half to death. His title on that Sunday morning was "Not by Sputnik but by Spirit."

When I was a divinity school student I would attend the evening services still flourishing in Boston's great downtown churches. Favorites included Dr. Theodore Parker Ferris, who held forth at Trinity Church, Copley Square, himself a worthy successor to Phillips Brooks in that pulpit, and I can still hear his voice when I read some of his old sermons. Often I would venture to Tremont Temple Baptist Church for a very different kind of homiletical fare, for there Dr. C. Gordon Brownville held forth with the passionate evangelism for which he and that Boston pulpit, "The Stranger's Sabbath Home," were famous. He preached for decisions, and it was not easy to resist the compelling altar calls to which his sermons inevitably pointed.

On occasion I went to Park Street Church, where Dr. Harold John Ockenga was in full cry. From that great pulpit on Brimstone Corner, as it was known, poured forth icy blasts of double predestinarian Calvinism. The sermons there were magisterial things, compelling attention if not affection, and listening to them was about as close as I wanted to come to eighteenth-century New England Puritanism.

Preaching's effect upon me was powerful, for I was moved not only by the language but also by the ideas that were generated; and in seeing how one man with a sustained effort could make words work, I cherished the thought that someday I might be able to do the same. This positive inspiration was modified by the negative examples of my college days, during which I think I heard some of the worst preaching of my life. I had a job as organist in the local Congregational church in those days, and thus for three of my four years I sat under the preaching of the local pastor. Organists have an automatic shutdown valve that goes into effect as soon as the minister begins to speak, but as a sermon-taster of long years, my valve didn't work, and so I was obliged to listen week after week to fairly miserable preaching. I remember to this day one particularly awful Lenten sermon series, the theme of which was "The Complexion of the Crowd"; and in succession we heard about those who were "Blue with Loyalty," "Purple with Rage," "Green with Envy," and "Black with Treachery." Lent was very long that year.

The worst preaching on a week-to-week basis, however, was in the college chapel, where attendance was compulsory at the three weekday morning services. On Wednesdays there was usually a sermon given by an accommodating local parson as the college did not have a chaplain, and those sermons invariably were Sunday hand-me-downs, cut and trimmed to the requirements of a short college service. The preachers tried hard, I imagine, to plumb the depths of their college listeners, but more often than not they failed, as the texts seemed irrelevant to the substance of the sermon, the illustrations seemed to have been taken out of a book of handy sermon illustrations, and the tone was either patronizing and condescending or pathetically aimed at pleasing young people who would not and could not be pleased. Those of us who sang in the choir were obscured from the view of the preacher and the congregation by the high walls of the stalls, and we customarily ignored the sermon and crammed for the next class. I, however, often could not resist a furtive listen, and with all of the arrogant bravado of youth I declared to myself that I could do better.

For the last thirty-two years as Harvard's preacher I have tried to make good on that boast. My congregations are not compelled to hear me, yet I am under compulsion to give them the best that I can, week in and week out. Never have I preached a sermon in The Memorial Church that I first preached elsewhere, for I resolved early on that my congregation would get the best of my first efforts. I would preach to their situation as I came to know it—not abstractly or generally—and I would always preach to them, especially to the students, as I wish I had been preached to when I was in college. Those convictions, together with my desire to make words work and my persuasion to connect the living faith with the living condition of honest, smart, but confused people, shaped my agenda as a preacher.

That agenda may provide a guide to the sermons in this collection. I begin every one of them with a biblical text, which I use as a centering device for the development of thoughtful listening and thoughtful speaking, and also as a pedagogical device intended to reacquaint my listeners with the central texts of our tradition. The text is the way into the Bible, and the means beyond the Bible to the good news—the gospel—and the good life. In the days of my youth, when I listened gladly to Ferris, Brownville, and Ockenga, and modest preachers in my hometown church, a generic knowledge of the Bible could be assumed for even unlettered men and women knew one book; and that one book was the Bible. Its metaphors and similes were the stock of common conversation, and people had committed vast quantities of it to memory.

Today, however, for many of those to whom I preach, the Bible is a lost book written in a foreign language for a different age, which is thus another reason for focusing on Scripture. The purpose of preaching is to reclaim an informed people for the Bible and to reclaim an interpreted Bible for the people, and that task I find to be my greatest and most satisfying challenge.

The sermons in this book are ordered both by the themes of daily life and by the passing seasons of the liturgical year. These organizing principles are important, for preaching that does not respond to the needs of the human condition is irrelevant, no matter how scholarly, pious, or eloquent it may be. Hearers listen from their situation—their "social location," as they like to say in the academy—and the preacher who ignores this deserves to be ignored. Hence preaching deals with such fundamental human themes as identity, anxiety, desire, fear, greed, love, and death. In an academic community, people are remarkably insecure about themselves, and so the questions of value, esteem, merit, and worth are addressed; and beyond the academy, as the preacher in Ecclesiastes puts it, vanity is an all-consuming subject. The Bible speaks to these and to many other themes of the human condition, reminding us that despite our congenital egocentrism, there is nothing new under the sun. It is a form of reassurance, somehow, to know that wherever we are, others have been there before.

The sermons in this volume also take seriously the ordered rhythmic motions of the Christian liturgical year. We begin with the church's new year at Advent, and we move from there through to Christmas, Epiphany, Lent, Easter, and Pentecost, with many of the church's holy days and saints' days commemorated in the preaching. Over the years of my ministry I have noticed an ever-increasing appreciation of this old Christian calendar, which is a far cry from the so-called liturgical year of my bare-bones Protestant faith that acknowledged only Christmas, Easter, and perhaps Mothers' Day and Children's Day. The liturgical year gives order and form to formless time, and provides a familiar landscape that is reassuring in its routine.

Early in my ministry, I remember wondering what I would have to say when my second Easter or Christmas rolled around. Our old professor of public speaking at Harvard had warned us many years before, "Be careful not to try to say everything you know in your first sermon, for you just might succeed." Having told the story of Christmas or of Easter once, what would there be left to say?

Well, while the story itself never changes, both I and my listeners do change, and while Christmas and Easter and the other seasons come around with relentless reliability, as yet I have never preached an old sermon or wondered what to say anew. Why? Not because I am extraordinarily clever, but because I am never where I was "then," and am always where I am "now." In other words, the interaction between season and sermon is always a transforming experience that moves us beyond where we once were. I find it very difficult to read, much less to preach, old sermons of my own, not because I repudiate the ideas expressed in them, but because, valid as they may have been at one time, those ideas have been modified by new circumstances and changed occasions. I tell my students in preaching that it is always easier to preach a new sermon than it is to rework an old one, no matter how successful the old sermon may have been in its moment. They don't believe me, but it is true.

So, this collection of sermons comes out of all the experiences and connections I have discussed above. I share them now with a wider public than that for which they were first prepared and preached, not as exemplary examples of the preacher's art but as a record of one man's preaching to one congregation over a long period of years. The hope of these sermons is always that the word will work for the transformation of the listener, or reader; and that in making words become flesh, somehow all language and words will be made real in the lives of hopeful people.

We live in difficult, demanding times, with a new anxiety upon us, and gone are the easy bromides of a simpler, more insular, self-satisfied age. What we need today is strength for the journey, the means of getting from where we are to where we would wish to be. Strength for the journey of life is what preaching is about; and my ardent hope is that in all of the journeys that the readers of these words may be called upon to take, these sermons of mine might prove helpful and useful, and might guide many to the word of life and the word become flesh, full of grace and truth. In the famous articulation of the British preacher H. E. Farmer, I subscribe myself as a willing servant of the word.

It gives me great pleasure to dedicate this book to two dear friends with whom for over forty years I have had the joy of sharing the best of Bates College. Milton Lindholm was dean of admissions at Bates, and, along with more than half of the living alumni of that college, I am grateful that he took a chance on me. He invested in my future, and the harvest has been a rich friendship, of which this book is but a small token of affectionate regard. Sharing the journey with Milt and his wife, Jane Ault Lindholm, continues to be fun, and I thank God for them.

Peter J. Gomes

Sparks House
Cambridge, Massachusetts
November 2002

PART ONE

Sermons on the Themes of Daily Life

Surplus and Substance

Text: For all these have of their abundance cast in unto the offerings of God; but she of her penury hath cast in all the living that she had.

—LUKE 21:4

My text is the fourth verse of the twenty-first chapter of the gospel according to St. Luke, where our Lord makes a comparative statement and an absolute judgment.

Those of you who were here last Sunday know that I spoke of that nameless, infamous woman in the gospel who anointed Jesus' feet and washed them with her tears, and if you wanted to, you could say that that sermon was about sex. Next Sunday, on All Saints' and All Souls' day, we will speak of the faithful departed, and you might think that that sermon will be about death. Today, in the account of the widow's mite from which our text is taken, it is obvious that we are speaking about money, or so it would seem. If we had Madison Avenue values here, or even the sensibilities of talk radio, we could advertise this as a series entitled "All You Need to Know About Sex, Money, and Death"; but then, there is more to each of these sermons than any of those.

We have heard many times this story of our Lord in the Gospel of Luke:

He looked up and saw the rich putting their gifts into the treasury, and he saw a poor widow put in two copper coins, and he said, "Truly I tell you, this poor widow has put in more than all of them; for they all contributed out of their abundance, but she out of her poverty put in all the living that she had." (Luke 21:1–4)

Or, as the King James version puts it:

And he looked up, and saw the rich men casting their gifts into the treasury. And he saw also a certain poor widow casting in thither two mites. And he said, "Of a truth I say unto you, that this poor widow hath cast in more than they all: for all these have of their abundance cast in unto the offerings of God; but she of her penury hath cast in all the living that she had." (Luke 21:1–4)

Most of us have grown up with the story of the widow's *mite,* and we know that it means a small denomination of ancient money, but as children we hear before we read or spell, and so as a child I thought that the story was about the widow's *might*—a modest but useful preaching point. Our Lord said, "This poor widow has put in more than all of them; for they all contributed out of their abundance, but she out of her poverty put in all the living that she had." Now, the context for this, in the preceding chapter of Luke, is Jesus' criticism of the rich and visible believers, the Pharisees— the rich, the powerful, who liked to wear long robes and stand in public places, and made much of their piety and of their philanthropy and good works. In one sense this is just more of the same: criticizing the establishment—those people for whom doing good works and giving good gifts doesn't cut anywhere into the substance of their being. People give who can afford to give. Here, the story contrasts them with one who in Jesus' eyes cannot afford to give, and therefore gives everything that she has.

There are times, I think, and this may be one of them, when we wish that the text were less clear and more ambiguous. It would be helpful in this text, for example, to discover that there are several nuanced hidden levels of meaning whereby it does not say what we think it says. It was Mark Twain, more cynical than devout, who said, "It is not what I don't understand in the Bible that troubles me, it is what I do understand." This is one of those texts: we get it. We can and we do understand the text about the widow's mite, and that is the trouble. It troubles us, I suggest, on two counts, with the first in the context of a much larger anxiety that we Christians have, which is that we are troubled when we talk about money.

There! I caught you. I can see you already frowning and freezing up, already grabbing for that part of you that is most important to you, holding on, thinking, "Here we go again." We don't like to discuss money in relationship to our church or to our faith or to our religion, although we will talk about it as far as the national debt is concerned, we will talk about it as far as taxes are concerned, we will talk about it as far public expenditure is concerned. We don't want to talk about it in terms of our religion or our church or our faith, however, because somehow, somewhere, somebody has told us one of the few religious principles that we remember, which is that religion is "spiritual" and money is "material," and that never the twain should meet—especially in church. Hence ministers, particularly those of the more respectable "mainline" churches, those churches from whom most of you have fled for the time being in order to come here on Sunday morning, are usually embarrassed to speak of money; and at best devote a few minutes on one Sunday a year, supported by a phalanx of sympathetic laypeople, to little homilies on "stewardship." Very subtle, artfully produced letters and cards are given that, if you are lucky, will not mention money or need or giving at all, and most congregations are equally embarrassed and annoyed by even these little subtleties. You should be grateful to me that I am not going to preach about money on Stewardship Sunday in November, because I am speaking about it today; and you don't have to stay at home on Stewardship Sunday, because the sermon traditionally reserved for that day is the one that I am giving you right now.

It is not that combination of the spiritual and the material that is the source of our chief discomfort, I would argue, and not so much that we dislike or even distrust the mixing of the spiritual and the material. The honest reason that we are dissatisfied is that in most cases we are very much attached to the material and do not wish to be persuaded to part with it either by Jesus or by a preacher. Our text this morning permits us to talk about money apart from that annual Sunday on which we appeal for a lot from a lot of you—to defang the subject, if you will, and to express your legitimate fears about your claim on your money and your money's claim on you, and to do so in the context of what the gospel teaches and what Jesus preaches.

I have said that our first anxiety about this text has to do with the subject of money and the mixing of the material and the spiritual, and we will come back to that later. The second anxiety has to do with what we know the moral of the text to be, and its obvious conclusion that Jesus approves of those who give more than *we* think they can afford. The rich, according to the parable, give out of their abundance, their surplus, their disposable income, which they can dispose of in charitable, benevolent, philanthropic ways, Jesus says; but the widow gave all that she had. Nondisposable income is what we can't get along without; and no one can give too much. So, when we hear the story of the widow's mite, our first sympathy goes out to the poor widow, who had no idea what she was doing and gave it all away, and now she will be an even greater burden upon the state, and those rich Pharisees will have to give even more to sustain her who could have sustained herself had she given only one copper coin instead of two. The rich give out of their surplus, says Jesus, but the widow gave out of her substance—that is, the essence of who she was. She gave all that she had, and, not simply content to describe the transaction, Jesus says that that is the better way: she has given more than all of them; in other words, no one is too poor or too constrained to give, and no one may give too much. We may not understand the principle behind this, but we certainly understand that it is this of which Jesus approves, and because of that, you and I are obliged to take it seriously.

Now, we may not understand the principle demonstrated here by the widow; we may not understand the notion that no one is too poor or too constrained to give, but the poor have no problem with this principle, and perhaps we can learn from them. By no means was my family wealthy when I was growing up, although they worked very hard to conceal from me the facts of just how poor we were. For my parents, poverty of means was an attitude to be overcome by wealth of spirit, and so we were rich but just didn't have very much money. I remember as an absolute principle of our household that when the monthly accounting of the family income came around, before the bills were considered— the mortgage, heat, food, and clothing addressed—the church money was first set aside, taken out of the file, sealed up in envelopes to be given in church, and put in the drawer so that we would not be tempted to raid it for necessities as the month went along. In the piety of my shrewd and very Yankee family, God's money was taken out first, for of course it was God's money and not ours, and only after that was given were the needs considered for which my father and my mother, and eventually I, had worked so hard.

It was not through pride that my parents did this; it was just their life-long practice for it was what Christians did, and somehow, with so economically unsound a practice, they nevertheless managed week after week, month after month, and year after year. They were not by nature charitable or philanthropic; it was not their habit to look down the list of appeals in the newspapers, or on the radio and eventually on television, to decide where they were going to spread their resources, but they did make that point of first setting aside God's money out of their money; and they didn't think of themselves as doing a great thing but rather as doing the right thing as they understood the gospel to teach it to them, and the least that they could do. They understood and were not frightened, though I cannot say for certain that they never suffered, although I saw very little evidence of it; nor can I say that they were openly rewarded, with showers of blessings pouring down upon them through the open windows of heaven, as is promised by so many television and radio evangelists in the gospel of wealth. I saw not much effect at all. They weren't impoverished, and they weren't overly endowed with worldly riches; they simply had an honest relationship with money and knew that a significant portion of it did not belong to them but to God, and so, being basically honest people, they gave it back to God.

While my parents were not tithers, many were, and I grew up in a church where lots of people tithed. Now, probably among you this morning are some M.B.A.'s and even some Ph.D.'s who have never heard of tithing, and perhaps a few others of you as well do not know what it is, as either a theological or a biblical or an economic principle, and so I will explain it to you. The tithe is a tenth, and tithing is the old biblical principle, much approved of under the law of Moses, that 10 percent of what you have belongs to the Lord, and the first tenth is holy unto the Lord. The principle is that 100 percent comes from God; God wants you to keep and enjoy and multiply 90 percent, but 10 percent belongs to God. So, for every dollar you have, ten cents belongs to the Lord, before taxes—in the days before taxes. The tithe, in fact, may be thought of as the first tax. As all things come from God, according to the theory, all things belong to God, but God claims only 10 percent of it, for God's own work—which is basic, elementary economy.

In early Christian times and in the early church, it was out of the tithes of the faithful that the charitable work of the community of believers was performed. It was the tithe that founded and funded medical care and hospitals, funded schools, and provided for the sick, the afflicted, orphans, and widows, and for children and others unable to care for themselves. Social welfare, in which the church has always been concerned, was run on the principle of mutual responsibility, of which the tithe was the minimal expression. You could, and were frequently encouraged to, give more; you could not give less.

Perhaps it is because of the example of the charity of the poor, that I witnessed as a young man, that I believe that these principles still work today. I think it is easy to eavesdrop in this community upon the charity of the rich, for all the buildings around us are monuments to the charity of the rich. You know that old saying, "Old Harvard graduates never die, they just turn into dormitories"; and it is true that we see the charity of Mrs. Widener and Mr. Canaday and Thomas Hollis and all of these people around us. I grew up instructed by the charity of the poor, which is all the more compelling because they had so little to give.

In the little Bethel AME church to which my family belonged along with the few other colored families of Plymouth, Massachusetts, in those days fifty years ago, in addition to their morning non-colored churches, it was the custom—and I have written about this elsewhere—to take up the offering not as we do it here in The Memorial Church or in most churches, but by having the people proceed to the communion table at the front of the church to present their monetary gifts before the stewards, who counted the money as the gifts were put down. This would be done during much singing and greeting; it would be sort of a combination of the offering and the kiss of peace, if we had the kiss of peace here. You'd come down the center aisle, there would be a table there, there would be stewards there, you'd be greeting them, they'd be greeting you, the church would be filled with singing and joyous music, you'd go back to greeting people on their way up, and the stewards would be doing a running tally. Then the music would stop and they would announce what the total was, saying, "We need fourteen dollars and forty-four cents, and we're going to do this again." They would do it again and again and again, calling the people forward until the day's goal had been met—and no one could leave until it had been met or even exceeded. Only then, when there was reason to do so, would we sing the doxology. These were people who had next to nothing, poor people giving out of their substance and not out of their surplus, giving that which was essential to them, who had enough confidence in themselves, in their church, and in their God to place the material at the disposal of the spiritual, and it worked: the church is still there.

In the matter of our text, all the biblical scholarship tells us that widows in biblical times were among the most vulnerable and marginal members of society. In that age of a patriarchal society, where a woman's status depended upon her relationship to a man—father, husband, or son—a widow often had fewer rights than a male child, and less freedom than a female child. Her source of protection and security was gone, and so too such financial independence as she might once have enjoyed. Surely there were rich widows, but not many, and not often do they play a role in Scripture. Widows in the New Testament are vulnerable and poor, and Jesus and St. Paul both specifically enjoin believers in the early Christian communities to look after widows and orphans, to visit them and take care of their needs—for they had no safety net but the community.

So, when our Lord invokes the example of the poor widow in St. Luke's Gospel, it is of the same moral effect as his commendation of the woman who crashed the party in last Sunday's Gospel: he again uses the marginal to drive a point to the center. He takes people on the outside edges of society and culture and social and economic security, and he uses them to drive the point that is central to his understanding of his gospel, and to what he wants you and me to understand about the gospel. The point is that if she, the poor widow, can do so much with so little, what more then can be expected of we who have so much? That is the point that cannot be evaded or avoided in this lesson about surplus and substance.

Our Lord is worried here not so much about financial formulas or "scales of gifts," as they like to say in the Development Office; he is speaking, rather, of the place in which one places one's ultimate trust, and of the means of expressing that ultimate trust, which is what we call faith. In other words, the woman who gave two coppers out of her poverty decided that she was not going to be defined by her poverty, or limited, but rather that by her total generosity she would be defined by her confidence in God's work and her total gratitude for God's grace. She who had received all was going to give all. She is an example of the expression "Those who have suffered most have most reason to be both grateful and generous." She thought in terms not of what she did not have, or even of what she lost, but of what she had; and out of a sense of gratitude disproportionate to all of her means she gave it all to God, thus attracting Jesus' attention, and ours.

We might be able to take this text more seriously if we knew what happened to her, but we don't know what happened to this poor widow, whether blessings attended her way, or whether she was thrown further upon the mercy of others. Did she win the lottery? *Bingo!* "A million coppers for you, my dear, as long as you live." Did a rich man marry her and provide economic security for the rest of her days? Did somebody say, "You can't be allowed to do this. Let us replenish your supply of this world's goods." It would be helpful for us to know if it all turned out well, that there is no risk to giving it all away, and that you don't have to hold on to just a little bit against a rainy day. Alas, we don't know what happened to her, there is no secret text to tell us, and there is no reassurance that she did not suffer for her extravagant act of generosity.

This is not an essay in sociology; this is not a *quid pro quo*. This is a moral tale whose details are meant to point up a larger principle and a larger issue, and if you think that the moral is that the poor should give even more than they do now, then you have missed the point, for this is not so much about those who can't as it is about those who can and yet do not give in proportion to what has been given to them. Those who do not give in proportion to their substance have every reason to be worried about this particular story. The widow is used to cast a light upon the rest of us, rich and not so rich alike, to consider by the light of her example and of Jesus' commendation just what we ought to be doing with our money, and what ought to be our relationship between our money and our faith. If money talks, what does it say about us and about our faith?

For most of us looking for a way out, it is easy to be lost, and convenient to be lost in the obvious extremes of this parable. Few of us are as poor as the widow, and few of us classify ourselves among the mighty rich, although among you there are both rich and poor. Most of us see ourselves in neither category; we just try to get along, to do the right thing with as little impact upon our pleasures and our resources as possible. Ambrose Bierce said that a "Christian is somebody who lives a life of virtue insofar as it is not incompatible with a life of pleasure." I know many who say, "I will be charitable when I am rich . . . or richer," or "I cannot afford to act upon my more generous impulses." Often I see seniors in the College who are asked to contribute something to the annual College Fund as they make their way out of Harvard, students who have received far more than they deserved both from the living and from the dead, and many of these young people have already crafted the artful questions and answers of their elders, saying that on a cost-benefit analysis of the situation they don't feel that they are yet in a position to pay a portion back to Harvard because they've already paid so much in to Harvard. It starts in this sort of stingy charity that says, "When I make my pile, then I will consider giving something from it." This story is meant to shame those kinds of stingy impulses, and to say that giving comes not out of surplus and convenience but out of substance and opportunity. I spend a great deal of time asking people for money, and I have heard all of these excuses, some of them even from some of you.

What our Lord wishes us to understand is that giving is concerned not so much with the size of the gift as it is with an attitude toward life, toward self, and toward God. If you understand that life itself is a gift from God, if you understand that you are meant to express God's self-giving life in the world, and if you are confident and hopeful that God will sustain you in wealth and in poverty and in everything in between, then you will see life as giving and not as holding. You remember what Churchill said, himself always worried about money and not famous for his charity? "We make a living by what we save, but we make a life by what we give." When in three weeks' time we commemorate our benefactors and our war dead we will not remember what they saved—whether it was their money or their lives; we will remember what, and that, they gave.

Now, let me not flatter you by suggesting that you don't know what this is about, for I know that you know all of this and that there is not a new thought or a new syllable here; you have heard it all before. The first lesson, from Micah 6, says it all: "He has showed you what is good." God has already made clear to believers what is expected of us in our attitude toward life, toward self, toward God, and toward others. You know this. What then is the proper response to all of this? Do I want you to sit down and write out a new check or a new will, or both? Do I want you to come forward as I receive and count your contributions to the work of this church?

No, not at all. We don't want so simplistic a response as that. I want you to think about the gospel. I want you to think about the life that you have been given by God through his great mercy, and about what is most fearful to you, and what is most precious to you, and about those things in this world for which you are most grateful. I want you to think about your fair share of your material responsibility in God's world, to this church, and to other agencies of good work. I want you to consider—not just today or tomorrow, but as a part of your thinking—your giving not in proportion to what you have but in proportion to what you have been given; and I want you to conduct this little spiritual audit in the quiet and odd moments of your lives over the coming weeks and days. If you begin, my good friends, to reconsider how to live your life with these concerns in mind, I would be willing to speculate that you will find your life increasingly worth living; and that is exactly what our Lord has in mind for you.

Blessing: Can You Take It?

Text: But seek ye first his kingdom and his righteousness, and all these things shall be yours as well.

—MATTHEW 6:33

"All these things." What are "all these things" of which St. Matthew speaks? Well, they are all of the things about which you and I worry; all of the things about which we are anxious, anxiety driven; all of these things, and more, that Jesus stipulates as we move through the sixth chapter of Matthew. What we shall wear, what we shall eat, what we shall drink—and, if we want to translate that into a contemporary list of anxieties: what will people think of us, what will we think of ourselves, where shall we be after June, where shall we be after lunch? What shall I do with what I have? What can I do about things I haven't? These are the things about which we are anxious, and Jesus makes it very clear: don't worry about these things; seek ye first the kingdom of righteousness, get your priorities together, and your perspective will improve. "Seek ye first his kingdom and his righteousness, and all these things"—food, drink, raiment, job, reputation—"shall be yours as well."

I think that if we took a survey of how other people in other religious traditions look at Christians we might observe, on the basis of at least the way we act and what we say, that they see that we are a religious people driven by our anxieties. The fuel of our faith is what we are worried about. We are united with one another by the frowns in our foreheads: that is what it would appear to be that drives the Christian faith. Listen to our prayers: I make them, you make them, they're made for you. God, give me this. God, spare me that.

God, help me through this. When we gather together to worship or to celebrate, what is it that we share more than anything else? Our concerns.

My little Baptist church in Plymouth keeps fiddling with its order of service, and one of the fiddlings that it has done most recently is to add, at what used to be the time for notices and prayer, a thing that is called "Celebrations and Concerns." Now, you can figure out my reaction to that, of course, but I noted while I was playing the organ for my church last summer for the months of July and August, when I had plenty of chances to observe divine worship from the other side, that when it came time for the concerns and celebrations of the congregation there were infinitely more concerns than there were celebrations. People were concerned about Mary's illness, Fred's pickup that needed a new transmission; they were concerned about folks in the nursing homes and in the hospitals, as rightly they should be. They were concerned about the number of volunteers they needed to run the fair and didn't have, and they were concerned too about Bosnia, and about our political and cultural life; and every once in a while someone, realizing that we were heaping up and accumulating these concerns, said, "Well, we ought to be thankful for something." We waited, and there really wasn't anything for which to be thankful.

Somebody observing us would say that we were driven by our concerns, by our worries, by our anxieties; and that is why I decided that this Lent I was actually going to preach a sermon about blessings—blessings that you and I have received, a state of blessedness in which we already stand without asking for a single thing. So I was driven to this marvelous text in the Sermon on the Mount, where Jesus says, "Seek ye first his kingdom and his righteousness, and all these things"—these blessings—"shall be yours as well," and I want to tip off the secret of this sermon right at the start by saying that these blessings have already been received. You are already the beneficiaries of them; we already have them. Intercessions long since made have been answered, as there is no one within the sound of my voice this morning who is not capable of standing up and blessing the Lord for what she or he has received. It is that perspective on blessing that is meant to drive out anxiety.

That is easier said than done, I know. Preachers are supposed to say things that are easier said than done. I do it all the time, and this is no exception. I have a particularly vivid illustration of how easy it is to say this in the face of the impossibility or the impracticability of convincing others of it. I've told you, I think, this story before, but it's good enough to tell again. Whenever I hear or read this wonderful passage from Matthew, I am reminded of the time I took it as the basis for a commencement talk to the Brearly School in New York City, now about fifteen years ago. If any of you know about those girls schools in New York, you know that they're pretty tough places, and that they pride themselves on significant distinction and achievement; if there are any Brearly women in this congregation this morning, please let me see you first so that I can duck out the door.

Brearly is a remarkable place, and I was invited to give the commencement talk on a weekday morning in the Brick Presbyterian Church, a place filled with proud and anxious parents, and anxious but somewhat relieved girls. I took as my text Jesus' words that you heard this morning in the second lesson: "Therefore, do not be anxious about your life," which I translated roughly as "Relax." Then I went on, inviting them to take time to smell the roses, consider the lilies of the field, and so on. It was, I think, a good reading of the text, if I say so myself, and a good sermon for such an occasion, and the girls liked it—at least they told me they did, and I believed them on the spot.

One of the fathers, however, was not so pleased with what I had to say. He came up to me with the crazed look of a man who had paid one tuition bill too many, and he looked me dead in the eye and said, "That was utter nonsense, and not only was it utter nonsense, it was irresponsible nonsense. It was anxiety that got my daughter into Brearly, it was anxiety that got her through Brearly, it was anxiety that got her into Radcliffe, and it will be anxiety that will get her into the law firm of her choice." So said he to me.

This guy had a problem, and it wasn't just with me or just with my sermon or just with Jesus. I was tempted to tell him, "Oh, get a life," and to stop using his daughter's life as his own, but that would have been rude. So, to give him the ultimate Christian insult, which I knew would turn him into mush, I said, "God bless you," and I left.

Anxiety, as that parent recognized, and as I have observed in all my years here, is a habit that is hard to break, and that is largely because there is so much about which to be anxious. Global warming and El Niño have made even the weather, which used to be a safe topic of conversation, a minefield of anxiety and turmoil, and everyone here this morning has his or her own private preserve of anxiety. You brought to this church this morning some uncultivated, some old preserved corner of trouble or sorrow or sadness or fear that you simply cannot get away from and that you will not let get away from you. Some of us are even defined by our anxieties: tell me what worries you, tell me what's on your mind, and I will tell you who you are, and know more about you than that I need or care to know about you. It is so easy to be defined by our anxieties and by our worries.

Now, as the gospel points out today, our Lord is not indifferent to our anxieties and our needs; he doesn't dismiss them in some kind of platonic ideal that anxieties don't exist. He knows that you have these needs; they are not unknown to God. Did you think that God does not know that you have reason to be worried about your grades? Of course not; God hopes you will do something about it. God knows what your needs are. God knows our anxieties about the state of the world, the state of our health, the state of our soul. God knows all of those things, and it is not a matter of ignorance but a matter of priority and of perspective. Jesus is not indifferent to or unaware of your anxieties, but at the heart of the most important and systematic of his teachings in the gospel, the Sermon on the Mount, his most reflective and expanded utterance, he tells us that we ought not to worry about the things that worry us, that we ought not to be defined by our worries and our anxieties. He tells us that we ought to focus on God and on God's righteousness, and he tells us that if we give God priority we will gain perspective and everything else will fall into place. One of the real things that will fall into place is that we will realize how much we have already been given, how blessed we are even at this very moment, how endowed, how rich we have been made by God. That is why, as the psalmist said, and as we read in Psalm 103 and sang in its paraphrase in the hymn before the sermon, we "Bless the Lord, O my soul, and all that is within me bless his holy name"; and the most important verse: "Bless the Lord, O my soul, and forget not all his benefits." Christians suffer not only from anxiety; they suffer from amnesia, forgetting all his benefits.

To give God priority and to gain perspective requires a reordering of the way we think, and an attitude adjustment on the part of believers such as ourselves. The way to begin to make the adjustment, the way to refocus our spiritual energy, is to consider not what we need as the beginning point of our spiritual lives, but what we have received. That sounds very simple, but I know from you and from my own experience that usually the point of our beginning is what we lack, what we want, what we desire, rather than what we have, what we have received, and how we ought to respond initially to those blessings. We are meant to consider not what we want God to do for us or even what we want to be able to do for God or for ourselves or for others, but rather what God has done and is doing for us, to which we can testify with our lips and with our lives.

It is for that reason—and I hope some of you have observed it—that I have inserted the General Thanksgiving over the course of this year as a standard practice at the close of the Prayers. Some of you will have observed this as just one more clipping from the Book of Common Prayer, a sort of yielding to my High Church tendencies, imposing yet more Cranmerian prose upon you against your better judgment, and all of that, and you would be right. There is another reason as well, however, and that is to remind myself and my fellow clerics and you that if we are not careful our prayers become laundry lists reflecting our anxieties instead of our convictions and our blessings. One way to do that is to make sure that no matter where we are on Sunday morning, and what we bring to the Lord's table, and where our hearts have been dragged through the mire and come with us with heavy burdens upon them, the one thing we will not neglect to do in our public worship here is to give thanks to God: "We bless thee for our creation, our preservation, and all the blessings of this life." A good place to start. We bless God for the fact that we *are*. We may not be what we used to be, we may not be what we're going to be, but we *are,* and that is source number one for blessing and thanksgiving. "We bless thee for our creation, we bless thee for our preservation. . . ." You're still here. Not only *are* you, but you *still* are. You're still here. We have been spared.

In the black church in the country, in the old oral tradition where folks would stand to "put up a prayer," as they called it, to God, they would put up a prayer that had an almost formulaic routine to it: "We thank you, Lord, for allowing us to rise from our beds this morning in our right mind." That is how those old black folks, who had so little for which to be grateful, began their prayers: "We thank you, Lord, for allowing us to rise from our beds this morning, and in our right minds, more or less.". . . creation, our preservation, and all the blessings of this life. . . ." That is why we say the General Thanksgiving, and if you can't join in any of the other prayers, that is the one that you ought to say morning, noon, and night. That is why this morning I want to talk about "blessing," and to ask if we know how to respond to God's blessings in our lives, and if we can take the blessings that God has heaped upon us. For I am convinced—I am persuaded, as St. Paul says—that the way in which we are enabled to "seek first his kingdom and his righteousness" is to consider what God does, has done, and is doing to, through, for, and with us. Blessing—yours and mine—is the word for life, blessing is the word for Lent, this morning.

The Continental reformers, the Calvinists of the sixteenth and seventeenth centuries, used the Seven Last Words of Jesus from the cross as a sort of moral syllabus by which various qualities were invoked for each of those words. For example, last Sunday I preached to you on intercession, and that came from the second Word, where Jesus intercedes on behalf of the penitent thief; and the third Word was always called the Word of Blessing, because it is the Word in which Jesus commends Mary to John and John to Mary: "Woman, behold thy Son; Son, behold thy Mother." This was thought to be a Word of Blessing, and it is instructive because it comes in the context of the most terrible agony imaginable—the death of Jesus Christ, witnessed by his own mother and his dearest friend, each of whom will be deprived of his presence. So when Jesus commends each to the other, the woman to the son and the son to the woman, he is in some sense giving evidence to the ultimate meaning of the word *blessing,* which is the presence of God. He is to be absent from them, but he is to be communicated and always with them, in their presence each to the other. They will each bless the other because in each will the other find the presence of God. At the foot of the cross, at those dreadful three hours, there is given the word of blessing that indicates that there is no circumstance, no place, no condition from which God is absent; and if God is not absent but present, God is blessing that situation. That is important for us to realize. Again, I know that that sounds easier said than done, and it is for at least three reasons that most of us have problems with the concept of blessings:

1. First, we find it easier to believe bad news rather than good news. Bad news we equate with reality; good news we regard as the exception to the rule. Isn't that usually the case? When the telegram comes, you don't say, "Hurrah! Something good has happened in the world and someone can't wait to get that good news to me." When the telegram arrives, or the phone call comes in the night, we know that it is bad news; we steal ourselves for it and prepare to get it. When good news comes we are incredulous: "How can this be?" Even undergraduates living in an exotic semi-real world, when they get grades back, say, "Oh, I *got* a 'B,' though hardly anybody gets Bs

here anymore," and with not a very great deal of pleasure or satisfaction. If they get an A they will say, "She *gave* me an 'A.'" There is a certain incredulity there too because they didn't deserve it; they wanted it, but they didn't deserve it. We expect bad news, and therefore we are not altogether convinced when good news comes our way. That is one of the reasons we have trouble with this concept of blessing: we're not quite sure what to do with it.

2. Second, anxiety is a human habit. That is what preserves us, that's what keeps us going on, that's what keeps mothers in business. God doesn't have time to worry about everything, and that is why, as the old saw goes, he invented mothers. In the case of the Brearly School he also invented fathers to be anxious and nervous, and my anxious father in New York had more evidence on his side of the case than I had on mine. Those who take time to smell the roses usually take longer to graduate than those who do not take time to smell the roses; those who take time to consider the lilies of the field have little time to shake the earth and will never own the field; those who are anxious but not willing to consider blessings are determined to make blessings happen, fueled by anxiety.

3. The third problem we have with blessing is that a blessing properly received requires a sense of gratitude, and gratitude, as Dorothy Parker once observed, is the "meanest and most sniveling attribute in the world." You know what she means: it is tiresome to be grateful to someone. If somebody has done you a kindness, the kindest thing that that somebody who has done you the kindness can do is to get out of the way, disappear, so that you don't have to be grateful to him, tied up hand and foot. Gratitude is a "cold" virtue, by which I mean that we do not enjoy being grateful because it places us in a relationship of obligation. In the language of deconstruction these days, it is a power relationship. If I do something kind and nice and gracious to you, it is not because I like you, and it is not because I'm kind and gracious; it is because I'm exercising power over you. If I hold the door for you, it isn't because I have to hold the door for you but because I'm condescending to hold the door for you, and therefore you should be grateful that I bothered to do it. That is why people get anxious when other people

do little acts of kindness toward them: they know that this is just weaving a chain of obligation, powerlessness, and indebtedness. Little acts of kindness are best unremembered, because they are interpreted in this cynical world as forms of ingratiating intimidation, even of power trips, and a form of moral manipulation.

For all of these reasons it is easier for us to address God with our anxieties, our concerns, and our lists of wants and needs and fears than it is to stand before God in thanksgiving for our blessings.

I want to suggest, however, that the concept of blessing is not so much for us the contract theory that we heard so beautifully described in the Book of Deuteronomy read for us by Professor Herschbach this morning. It is not so much the contract theory—that is, that if we are good, we will get. Blessings are not rewards from God for services rendered. Blessings are ways in which God allows us to see God and, even more important, to gain such a perspective, such a vision, such a view of God and of ourselves that we will realize that we have no basic reason to be anxious, and can indeed "seek his kingdom and his righteousness," knowing that all else will take its rightful place. A blessing is not a reward; it is a means to realize who God is by what God is doing, and who we are to be so beloved of God.

To speak of a person as blessed is to acknowledge the presence of God in that person, and in that person's life. When the angel Gabriel, for example, saluted Mary as "blessed among women," he was acknowledging the unique presence of God in Mary, and in her life. God is with you, in you, for you; and when we say, "The Lord be with you," we mean that God's presence in your life is a sign of God's blessing. God is the source of blessing, and therefore to be blessed is in the first place to acknowledge the presence of God in your life and in your place.

When we think this way, then, we are meant to focus on those places in our lives where we have known and seen the presence and power of God. That is an exercise that you should engage in daily. Think of your own daily preservation, the little hints and guesses of the presence of God—whether in the corporeal world of a good meal, delightful sights, or a wondrous insight; or in an idea that comes to life: the signs, for example, that spring is coming, and that its color is red and not green, is a blessing, a hint, a sign of the presence of God not just in nature but in our own lives. You have your creation, your preservation, and all the blessings of this life for which to be grateful.

A blessing is also what God wishes for us—not just what he does for us, but what he wishes for us, what God desires for us in matters great and small. Is it not an extraordinary thing to consider that it is God's desire that good things should happen to us, and that we should have perhaps more than anything else an awareness of the good things that God has already provided us? This awareness is the sign of spiritual growth and maturity. God intends for you to be blessed, God intends for you to enjoy life. "What is the whole duty of man?" The dour Westminster Confession tells us, "To love God and to enjoy him forever." God means for you to be blessed. Your job is to forget not all of his benefits.

In my calling many years ago I once encountered a devout old woman I had known all my life whose whole universe had once been wondrously filled with great and glorious things. She had done great things, she had seen great things, and she had great things, but by the time she was coming toward the end of her days she had been reduced to the things she could arrange upon the top of her bedside table in the nursing home: her entire universe had been reduced to a few inches no larger than this pulpit desk. She had her Bible, a few photographs, some old mementos of family and friends—she had a universe in that tiny space. She said, "This is all I have left, and it reminds me of how much God has given me." Out of that scarcity came the rich sensibility of her blessings. She knew what it was to be blessed because she had not forgotten all of the benefits of God, and not having forgotten that, she therefore had her view in mind, she therefore had her perspective in order, her priorities in order; she had sought first the kingdom of God and of his righteousness, and all else had been taken care of.

Let me close with my favorite collect. Of all of the collects in the Book of Common Prayer, of all of those wonderful summaries that Cranmer translated and then perfected into English prose, it says all that I want to say this morning; and it is this one, which reads:

O God, who hast prepared for them that love thee such good things as pass our understanding, pour into our hearts such love toward thee, that we, loving thee above all things, may obtain thy promises, which exceed all that we can desire.

We are a blessed people blessed by a blessing and blessed God, and it is our joy to remember that every day of our lives.

Freedom, Choices, and Commitment

Text: Choose ye this day whom ye will serve . . . as for me and my house, we will serve the Lord.

—JOSHUA 24:15

That first lesson from Joshua is full of choices, options, and challenges. Joshua essentially says to the people of Israel: God has delivered you, God has brought you out of Egypt, God has done all sorts of tremendous and wonderful things for you. Now you ought to serve him in response. If you don't want to serve God, choose the ones you will serve, but "as for me and my house, we will serve the Lord." This is a sermon about freedom, choices, and commitment.

FREEDOM

I have been spending a good deal of time this past week with the Class of 1998, the freshmen, the newest members of the University, our future, our hope, and our promise. We welcomed them and their parents last Sunday, and in the seven days since then we have watched them go through the magical process of induction, introduction, and indoctrination that makes Harvard undergraduates out of nice high school students. It is a fearsome thing to behold, this transformation.

It is from them and from this process, however, that I got this morning's sermon for the opening of the new academic year, so I am grateful to them. The text from Joshua suggested itself, and the text was amplified by the issues that came to life in every conversation, every discussion group, and every casual chat with the freshmen. The issues are these: (1) What shall I do with my new freedom? (2) How can I make the choices I must make? (3) What is worth my ultimate loyalty? (4) To whom or to what shall I be committed? (5) To whom or to what shall I give my all?

These are not just freshman questions to be asked only by dewy-cheeked eighteen-year-olds at a loss for answers in a strange and foreign land. These are life questions. Even graduate students, G8 and beyond, even tenured professors, even sophomores are tempted by one or more of these questions, and it seemed to me that the first Sunday of a new term and a new year was as good a time as any to face them.

When I told someone earlier in the week the title of my sermon, he said, "What a lot of clichés to pack into one title, let alone into one sermon: freedom, choices, and commitment." I suppose I should have bristled at the pejorative tone of "clichés." Then I decided that there is nothing wrong with clichés, that in fact most of the clichés I know are annoyingly true. Although I don't sew, I believe that those who do sew know that a stitch in time *does* save nine. I do know that the early bird usually catches the worm, and that he who laughs last laughs best. It is better not to act in haste lest you repent at leisure, and handsome is as handsome does. So, a cliché is not necessarily a bad thing, especially if it helps you to remember a truth without which you would be in danger. Freedom, choices, commitment may have the ting of familiarity about them; they also point us to the truth without which Christians at the beginning of any enterprise—much less the enterprise of another academic year—will be in jeopardy.

Our lesson from Joshua gives us the scene, and paints it vividly. The children of Israel are wandering in the wilderness full of their freedom and no longer slaves in Egypt, but they have not yet become anything else. They are in midpassage, as it were, much like the college experience. They know freedom "from"; they have not yet experienced freedom "for." Joshua gives them a chance at choice, an opportunity to translate freedom into something else—for the essence of freedom is choice: "Choose ye this day whom ye will serve . . . as for me and my house, we will serve the Lord." The choice is an invitation to commitment, to an ultimate loyalty to the God who deserves that loyalty not in the abstract but in the concrete. God does not say, "Trust me and I will do great things for you." He says, "I have done great things for you: trust me." The choice is an invitation to an ultimate loyalty to God, who has already demonstrated ultimate loyalty to the people. The elements of freedom expressed in choices that lead to commitment are all in place, here in the twenty-fourth chapter of Joshua. How is it, however, that we speak of freedom and commitment in the same breath? Are they not opposites?

When marriages or relationships break down, more than once I have heard one or the other of the parties say, "Oh, I couldn't keep the commitment; I wanted my freedom." Commitment equals bondage, obligation, duty, responsibility. Freedom means "Free at last, free at last. Thank God almighty, I'm free at last."

I asked a freshman what she most liked about being away from home, and she answered, "The freedom." I imagine she meant the freedom to go to bed as late as she pleases, to get up as late as she pleases, to eat what and when she wishes, to dress, perhaps for the first time in her life, without comment or censor. There is even more freedom than that in an academic community such as this. You are free to attend or not to attend your classes. We have not compelled you to attend chapel services in one hundred and twenty-odd years. We have no truant officers here in Harvard College. You are free to blow your credit card with one blowout on food, or clothing, or entertainment. You are free to express the most outrageous and unfounded opinions, and even to write them and publish them daily. You are free to discuss books you haven't read, and to criticize people you haven't met.

Much of this college freedom is represented by the freedom of the *Catalog.* Here in the *Catalog of the Faculty of Arts and Sciences,* there are available to you more than ten thousand courses, seminars, and tutorials, and you are free, in theory, to choose any or all of them. With no limit and with ultimate possibility, true freedom ought to be known, cherished, and experienced.

Freedom: we love the word, the concept, the sound. My colleague in this faculty, Orlando Patterson, in his big book on freedom, calls freedom the most sacred of the Western concepts. We live for it, love for it, are prepared to kill for it and to die for it; and yet this freedom is not the unambiguous thing our moral shorthand is tempted to make of it. We all know stories of prisoners who are freed from their imprisonment only to find that their new liberty in the free world is more demanding and dangerous than their old life in jail, and who find themselves longing for the security of the jail cell.

We know of the countries of Eastern Europe that, liberated from the slavery of Communism, are having a hard time with the freedom of the free market and the obligations of the free world. Freedom is not all that it's cracked up to be.

We remember how the children of Israel, after their liberation from slavery in Egypt, complained of their freedom to die in the wilderness. Similarly, after a while even undergraduates complain that mere freedom "from" does not help them in the tasks of freedom "for."

The moralists of another generation understood what we contemporary Americans often forget: that freedom is not merely the absence of restraint. In the words of a nineteenth-century divine:

But what is freedom? Rightly understood,
a universal license
to be good.

Now, that is worthy of Noah Webster or Kahlil Gibran, and qualifies as a genuine cliché, the sort of thing William Bennett would print in boldface in the second edition of his book, *The Book of Virtues.*

Freedom, as every struggling nation and individual learns sooner or later, is a means and not an end, and the essence of freedom is not liberation, as we so readily suppose; both the essence and the expression of freedom is choice. You are free in order to be able to choose.

CHOICES

What is the one thing the unfree are unable to do? They are unable to choose. Slavery is the ultimate lack of choice, for to be a slave is to see no choice, to have no choice, to be unable to exercise any choice. Freedom implies and requires choices, and Joshua's great question in our text puts the test to the freedom of the people. "Choose ye this day. . . ." You have a choice. Your freedom is expressed in the face of your choice. So, as free people, choose.

We all have choices. I know those moments when we say, "I have no choice; I am trapped." If the essence of freedom is choice, however, then many of us know ourselves to be from time to time unfree, captives of circumstance or of the moment, or of conscience, or of ideology. Here in college that lack of choice can seem formidable: my parents want me to go to medical school and become a rich doctor for the honor of the family. How can I choose not to do that? My ethnic group insists that I affirm the group identity of which I am a part. How can I choose anything other than that? My colleagues are difficult and unproductive, unpleasant, and too close. What choice do I have but to respond in kind? The choices seemingly available to us are like those presented in Woody Allen's famous parody of a commencement address of a generation ago: "We stand at a historic crossroads. One road leads to total annihilation, the other to existential despair. Let us hope for the wisdom to choose wisely."

I would rather take the counsel of Dietrich Bonhoeffer than that of Woody Allen. It was Bonhoeffer who, while a prisoner of Hitler and awaiting his own death, showed that in his imprisonment he was free, because he exercised the essence of his freedom by choosing how he would deal with his imprisonment, his captors, and his death. He recalled Martin Luther's fighting lines:

> Let goods and kindred go,
> This mortal life also;
> The body they may kill;
> God's truth abideth still,
> His kingdom is forever.

It was said of Nelson Mandela that during all the years of his imprisonment in South Africa for conscience's sake, he was the only free man in that country.

To choose is to exercise the option to define how you will deal with your lack of options. In this we all have choices to make; we are in the constant process of exercising our freedom, whose essence is choice. We are free even to make bad choices and to make mistakes—even big ones—here. My old piano teacher once told me, "God invented mistakes so that we could learn quicker." That was a comfort to me, who had trouble with the C-sharp scale, and who did not always translate accurately the notes from the page to the keyboard.

In our text, the children of Israel could have chosen the lesser gods of their fathers, the gods of Egypt, the petty deities of their past and of their neighbors, the gods of the Amorites, but they are asked to make an informed choice. The gods of the Amorites had done nothing for them; it was the Lord who had defeated their enemies. It was the Lord who said, "I gave you land on which you had not labored, and cities which you had not built, and you dwell therein; you eat fruit of vineyards, and olives which you did not plant." In the opening of a new term we acknowledge that those of us who inherit this Harvard in 1994 are heirs of people who worked and labored, built and gave long before us. We enter into a city that we did not build, into a university we did not create, and we are beholden to the goodwill and labors, imagination and wealth of others, and ultimately of God. We remember this at the beginning of a new academic year, and in the University hymn we are about to sing in Latin. The translation is there, for you to acknowledge that obligation, and to see choices.

The children of Israel had a choice, and they would choose the God who had done great things for them, for they may have been willful, but they were not stupid. Their freedom consisted of making the right choice, and that choice is one of ultimate loyalty, ultimate commitment, of giving oneself over completely and totally to someone, something, worthy of one's utmost.

COMMITMENT

If the essence of freedom is choice, the object of freedom is commitment. How often have I heard the young say, "I want to find something to give my life to." Some see ultimate commitment to the family, or to business, or to the government, or to a profession. People join the military because they wish to be part of something that demands their utmost best, and that is to do something ultimate and worthwhile. People believe in God for the same reason.

I know that conventional wisdom says that we are anarchic, autonomous individuals with no sense of each other or of commitment, and that our ideas are driven by the idea of being number one, but I believe that this is not all of the story. I think that most of us are searching, and especially the young, for something worthy of our ultimate trust, our ultimate loyalty, that something worth submitting to. We hope that our heroes and celebrities will play this role for us and they fail; and the lyrics of contemporary popular music, particularly of rock and of rap, sing of the angst and terrible despair we feel when we discover that there is no one, nor anything, worthy of what we have to offer. Money, sex, power: we have sought them all, and we find that the example of those who have them all is not encouraging.

The most enslaved people are those who are bound to our constitutional guarantee of the pursuit of happiness, pleasure, satisfaction, and sensation. For such as these, and for those who aspire to join them, the notion of commitment as the object of freedom and the consequence of choice seems fantastical, revolutionary, illusory, sheer madness. Yet it is just such a sweet irony that is the essence of the Christian faith: to gain your life you must lose it, to be a winner you must be a loser, to be free is to choose to be committed.

Remember Willa Cather's line in her novel *My Antonia,* where she defines happiness as submission? "That is happiness;" she writes, "to be dissolved into something complete and great." To be "dissolved"—not to be affirmed, but dissolved. She chose that sentiment for her epitaph, and it is carved onto her tombstone in Jaffrey, New Hampshire.

You do not need to restrict such an epitaph to your tombstone. Life worth living is life lived in service of that which is ultimately worthy and trustworthy, and only in such service will we ever know freedom. That is the essence of Archbishop Cranmer's magnificent collect for peace, which says of God:

> O God, who art the author of peace and lover of concord, in knowledge of whom standeth our eternal life, whose service is perfect freedom. . . .

For the Christian, as well as for all of God's children, God gives freedom to choose the best, the ultimate, the highest. You are free to choose God. Tempted as we are to try our options on for size, none of the lesser gods will do. We have been given this new day, this new year, and this fresh word from the Lord to help us to make wise choices freely: the essence of freedom is choice; the object of freedom is commitment. Therefore, it is simple: give all that you are and have to him who is worthy of all that you are and have. Give to God nothing less than your whole life and all that is in it and within it, and then you will be truly free. Make the right choice, and then you will know that freedom that is perfect service.

> Choose ye this day whom ye will serve . . . as for me and my house, we will serve the Lord.

When They Think You're Crazy

Text: To this day I have had the help that comes from God, and so I stand here testifying both to small and great. . . .

—ACTS 26:22

Paul is on trial in Agrippa's court, giving testimony: "To this day I have had the help that comes from God, and so I stand here testifying both to small and great, saying nothing but what the prophets and Moses said would come to pass." His statement refers to the situation as outlined previously, and if you lose interest in my sermon cast your eye on the twenty-sixth chapter of Acts, and hope that as you read your part and I speak my part, we both come out together at a little past noon.

Quite some time ago I was seated at the high table at the Faculty Club, having lunch with my back to the door in the midst of the clinking and clanking and general hubbub that accompanies dining at high noon, when slowly I realized that the clinking of knives and forks against china, and the tinkling of ice in crystal water goblets, had stopped, and that there was an unaccustomed silence in the dining room. I turned around, and there stood a young student waiter with a tray of glasses, uttering strange wailing sounds. People at the tables had stopped gossiping, everyone listened to his inchoate speech, and when he started to speak in English, someone asked, "What's he talking about?" Another answered, "It's something to do with religion;" and the first said, "Oh . . ." and went back to his gossiping. The manager of the club came to lead the boy away to his office for a chat, and we never saw him again.

When they think you're crazy, it often has something to do with religion, and particularly with the Christian religion. This is perhaps an alarming proposition: *it is not natural to be a Christian.* Not clear? Let me put it another way: *it is not normal to be a Christian.* Still uncertain of what you have heard? *It is unnatural and abnormal to be a Christian. It is an act against nature.* Still uncertain? *It might even be illegal,* in that part of North Carolina represented by Jesse Helms, *to be a Christian.* It is contrary to nature to be a Christian: you may be tolerated, or you may be ignored and persecuted, or they may think you're crazy.

You doubt me. I can tell, for a preacher can always tell when a congregation takes exception to what he says. Some get up and leave, and that is always a relief; others remain, but fold their mental arms and say, "Show me, if you can or if you dare." So I will.

Remember the first lesson, read so well for us by my friend and colleague Dr. Allen Counter? You all remember the Beatitudes—the "Blessèds"—from Jesus' Sermon on the Mount? The Beatitudes are probably, next to the twenty-third Psalm, the most familiar and beloved bit of scripture in the Bible. "Blessèd are the poor in spirit, for theirs is the kingdom of heaven; blessèd are they that mourn, for they shall be comforted; blessèd are the meek, for they shall inherit the earth. . . . ," and so forth.

A few weeks ago I saw a wonderful cartoon in the *New Yorker* showing people much like yourselves greeting the rector at the door of a church, obviously after a service. In the center was an enormously formidable woman on the arm of a tiny little man, and she is saying to the rector, with a hint of disdain, "And just when do you expect that the meek *will* inherit the earth?"

The joke of course is that neither she nor we expect the meek to inherit the earth, or much of anything else: the meek don't come to Harvard, for example; they are at Brown or at Yale. The rest of the Beatitudes, blessed and lovely as they are as the standard of Christian behavior, are not to be taken seriously by anybody of consequence, and those who do take them seriously live in small isolated communities where they eat bran and take cold baths, marry their cousins, and farm themselves into extinction. All that remains of those wonderfully meek Shakers who tried to take the Beatitudes seriously are a few songs and some modestly fine furniture. No, anyone taking this stuff too seriously is thought to be crazy. The normal, natural instinct is to protect one's interest, go with the flow, find the acceptable way, and stay in it. It is the "leadership" of our would-be leaders: of our president, who governs by polls, or of a Bob Dole, who says, "I'll be whatever you want me to be."

Someone, anyone, who goes contrary to all of this, especially when his own life is at stake and his reputation with it, is thought to be crazy, mad, having taken leave of his senses. He attracts attention and the notice of the crowd.

That is what happens to the apostle Paul. We encounter him this morning, in Acts 26, in one of the most famous trials in the Bible—or, for that matter, in all of literature—as he stands in a Roman court accused of blasphemy against the Jews, and hence guilty of crimes against the good order of the Roman state. He regards himself as simply following the heavenly vision whereby he met Jesus and turned his life around, and he stands accused of the abnormality of being a Christian in a world where such a concept is both dangerous and crazy.

Of what crime is he accused? According to the text, he changed his mind: he took up another set of opinions.

What is his defense? "Wherefore, O King Agrippa, I was not disobedient to the heavenly vision, but declared first to those at Damascus, then at Jerusalem and throughout all the country of Judea, and also to the Gentiles, that they should repent and turn to God and perform deeds worthy of repentance." What is wrong with that? Where is the crime? Paul is not advocating blood sacrifice, or conscientious objection to the state, or non-payment of taxes. He is advocating nothing nearly as radical, seditious, or dangerous as today's superpatriot militias of Middle America: this is no Randy Weaver, no Timothy McVeigh; this isn't even David Koresh.

Who is he? He is a man who has had his mind changed and who wants to change the minds and hearts and ways of others in the vision of Jesus Christ; and sometimes—not always, but sometimes—when you change your mind, "they" think you are crazy.

All of the people at the trial, the Jewish accusers and the Roman judges, would have preferred the "normal" Paul. Remember him? The "normal" Paul, the preconversion Paul, was the superzealous, overly ambitious young Jew who took it upon himself to persecute and prosecute people believed to be disloyal to the conventional wisdom. The "normal" Paul was the fellow who volunteered for missions to root out subversives and maintain orthodoxy among his co-religionists. The "normal" Paul was the one who voted to condemn in heresy trials, and who held the coats of those who stoned the apostle Stephen to death. The "normal" Paul was the zealous young spear carrier for his movement who asked no questions, questioned no orders, and did what he had to do by any and every means necessary. He was promoted in his movement, and he could have had a house in the suburbs and a good pension: all that was his *until* he was converted and lost his mind, found his soul, and became crazy in the eyes of the only world that once counted to him.

A footnote: what has always fascinated me about the most dangerous social movements of the twentieth century is the extraordinarily normal quality of the people attracted to them. Have you ever watched those films showing the thousands of people attending Hitler's rallies, wearing swastikas and going about their everyday duties in the Germany of the 1930s, before the war? What strikes me in the films is how normal they all look, like everyday German burghers, with no horns on their heads, no warts on their noses, and no tails between their legs. They look normal, and that is scary. They look the soul of ordinary, normal, and even decent people. We don't even have to go to Germany: last week I saw a television program on the rise of the Ku Klux Klan in the 1920s—the "Age of Normalcy," as Mr. Harding called it—in Indiana. Who were those people? Not rabid racists, wild-eyed revolutionaries, or deformed social misfits. They were so ordinary, so normal as to defy the imagination—the druggist, the butcher, characters out of Norman Rockwell and Robert Frost; and thus it was "normal" people seeking to preserve their "normal" world who put on white bedsheets and burned crosses and hanged black people in order to do so. That is normal, alas, and we understand it only too well.

Against such "norms" any Christian who actually believed that aspiring to the gospel was the only way to go would be seen as crazy—indeed, as a raving lunatic; such a person would either be ignored, or tried and put away.

Paul argued that all that he was and all that he wanted for others was that they should live a life of repentance and perform deeds worthy of repentance. That is what he says. "And as he thus made his defense, Festus said with a loud voice, 'Paul, you are mad, your great learning is turning you mad'" (Acts 26:24). Festus said, in effect, "You are *crazy!* You've *lost it!* Your learning is driving you away from common sense."

The case was so compelling that only a madman could make it. What the world called madness, however, Paul called the sober truth: "I am not mad, most excellent Festus, but I am speaking the sober truth. For the King knows about these things . . . for I am persuaded that none of these things has escaped his notice, for this was not done in a corner" (Acts 23:25, 26). "Normalcy," as that most normal of all American presidents, Warren Gamaliel Harding, once described the *status quo,* is the background—the ambient sound, as it were—against which an authentic, even modest, witness for Christ looks heroic, and even crazy. Can you think of a "normal" heroic person in history? Over lunch today while you are waiting for dessert or for the bill, try to see if you can name a "normal" person who has done something great and worthy of remembrance, and who was not at one time or another thought to be mad or crazy. I'll bet that the only candidate whom most of you will be able to come up with will be Forrest Gump, and that may tell us more about ourselves than we can bear to hear: our candidate is a "normal" person of the motion pictures.

When they think you're crazy, it may be because you are perhaps trying to do the right thing, trying to live by an ethic that does not quite square with this world. You are trying to do deeds worthy of repentance when all that is wanted is for you to put in your time and collect your pension.

In the remarkable account of Paul's defense of himself there is a telling moment when he almost persuades the judge, King Agrippa, that the abnormal way of Christ is the right way. Do you remember, at verse 28, where Agrippa says, "In a short time you think to make me a Christian"? Or, as it is written in the King James Version, "Almost thou persuadest me to be a Christian."

Some years ago, amid great controversy, I invited Billy Graham to preach here, and as his visit drew nearer and nearer, those who had been indifferent or hostile became more and more curious and interested. Finally, on the day of his visit, I received a call from Massachusetts Hall saying that the president would like fifteen minutes with Dr. Graham, if Dr. Graham could spare them. Well. What could this mean? I escorted Billy over to the president, and left the two of them together while I waited in the reception area. Fifteen minutes came and went, thirty minutes came and went, and then nearly an hour. Then the two of them came out of the president's office with much laughter and good cheer, and parted. As Billy and I walked back over here to the church, I asked him how it went and he said, "I felt like Paul before Agrippa, and I think I almost had him." *In a short time you think to make me a Christian. . . ."*

Now, why do I tell you all of this at the beginning of term? Why a sermon on Christian insanity? The answer is simple. Most of you young people at the start of the year want desperately to find a place for yourselves here at Harvard. You want to fit in and to not be odd man or odd woman out. You think you know the rules of the place, and you dearly want to follow them lest someone think you don't know any better. The temptation is so great to be ordinary, to conform, to be normal and not stand out lest people think you are crazy, that you won't dare to follow your heart or the heart of your faith. "Harvard is a place for the great nonconformists," we are told: "Look at Harvard Square and the zany variety of life in the pit in front of the Cambridge Savings Bank." Well, I have looked at "zany" Harvard Square now for twenty-five years, and just the other day I looked at all that creative insecurity in the pit, all those wild and crazy suburban kids play-acting in front of the Cambridge Savings Bank, and you know what I discovered? I discovered that I couldn't tell one from the other because they all looked, dressed, acted, and sounded exactly alike: so much for the infinite variety of Harvard, or of Harvard Square.

True nonconformity has nothing whatsoever to do with clothing or with hip counterstyles, or even with outrageous music, all of which in its outrage sounds like just so much elevator Muzak for the counterculture. True nonconformity risks being called "crazy" by the crazies. It is what was said of Theodore Parker, the radical Unitarian of Harvard Divinity School of a century ago: "From their orthodox form of dissent he dissented."

Paul's ultimate defense is not an argument or a plea but a relationship within which he stands against the world "*contra mundum,*" as the old saints used to say. "To this day I have had the help that comes from God, and so I stand here testifying both to small and great." We too stand in just such a relationship: that testimony is ours as well, and when we make it, as I know that we must and hope that we will, "they" may call us crazy, but we know that we are not alone, and indeed that we are in very good company.

The Quick and the Dead

Text: This is how one should regard us, as servants of Christ and stewards of the mysteries of God.

—1 CORINTHIANS 4:1

Before the time of many of you who are now members of the University, the streets outside of the Yard and in front of Memorial Hall—if you can imagine Canaday Hall not there—converged into an incredibly crazy pattern. Broadway, Cambridge Street, Kirkland Street, Oxford Street, and Peabody Street merged at the foot of the delta and in front of Phillips Brooks House, and to cross them was always a peril at any time of the day or night, but especially so when the classes changed on the hour during term. McGeorge Bundy, while dean of the Faculty of Arts and Sciences, once famously described this troubled crossing by saying, "The way to the Law School is only for the quick and the dead."

As was typical of Dean Bundy, he was both accurate and clever, but we must try to be more than clever, and equally accurate, when we speak this morning of the quick and the dead. The quick—that wonderful Anglo-Saxon word that describes the indwelling of life as a quickening, and the characteristic activity of the living as being quick about their affairs—are the living; and the dead, on this day of all days of the year, and in this place of all places on earth, speak for themselves. In The Memorial Church we have kept for many years this Sunday, the Sunday nearest to Armistice Day, November 11, as the day and the place where the living and the dead meet in intimate proximity, for our congregation today consists of the quick and the dead.

THE DEAD

Let me speak first of the dead, for they have pride of place here this morning and we should remember that without them we would not be here, and neither would this church. Last year, on November 11, 1998—the eightieth anniversary of the armistice that ended World War I in 1918, on the eleventh hour of the eleventh day of the eleventh month—I was by good fortune in London, in the very year in which a great effort had been made to restore the two-minute silence at eleven o'clock in the morning in memory of the war dead. Older generations remembered that two-minute silence as an incredible moment of silent observation, but modern times had begun to see the diminishing of the observance; and so in honor of the eightieth anniversary a major effort was made in the British press and in cultural agencies to get the country back to that moment of remembrance. On November 11, 1998, I found myself at the front desk of a hotel at that precise hour, and as I watched, clerks put down their pens, people sat quietly in front of their computers, pedestrian traffic came to a halt, the few men with hats on took them off, and even the ubiquitous elevator music was turned off. This apparently happened all over Great Britain, and it was very moving. It was most impressive.

At dinner that evening I was seated next to an English lady who asked if we had anything like it in America, and I reminded my friend that I served in a church whose entire identity came from the dead of the First World War. I didn't tell her how controversial the idea of a war memorial had been here in the 1920s, when President Lowell and Edward Caldwell Moore, chairman of the Board of Preachers, had proposed it. I didn't tell her that the students, through the pages of the *Crimson,* had said that for a memorial they preferred something beautiful like a column or useful like a new stadium, and found the idea of a church to be neither. "Compulsory chapel," they called it on the front pages, in bitter opposition to Mr. Lowell. Nor did I tell her of the controversy concerning what to do with the Germans who, although Harvard graduates, had fought for Germany and died in the war on the opposite side.

Were the Germans to be included with the other graduates, who died as their enemies? If they were included, would the character of the building be compromised? Were they to be excluded? Was this, then, to be a memorial to victory only, and not to peace? You will discover the solution on the north wall. I did not tell my table companion that it was the architect, Mr.

THE QUICK AND THE DEAD   37

Coolidge, and the president, Mr. Lowell, who decided on the noble principle that undergraduates should always enter this church not as they do nowadays through the west doors, but rather through the south doors from the new Yard, so that on their way to worship they would always pass through the Memorial Room, by the names of the dead, and by the sarcophagus entitled "The Sacrifice." There the young and the living would always thereby be reminded of the sacrifice of the 373 Harvard dead.

This Memorial Church, on Armistice Day, November 11, 1932, was dedicated to peace as a house of prayer for all people and in memory of those young men who, while a bright future beckoned, willingly gave up their lives that others might live in freedom. Less than a decade later we were at war again, and in 1951 the names of the dead of World War II were added to the south wall. For those of you who are statistically minded, it took forty-two weeks to carve the 13,651 letters that stand in memory of the 697 faculty members, students, and alumni of the University who died in World War II.

In 1976, tablets to the dead of the wars in Korea and in Vietnam were added to the north wall; and on this occasion next year, with the permission of the Corporation, it is our plan to unveil a new war tablet in memory of three members of Radcliffe College who served as nurses in World War I, and who died in that service. Of these three women—Lucy Fletcher, '10; Ruth Holden, '11; and Helen Homans, '13—it was written in *The Radcliffe Quarterly* in 1918: "They gave their lives for their country and its allies just as surely as if they had met death in the trenches." They who have had no memorial will have one here.

When the bell tolls this morning and we remember that on its lip are inscribed the words "In Memory of Voices That Are Hushed," we will be reminded that our memories are not only of voices that were hushed in battle or in war, but also of voices belonging to members of the University who have given particular service to this University Church since its foundation, for this is a commemoration both of the war dead and of benefactors. You will find their names listed, and we will read them aloud during the Act of Commemoration.

Perhaps some of you have read Professor Laurel Thatcher Ulrich's sharpish piece in the current issue of *Harvard Magazine,* where she speaks of women's invisible history at Harvard, and of what we should be doing about it. She is on the right track, but in her listing of unsung heroines I noted with some sadness that she had neglected to mention two women to whom we are indebted in this church, and whose names we honor publicly and gratefully every Commemoration Sunday. Few know that it was a woman, Caroline Plummer, who in 1855 endowed the professorship upon which I sit. She had little to do with Harvard, but as a memorial to her brother she established a professorship whose incumbent was to have charge of the University Chapel. She lives on in the eight of us who have served in her name: Miss Plummer's history is not forgotten here, nor have we forgotten her, or her gift.

Nannie Yulee Noble, who in 1898 established the William Belden Noble Lectures in memory of her husband, is another woman to whom this church and university stand in great debt. The leading theologians of the twentieth century from around the world have served here on Mrs. Noble's foundation. She is not forgotten here, nor her name obliterated from our memory.

The most recent of the dead whose names we record today in our thanksgiving is my predecessor, Charles Philip Price, the seventh Plummer Professor and Preacher to the University, and himself a veteran of World War II, having served in the navy. He died just a few weeks ago in his eightieth year, much too soon for those of us who loved him. I owe my presence among you today, and in all of the twenty-five years before today, to Charlie; and many of you here and within the sound of my voice elsewhere owe him a debt of gratitude as to a faithful pastor, preacher, professor, and priest. William Alfred, the poet-playwright also just taken from us, wrote in his *Agamemnon,* "It is a fearful thing to love what death can touch." Such is that fearful and lovely thing we name today with our wreath of laurel, our silence, and our tolling bell. This is the place where the quick and the dead meet.

THE LIVING

What, though, of the living? How shall we speak of the quick? A memorial is of no use if there is no one to do the remembering; and Mr. Lowell understood, as his critics did not, that a worthy memorial to the dead is one in which the dead and the living are mutually engaged.

I think, for example, of the memorial services that the College classes hold at the time of their fifth reunions, having watched every year since 1970 as they have returned to Cambridge and to this church to come to terms with their own mortality, and to effect, insofar as they are able, a reunion between the quick and the dead. Usually at the fifth reunion there are few deaths, and all of them are tragic, all of them untimely, for death is an unwelcome and unfamiliar intruder upon life: at the sixty-fifth or seventieth reunions, however, there are invariably more dead than alive. All the way in between those numbers I watch as each generation tries to cast the balance between memory and hope. The younger classes—those before the twenty-fifth reunion—tend to be dutiful about the memorial service, and look upon the dead as an exception and the memorial service as at times raining on their parade. The older classes, however, know for whom the bell tolls, and that a reunion is truly a reuniting of the living and the dead, a putting back together of a memory. Secular and cynical as Harvard graduates tend to be, they nevertheless understand implicitly the doctrine of the communion of saints. The older you get, the clearer it becomes.

We have spoken of the dead, we have spoken of the quick, but what about you? What about you who are here today? There is *you* to be put into this equation. Many of you, praise God, are here regularly on Sundays and at the daily service of Morning Prayers, Monday through Saturday, and many of you find your way to the many occasions that call people together here in this University Church. You the living inhabit this space, you by your presence make certain that these are not mere ghostly ruins. The children downstairs in the church school—your children, your grandchildren, your great-grandchildren—and the undergraduates on either side of the screen, the young and old from near and far who share in the worship of a living God—all of you by your presence, your prayers, and your praises help to make certain that this place will never be simply a memorial to the dead, a tabernacle to people who are no longer here. You know what it means to be joined in the communion of saints, of friends on earth and friends above.

As your minister I have watched and shared for now a quarter of a century in this intimate relationship between the quick and the dead. I have watched the generations come and go, I have married many of you, I have baptized and dedicated you and your children. I have called upon you in times of sickness and of hospitalization, in times of joy, in times of celebration, and I have buried far too many old friends and colleagues. We have been together in good times and in bad, we have celebrated and we have mourned, but above all we have never forgotten the sacrifice of our dead nor the promise of our young. These are the things that have kept us together and that nourish the fabric of this space. This is not merely a memorial; this is the place where the living and the dead meet.

THE MYSTERY

I cannot speak for my predecessors as Ministers and Plummer Professors in this place, but, as for me, I wish to be thought of as St. Paul asked the Corinthians to think of him: "This is how one should regard us, as servants of Christ and stewards of the mysteries of God." A mystery, as we know, is not a problem waiting to be solved but an experience into which we are invited to enter. Mystery is not an *argument* for the existence of God; mystery is an *experience* of the existence of God, and that experience is what happens when the quick and the dead meet with one another and with God. The ministers in this place can rightly be described as servants of Christ and stewards of the mysteries of God.

At the center of our existence is the mystery of whose we are, and of what we are meant to be and to do.

At the center of our lives is not a collection of satisfying facts but a deepening mystery that deepens as we grow older.

At the center of our faith is a mystery that transcends all the facts of religion: that God creates us, sustains us, and redeems us so that we may both live and die on purpose.

At the center of this college stands a church in which the quick and the dead meet on intimate terms—and never more so than today—with God and with one another, a mystery beyond all measure.

For all of this, and for all of those who although now dead yet make all of this possible, all that we can do is to give grateful thanks to God.

The infinite always is silent
'Tis only the finite speaks;
Our words are the idle wavecaps
On a deep that never breaks.

We may question with wand of science,
Debate, decide, discuss:
But 'tis only in meditation
That the mystery speaks to us.

JOHN BOYLE O'REILLY

Desire

Text: As the hart desireth the waterbrooks, so panteth my soul after Thee, O God.

—PSALM 42:1

Ordinarily my text is taken from one of the two lessons for the day, but this morning I take it from the psalm we read, which was sung in splendid paraphrase, because it is a hinge point, a bridge between the two lessons. Therefore we have as our text, "As the hart desireth the waterbrooks, so panteth my soul after Thee, O God."

Also, usually my sermon has something to do with a biblical story, a point of doctrine, a point to take seriously, or a moral exhortation to either do something or stop doing something. This morning it has nothing specifically to do with any of those, for I wish to talk about an attitude, about something you feel, something you know something about because you have experienced it or it has shaped your lives. This morning I wish to talk about *desire,* a word that is seductive, a slippery word, a wonderful word; and I know that I have never before preached a sermon on desire, for I looked it up in my ample files from twenty-six years of preaching in The Memorial Church, and it is not there.

Now, I am evidently not the only one interested in the subject of desire, for, as you know, we post the titles of sermons to be preached in this church onto a signboard by a pillar outside, and one day this week when I looked up to see the poster, it had gone missing. Someone or something had stolen my sermon, and I looked all around, hoping that I might see it, and then I did! There it was, posted in a freshman window. I thought to myself that I must look into this, so I went over to the glass and knocked:

"Let me in, please," I said to the boy who came to the window, adding, "Where did you get that sign?"

"Boy, isn't it great?!" the boy replied. "My roommate pinched it off the church!"

"Do you know who I am?" I asked.

The boy had the presence of mind to say, "No, but I think I'm going to find out . . ."

I pointed to my name written on the sign, and said, "*I* am *Gomes;* and the price you will have to pay for this mischief is to post all my signs for the rest of the year, and you and your roommate must come to church."

There is something elusive about the word *desire,* something that is not contained in the words *want,* or *need,* which is closer, more akin, to the word *longing.* When a lover says to the object of his love, "You are my heart's desire"—that is, if people still speak like that other than on Valentine's Day and in soap operas—you don't get a sense of conquest or of achievement, or even of accomplishment; you get a sense of need so great that it is worth defining one's life in pursuit of it, and always with the sense that one might not get it, and surprise if and when one does.

"Ambition" is the sense of the word *desire* as the psalmist in Psalm 42 uses it, as we read this morning, where he uses both desire and longing to express what the soul seeks in its pursuit of God. Psalm 42 bears careful reading, and listening. I once heard a seminarian give a Morning Prayer talk on Psalm 42, in which it was clear that he thought that the "hart" of which the text speaks was that vital blood-pumping organ, the seat of human emotions. "The heart has its reasons," I thought, "but this is not one of them." Perhaps because I come from Plymouth, Massachusetts, I have always known that the hart, or red deer, is not a metaphor for love but a real living being who needs water in order to live, and who must spend his days in search of it. "As the hart desireth"—longs for, craves, cannot live without—"the waterbrooks, so panteth my soul after Thee, O God."

Desire is so tender a word, so erotic when used in the language of love. We sing, *Jesus, lover of my soul . . .* where the lover is seeking the ultimate possession. The lover of God is one who cannot live without the love of

God, and whose life consists in seeking out God: the lover of God is defined by the pursuit of God, for going after God with all of his heart is at the heart of the notion of desire. Desire is not easy for us to define or to comprehend these days, as when we confuse it with lust in the sense of "I lust after a Lexus," or "I want all the money that money can buy." Desire has a hint of unbridled ambition, and the Puritan in us warns us to keep our desires in check or to check our desires at the door.

Desire is also difficult to talk about because we understand that a desire must be translated, almost immediately, into an achievement. For so many of us, and so for the spirit of this age, desire is canceled out by gratification, and this is the formula: "I want" equals "I get." Longing is un-American; it doesn't appeal to our need for instant and immediate satisfaction. One of the principles of modern social relations is that to long for something, to want it very badly without getting it straight away means failure, disappointment, and frustration. Thus it is hard for so many of us to realize that the essence of the relationship with God is *not* immediate satisfaction, instant gratification, and the settling of all the matters on our personal agenda. Rather, the essence of the relationship with God is the longing for, the desire for, that relationship that in itself is good. Most of us are here not because we have all our needs fulfilled, but because of our inarticulate need or desire for God: we know enough to know that we want it fulfilled.

In other words, lest I lose you, let me make it clear: the essence of the relationship with God is not in having God, but in seeking God—although not all who seek God are here this morning. You and I are here not because of what we have but because of what we desire. The essence of the relationship with God is not possession but pursuit, and those equally difficult words *patience* and *perseverance*. Any church, any preacher, anybody can sell a religion or a God who delivers the goods on time, who pays the bills, gives you pleasure, peace, and security, and who is at the other end of the dial or prayer wheel, or mouse: there is no problem with filling TV studios or crystal cathedrals. Who would not be satisfied with a God who, when asked for a car, gave one; who, when prayed to for peace, delivered it; who, when asked for peace of mind or strength of will, gave it? This reminds one of the African proverb that says, "When I pray for bread and get it, I think about bread and forget God. When I pray for bread and don't get it, I think about God a great deal." We pray for bread and we have not got it; we are driven to longing, desire, and hope.

It could be that the answers to our prayers obscure the one whom we seek in prayer: it could be that desire is God's way of getting our attention by not necessarily providing what we want as spiritual consumers—"God, I want you to desire me"—but rather what we need in order to live: our heart's desire. I am reminded of that old line, "Death is nature's way of telling us to go slow."

That, I think, is the sense of both of this morning's lessons. In the first, which Dean Knowles read for us, we begin with a dangerous economy which would horrify my colleague Jeffrey Sachs and those in the economics department and in the Kennedy School: that those with no money are invited to come and eat. This idea throws the economic determinists, not to mention those who worship the market, into a fit. The point, however, of Isaiah is that the human economy is so often wasted on that which we think is sufficient, but which really is not. "Why do you spend your money for that which is not bread, and your labor for that which does not satisfy?" Your money should be used for something more lasting.

The delusion of a consumerist world is that the world can be satisfied by that which it can buy and consume. The American dream, which our politicians massage and manipulate for their own very selfish purposes, appears to be based on the premise that we should aspire to acquire more and more, that every generation has the right to more than its predecessors, and that somehow in getting and in spending, as Wordsworth once put it, "we shall all be saved."

Our pundits, pollsters, and politicians, and even many of our people, don't seem to get it: as long as the so-called American dream is the desire for tin-pot economic and material success together with an entitlement and an attitude, that dream will turn out to be the nightmare it has become for so many, and we bless God that it remains an elusive nightmare. People will beg, borrow, and steal to claw their way into that material dream, and when all is said and done they remain unsatisfied, unfulfilled, and ill-served. What else can explain the paradox that the richest, most powerful, and most Christian nation on earth—that's us—is also the most unhappy, anxious, and spiritually insecure nation on earth, all at the same time? Could it be that he who dies with the most toys does *not* win?

I think that most of us in our heart of hearts secretly know this, and I also think that while we can easily be diverted and tempted by the lesser gods of the market, those things on which we spend our money but that do not feed us, those things for which we work so hard but that do not give us pleasure or satisfaction, we know that none of this is the real thing, that none of this lasts, that none of this is really true. As a cynical friend of mine once put it, "Therefore dis-ease, unquietness, wealth, and power will do until something better comes along."

Most of us desire that something better: to put it simply, we long for God; we desire to know the reality of the Spirit as the only thing that will sustain us. Note that I have not said that we wish an understanding of God, or a knowledge of God; I have said we have a *longing* for God, a *desire* for God. We are tired of the tacky, the trendy, and the second-rate. We know frauds when we see them, especially when we look into the mirror every morning. If we have a fundamental craving, an unuttered, fundamental desire of the heart that transcends everything else, it is the desire to know the living, loving God. "O that I knew where I might find him," says Elijah in the oratorio that bears his name. We want, we desire, we long to accept the invitation of Isaiah in this morning's lesson: "Seek ye the Lord, while he may be found. Call ye upon him while he is near."

Coming to church is not a celebration of our captivity of God. Coming to church is a proclamation of our continuing search for God. Coming to church proclaims that we have not been taken in by the fern-bar quality of life that passes for reality. Coming to church testifies that we are dissatisfied with the second-rate and the second-best. Coming to church is an affirmation that our desire, our heart's desire, the profound, inarticulate, *groaning* desire—as Paul said—for the love of God, has not been satisfied or seduced by all the gaudy tricks and pacifiers of this tedious age. We know that there is more to it than this, and we want it, and what is more, we *need* it. "As the hart desireth the waterbrooks, so panteth my soul after Thee, O God."

The longing of the soul after God is in itself a good thing: the ache, the hope unfulfilled, is a good thing; we are not to be seduced by satisfaction, nor are we to think that the only choice is between success and failure. Longing, desire, for that which is good, for that which is God—longing, desire, is that which keeps both failure and success in perspective and at bay. We must understand that the desire for God is God's means for us to find God. Now, I know that that sounds like a tea-bag or fortune-cookie aphorism, but it is true: *The desire for God is God's means for us to find God,* or, again, *The desire for God is God's means to God.* That is what Isaiah means when he says, "Seek ye the Lord while he may be found, call ye upon him while he is near."

Now, there are ethical and moral demands here: let the wicked forsake his ways, and the unrighteous man his thoughts—and that is all well and good. We spend a lot of our time thinking about what we ought to do, what is right, what is wrong, what is good, and what is bad, but this is *not* where the emphasis begins, or where it is to be found in today's lesson, for goodness, virtue, and morality are all consequences of the good desire for God. You cannot be good in the absence of the desire for goodness. Virtue begins in the desire for God: in other words, if what you seek is right, then righteousness will follow. Start with this desire and your life will take shape from it.

This, then, is an invitation to a sense of divine discontent, for desire is a discontent, a dissatisfaction with things as they are or as they appear to be. To desire God is to acknowledge that we do not have God, and that we know at the same time that we want God: desire is to seek after that which we do not know but know enough to know that we need.

As Augustine once put it, Christians are people with restless hearts who know no satisfaction, and who cannot be distracted by anything less than the experience of God. Desire, thus, is not to be contained, or bought off, or bribed. The desire for God is nothing less than the fuel of the soul: it keeps us going, and coming, and going again. Like the frightened hart that needs water to live and whose life is spent in pursuit of it, so do we long for desire, the living water by which God sustains us. There is a saying: "Tell me your ultimate desire, and I will know all that can possibly be known about you." We are not what we have, we are not what we know, we are not what we do, we are not even what we eat. We are what we desire, and the people of God are known by their desire, insatiable and unquenchable, for God. That distinguishes us from everyone and from everything, and makes us impatient with ourselves, with the world, and with things as they are; and zealous to satisfy ourselves for the living God. "As the hart desireth the waterbrooks, so panteth my soul after Thee, O God."

Does It Work for You?

Text: I am come that they might have life, and that they might have it more abundantly.

—JOHN 10:10

It is useful to remember that in the second lesson, when Jesus extended his metaphor of sheep, shepherds, and sheepfold, his listeners didn't get it and so he repeated it; and this universal lack of understanding is why we have continued to preach on it for these thousands of years.

We focus this morning on John 10:10, which is perhaps one of the loveliest verses in all of Scripture and certainly among my favorites. The words of our text are God's stated intention for us in Jesus Christ, and the promise of the abundant life, life lived fully, with the promise of more to come, so that we can imagine it not as nasty, brutish, and short but rather as abundant and overflowing. The thief, says Jesus in the gospel, comes to do harm to the sheep, to steal and to kill and destroy, whereas "I am come that they may have life, and have it more abundantly."

That is God's stated intention for us; it is not obscure or lost, for we are the sheep of his pasture, and we ought to be able to rejoice in that blessed assurance. The question, however, of the minute is, Does it work for you? Does that blessed assurance, that statement of God's intention for an abundant life, that essential promise of the Christian life—does it work for you? Does it make any difference in your life? Does the Christian life work for you? Does it work every day?

Where did we get such an idea? The question was prompted somewhat by the beehive of activity in this church over the course of the past two weeks when we have been host to Harvard Hillel's Reform congregation for the Jewish High Holy Days, and by a question put to a Jewish friend by a person who asked quite sincerely, "You Jewish people have been among the greatest-suffering people in all of history. You have never relinquished your faith, and in these Days of Awe you spend all day in services. Does it work for you? Why bother? History would seem to suggest otherwise."

An observant Jew would reply with the precious aphorism that I have come to love: "It is not the Jew who keeps the Holy Days, but the Holy Days that keep the Jew." That is just a little too facile, too slick, for us Christians, I think. The question, Does it work for you? is not quite so easily answered by ritual observance, and most of us would not dare to ask the question of ourselves, for we might very well fear that we would not like the answer, or that we might find it disagreeable.

An illustration of this I read in the *New York Times* during the dog days of August, which some of you may have read as well, of the neighborhood grocer in a rundown urban neighborhood in Newark, New Jersey. A black man and his wife, after listening in their church to the gospel over and over again and trying to take it seriously, decided to do the Christian thing and translate Christian principle into business, to behave as good neighbors, and to stop selling tobacco, alcohol, or lottery tickets in their store to the poor who could barely afford to buy them. Guess what happened? You can guess. They nearly went out of business; they may in fact be out of business by now, although there has been no story yet in the *New York Times* about their successors; and they were ridiculed by the very neighbors and family and friends whom they were trying to save, and laughed at for trying to mix religion with business. They were small-timers, this mom and pop— amateurs who should have learned from those Christian businessmen in the boardrooms of America who fill the churches on Sunday and the boardrooms on Monday, and who are there and will remain there because they know that it is neither possible nor smart to mix business with the Christian faith.

Does it work for you? If you asked that New Jersey Christian couple if it works for them, theirs would be a sadder and wiser answer today.

It has been said to doctors, "The trouble with you doctors is that you spend so much time with sick people!" My own time is not filled with positives, for few clergy hear about their people's successes. You come to us with all of your junk, all of your failures, and it doesn't, indeed, work for most of you, the pathological failures who come to church to be with other failures. Most of us today know more of life's failures than its successes, even in this community dedicated to the fine art of success. Perhaps it is a part of the malaise of the time, at the end of the millennium. A recent poll asked a sample audience, "What is the greatest danger of our age, ignorance or apathy?" Half of the respondents replied, "I don't know," and the other half, "I don't care." When I talk to alumni and read the class reports I feel I am peeling an onion, for people have not got it.

One of my English friends, admittedly not a fan of the late Princess of Wales, in a recent letter in the aftermath of the collective hysteria of the English people and others in reaction to her death, commented that most people seemed to identify with her manifest failures in life, with the things that didn't work for her. In the name of "vulnerability," she gave permission for people to acknowledge their failures, their imperfections, their lack of wholeness, and because the whole world is full of failures, the whole world mourned. In her death, he said, we celebrated a life that seemed to work but really didn't, and we did so because that is more often than not the case with ourselves. It *seems* to work, it looks good to me, it sounds good, but it isn't. Remember that book of Erma Bombeck's some years ago? She called it *If Life Is a Bowl of Cherries, What Am I Doing in the Pits?*

How do we reconcile God's clear intention for us in our text—his desire that we should experience the abundant life—and our own experience that life is more often empty than full? That is the question, and we dare ask it, we dare stir up the embers of our own anxiety, because I believe that we can have confidence in at least two answers that Scripture provides in the lessons this morning.

In the first lesson, from Ecclesiastes, we are asked to "Remember thy Creator in the days of thy youth." However you define yourself as a youth, this has your name on it. Why should you do so in your youth, while you are as young as you are now? Because now is the time when you are at the peak of your mental and physical prowess, and because if you don't do it now you won't be able to later. Now is the time that all of your powers are at their highest. Remember now your Creator, remember now God, while you are still young enough and alert enough to do so, while you still have your faculties, before the evil days come, before you are so overwhelmed by experience that life will seem like one long and unavailing struggle. I will give you an anatomy lesson about the physical plant: do it now before your legs go arthritic and your back hurts, before your eyes begin to fail and your teeth fall out, before you lose your hearing and it is always autumn and never spring. If it is true that we reach our sexual peak at fourteen and our intellectual peak at nineteen, then many of us are on our way downhill. That is what Ecclesiastes is saying—that, contrary to popular rumor, youth is the time to remember God. Youth is the time to remember from where and from whom you came, and you should do it now while you can, for it gets harder.

We think of memory as something only for the old people whose lives are in the past, who can't remember where they put the car keys yesterday; but what the old most often remember are the things of their youth. The young think they have so little to remember, and they have, and that is why it is all the more precious to cherish. The young remember the smell of their mother and the sound of their father's voice. They remember both the slightest slights and the smallest praise. Ask the children downstairs in the Sunday school what they remember, and they will overwhelm you with detail. Among the things that they are meant to remember is their Creator, and perhaps more than anything else the purpose of that memory is to recall to the forming mind how we go from one side to the other, how we pass through the valley, great or small, or, as the black gospel song puts it in the immortal voice of Shirley Caesar, "How I Got Over."

The Remembrance of Things Past is not just the title of an interminable novel; it is the first work of a Christian, and one is never too young to begin it, for providence has been at work from the beginning; indeed, our very beginning was a work of providence, and one is never too young to remember the providence of the Creator.

Perhaps it is right that James M. Barrie, the author of *Peter Pan,* the story of the boy who would not grow up, should give us this useful thought about remembering: "God gave us memory," said Barrie in 1922 in an address to some college students, "so that we might have roses in December."

Earlier I said that there were two uses of memory that are meant to help us in the gulf between God's promises and our experiences, and this is the second: to remember what God's promises and intentions for us are. "I am come that they may have life, and have it more abundantly." It is God's intention that we should flourish. When people ask me how I am, I always answer, "I flourish!" It puts them off, they don't know what to say; but I am more than just "Okay." I *flourish!*

Now, it is a dangerous thing to say that to a congregation of American Christians, for by saying it we assume that God means the same thing that we mean by *abundance* and *flourishing,* and that therefore ours is the gospel of more, and the text of it is, "He who dies with the most toys wins." We know the gospel of secular prosperity: as The Reverend Ike used to say, "The best thing you can do for the poor is not be one of them." We know what "success" means in a sensation-saturated culture, and we want our share in it.

Last Sunday Dr. Willimon preached tellingly on the text "A good name is better to be chosen than riches"; and afterward at the door I heard one of you undergraduates ask, "Well, why can't I have a good name and riches too? After all, that's why I came here."

I am not knocking material success; I am not St. Francis of Assisi. Money is not a sin, but it is a problem—and that is why I try to help you to "solve" it every week!

For Jesus abundance is fullness—that is, the lack and absence of anxiety, fear, or terror, for those things have been driven out by peace, joy, and love. The abundant life of which our Lord speaks with special reference to his sheep has more to do with security than with prosperity. It is dangerous for a sheep to be fat and complacent and unable to move quickly, and the shepherd vows to protect it from itself and from everything and everybody else.

How do we know that security is not the same as wealth? Think of all the prosperous people you know. The merely prosperous are never secure: they always want more; they always fear that they will lose what they have; they live lives of perpetual anxiety. Look at the prosperous suburbs; look at the gated communities. Are they keeping people out? Are they keeping people in? The rich invest in security systems. This is not that state of nerves to which Jesus calls us, and which is God's intention for us, for God intends us to know what elsewhere in Scripture is called "fullness of joy."

That, then, is God's stated intention, and that should be our aim. Our ambition should be the abundant life that Jesus intends for his sheep, that peace that this world can neither give nor take away, truly that peace that passeth understanding.

How do we get it? We aspire to it, we work for it; we accept that in this life anything that is worth having is worth struggling for, and that by our aspirations, not by our achievement, shall we be known. How do I, personally, wish to be remembered? Well, I will tell you. I could list things the way that Thomas Jefferson did, but I will simply tell you that I want to be remembered as one who failed grandly, that I grasped at great, good, and holy things for God, and that although I didn't achieve them, I was ennobled by the effort; and, like Sisyphus, I wish to be imagined as happy in the process. This is what Albert Camus means when he writes, "The struggle itself toward the heights is enough to fill a man's heart. One must imagine Sisyphus happy."

I was brought up on a rather Spartan regimen in our little junior high school in Plymouth, Massachusetts, and we had a school song that I've quoted to you before. It's not in the present edition of the *Harvard Hymnal,* but I guarantee it will be in the next one. It looked at us young people in a world not of our making, with struggles not of our design and with failure surely ahead of us, and it said, "Be strong! We are not here to play, to dream, to drift. / We have hard work to do and loads to lift. / Shun not the struggle: face it! / 'Tis God's gift."

Well, does it work for you? You've had thirty-five minutes to consider that question—which, after all, is perhaps the wrong one. The right question is, Is it worth working for? Do you work for the Christian faith? Will you work for it, live for it, struggle for it, fight for it? We are not a work in progress but a work in faithfulness, and what we strive for and seek in Christ, that peace and security of the full and abundant life, sustains us even as we search for it. That is why they call it the gospel, the good news, and that is why and how it works.

Beyond Excellence and Fairness

Text: He has showed you, O man, what is good. . . .

—MICAH 6:8

Often in the choosing of texts it is a conceit of the preacher to try to find as obscure and unfamiliar a set of verses as possible with which to bedazzle the faithful and the confused. That, however, is a luxury for later in the term. In the beginning of the term, it struck me as essential to give out a text with which most of you appear to be intimately familiar. You've heard it before, you know what it says, you know perhaps where it is going, so at least we ought to start out in the same place and on the same page. Hence my text for this opening Sunday of the new academic year, the eighth verse of the sixth chapter of the book of the prophet Micah: "He has showed you, O man, what is good." Did you notice that I didn't even have to spell out what the prophet Micah said? I have just used that phrase, "He has showed you . . . what is good," because you can fill in the blanks, and I will give you a little help along the way.

Before we get to the prophet Micah, however, we must acknowledge where we are, and we are wonderfully at the start of another academic year. When the great John Finley, long-time Master of Eliot House, and Eliot Professor of Greek, retired some twenty-five years ago, he was asked what was the thing that he most missed about his active service. He answered, "The vacations." I have had a good vacation, and I hope that many of you have also, for the glorious thing about vacations is that they are merely the sets of punctuation marks that augment our vocation, our work that brings us together here; and the start of it is a wonderful season.

Last week as I walked among the freshmen of the Class of '05 at Freshman Registration, amid absolutely splendid chaos in the Yard, with everybody selling everybody else a bill of goods and everybody willingly buying it; and as I walked among the new students in the Divinity School, a little longer in the tooth but equally eager and pleased to be here, I was reminded of an apocryphal sign placed at a registration desk of the Law School at about this time of year many years ago: "Kindly check your enthusiasm at the door." Despite, however, the natural cynicism of the old-timer—"Been there, done that, heard it once, heard it again"—perhaps the promiscuous energy and excitement flowing around this place at this time of year are indeed contagious. People who were old and worn out, sad, flaccid, and flabby in May and June are now suddenly like watered household plants placed in the light, and the frustrations of May and the failures of June are forgotten and we are all freshmen, all members of the Class of '05; and we all have clean slates, sharpened pencils, cleaned-up Palm Pilots, and the resolve to get it right this time. Light, brightness, and energy are the signs of these days; we have a new president to go along with it all, and we are officially off and rolling, in our three hundred and sixty-fifth year, at 8:45 on this coming Wednesday morning. So, hurrah! Happy New Year! Welcome! Welcome back!

A few years ago, after a Sunday sermon I preached as a guest in Sage Chapel at Cornell University—high above Cayuga's waters, as you know—I had the pleasure of lunching with Cornell's then new president, Dr. Hunter Rawlins. Over the soup he told me that in his opening weeks as president he was trying to find what essential values held together a modern research university such as Cornell. What could members of the modern research university agree to as defining operating principles? He told me that, after considerable research and investigation and inquiry among the high and the low and everybody else, he could come up with only two immutable principles by which the university would be defined. Those two principles were *excellence* and *fairness*. Those were the only two values that even a quorum could agree upon in the modern university. He did not say this with satisfaction, I hasten to say, but with a sense of a weary coming to terms with the nature of modern academia, and the nature of the place over which he had been chosen to preside. It was not to truth or to beauty, not to goodness or even to light or to wisdom or virtue that the modern research university could commit itself, he found, but to excellence and fairness.

Now, we can all agree that everything must be excellent, for we are all the result of some excellent process: the excellent admissions process, which was excellent enough to choose you, and not him or her; the excellent tenure process, which was wise enough to keep us, and not her, or him; the excellent resources that we try to provide here; and the excellent environment. Who wants to concede to a "B" when we are entitled to an "A"? Who wants to concede to second-best when we are entitled to first-best? We all honor excellence. We are the best, the top, and arguably without peer. When Harvard searches for professors, the mandate is not to find just the best for Harvard but the best in the world, which to the distress of many an assistant professor usually means someone from far, far away. Excellence: we live with it every day, and it is a cold and demanding companion; and what could be wrong with fairness? Every little child in a moment of temper, when life doesn't go the way he or she wants, cries, "It's not fair!" It is the ethic of the playground, the ethic of the sports field, the ethic of science: we want to make sure that everything is done fairly and properly, which of course means the supremacy of process. Think about that. If process is supreme, then those who are ultimately supreme are those who control the process of fairness, whatever it is. Think about that when things seem unfair to you.

So, we have our standards and our procedures, and by these two we are defined. Apparently not well enough defined, however, if you read the *U.S. News and World Report* of last week, for there is now more excellence and fairness in Princeton, it seems, than in Cambridge; but everyone is entitled to a consoling myth, and they perhaps need it more than we do. Excellence and fairness aside, however, the university, and this one in particular, once aspired to something more than mere excellence and fairness, important as those are; the university once aspired to greatness, and understood that greatness cannot be achieved without goodness. It was understood instinctively. Universities in general, and our own in particular, once upon a time were unambiguous in claiming a moral mandate for what they did and who they were. It was no parochial accident that our founders claimed this University not simply for an abstract truth such as the "truth" one gets when two and two equal four. They did not claim Harvard for that truth.

Rather, the VERITAS that adorns every printable surface around here was a truth that had both a personality and a public dimension—"Truth: For Christ and the Church": VERITAS: CHRISTO ET ECCLESIAE.

There is a rumor about, and fanned in certain quarters, that this University has long since abandoned its ancient motto and is conformable only to VERITAS. That simply is not true. The seal by which the President and Fellows of Harvard College continue to conduct their business is still the seal that says VERITAS: CHRISTO ET ECCLESIAE. One cannot undo the past, and in this particular case one ought not to undo the past. The university—and this University in particular—is in the business of goodness and virtue personi-fied, and not simply in the bottom lines of fairness and excellence. Christ and the Church were an essential part of that truth to which Harvard and the generations of its children were committed. At least once a year, in a public place at a public time—and this is that space and this is that time—we enun-ciate this boldly for all to hear. Truth for Christ and the Church is not here by accident or by sufferance; it is here by design and intent.

Now, I've been around here long enough to know that this particular fact constitutes an embarrassment to many of our colleagues and friends who would shape the modern university into a "think tank" of neutral, international excellence and fairness. I remember a dean of the Faculty of Arts and Sciences, one whom I continue to count as friend and colleague and whom I have always admired, who, pointing to The Memorial Church from his office in University Hall, once said to me, "Beautiful building, but if we were starting over, I think we wouldn't put it there." We are *not* start-ing over, however, and we are here, and we're not going anywhere.

Indeed, as a symbol of Christian truth—the unity of mind and spirit and the assertion from our own tradition and from that of many other religious traditions now happily represented in this University—we are here to remind Harvard of a dimension beyond its own self-interest and self-perception. Our Puritan predecessors were no friends of the Jesuits, but they would have appreciated the Jesuit ideal that says that the purpose of an education is to combine academic study and personal formation with pub-lic virtue, public service. That is what an academic institution worthy of the name is all about—not about simply plowing up new information, not about simply storing up old information, not about simply keeping people who make new information; rather, the purpose of an institution of this sort is academic study, personal formation, and public virtue.

One of the reasons I wanted so much to have our tower and spire lighted at night, as we began to do on New Year's Eve on the millennium this year, was to provide a vivid, powerful symbol that we stand here to remind the University of a higher dimension and another direction. You should go out into the Yard at night sometime. The Yard is cast in Stygian darkness; there are little glimmers of light that reach only halfway down the steps of Widener Library—an appropriate symbol, it seems to me—and you can see only one foot in front of the other. The Yard is cloaked in darkness, save for a shaft of light that rises out of that darkness and points up into the heavens; and that is what this place is about morning, noon, and particularly at night. It invites you to look up, and out; and I should like to think that freshmen huddled in these brick Quonset huts around here, who are from time to time longing for a dimension beyond the tiny little blue screen of their personal computers, might find a greater light and a brighter dimension. I pray God that that is so, and if it is so, it is well worth the electricity bill.

Now, this lighting and this building are not to impress or overwhelm our godless friends, who are beyond being impressed or overwhelmed, and certainly not by the likes of us. They are not easily impressed by signs or symbols, metaphors or tropes, and this, therefore, is not for them. It is to remind *us* of where we stand and for whom we stand; and that we must constantly take a stand for truth, for Christ and the Church. That tower, this church, and our faith point beyond mere fairness and excellence. They make us aliens in an alien land, they make us stand out from the crowd, and they make us hold the crowd to account.

Well, I can hear you thinking that all of this is very well and good, but can we give a content to it? After all, metaphors, signs, and symbols point to something: what can we find at the end of this direction? We can, and we do, give a content to it. It is as clear as the lessons we have heard read this morning, and we already know what it is. The prophet Micah is called one of the "minor" prophets, which is because he is measured by the usual University standard of output. His is a thin little book, so it must be a minor prophecy, whereas the big books of Isaiah and Jeremiah and Ezekiel, the so-called major prophets, are heavy-weighted, tenurable books. Poor little Micah's work is a review or an abstract or an article, but in that little minor prophecy there is a huge package, a huge wallop for us. He tells us that God has made no secret of what it is that God wants from us. God has made no form of esoteric hidden wisdom or knowledge or gnosis available only to the theologians and philosophers; he has made it crystal clear, breaking all the boundaries. What does the Lord require, or expect, of those who choose him, and whom he has chosen? Very simply, he says that we are to:

1. Do justice

2. Love kindness

3. Walk humbly with our God

Do you notice that those are all verbs? They are not adjectives or even nouns; they are action words. We are to do justice, not simply to take justice; we are to love kindness, not simply to love the idea of being in love; we are to walk humbly with our God, not simply to speculate on the nature of humility. Those are meant to be practical skills applied to each of us by each of us, for all of us.

The people to whom Micah wrote these words were very good at talking and speculating and gesturing and making symbolic actions. Liturgical correctness was their great preoccupation. They could, and they did, put on a great show; but amid all of that they acted as if they hadn't a real clue what it was that God simply and clearly asked of them. That is why Micah virtually *roars,* "Don't give me your ceremonies and rationalizations, for you know what God wants from you: he wants mercy, kindness, and humility. How much simpler do I have to be?"

Those qualities were in as short supply then as they are now. No job description, to my knowledge, contains among its list of desirable qualities those of mercy, kindness, and humility. We are currently looking for a provost in the University, and nowhere in the *Gazette* have I seen those qualities displayed as admirable qualities in an effective provost, and we all know that persons displaying those qualities are likely to prove themselves temperamentally disqualified for appointment. "Too nice" will be the phrase generally used, as we proceed to the next candidate.

Some years ago I was on the commencement platform of Duke University with Jimmy Carter, I as baccalaureate preacher and he as commencement speaker, and we were both to be honored with honorary degrees from the Harvard of the South. Trying to make small talk with President Carter, I said, "My gosh, you certainly have earned the moral accolades of the century with your conduct as ex-president and all the good works that you do." He smiled rather sweetly, and said, "If all the people who respect me today had voted for me yesterday, things might have been considerably different . . ."—and different they might well have been. Just think about what might have happened. As president he exemplified mercy, kindness, and humility out of his genuine Southern Baptist piety, and what did we think of that? We laughed at him, and we thought him "unpresidential." If everybody today who respects Jimmy Carter had voted for him the second time around, the course of American history might very well have changed. That is probably why we didn't vote for him: we couldn't risk the change. We couldn't afford the change. We dare not have a real Christian in public office.

Religious values might compromise the educational mission of the modern university. I hear that idea often, and from very intelligent and powerful people here and elsewhere. We are in the "knowledge" business, they say, not in the "virtue" business, and knowledge unites while virtue divides. Thus the secular religion of the academy becomes "knowledge"— the making of it, the discovery of it, the preservation of it, and the dissemination of it.

Then there are people who actually believe that the more we know, the better off we will be, and the better kind of people we will be. There is the view that knowledge not only is itself a virtue, but that it inculcates virtue. Knowledge is moral, and thus the way to virtue, at least in our College, is through a neutral intellectual process called "moral reasoning." Many of our undergraduates are seduced into the notion that moral reasoning—a course that they are required to take in the Core Curriculum—will make them better people, and they are surprised to find that it does not. Had our Harvard students had the benefit of listening to Sheldon Krimsky give a Phi Beta Kappa talk at Tufts last spring, which was abstracted in the *Boston Globe,* they might have heard a question that frequently eludes them here. Krimsky asked Tufts's brightest and best:

> Are more educated people likely to lie less? To express more humanitarian values? To be more beneficent to others? To show more empathy? To make more complex moral decisions? I don't think so.

Smart people are not necessarily good people, for knowledge may be power but it is not virtue, and smart people often do wicked things. On any intellectual or cultural scale Hitler's Germany would be at the top of the art and culture sweepstakes. Art collectors, philosophers, connoisseurs, and aesthetes, the Nazis were also the scourge of the earth, and it was the conceit of their urbanity, indeed of their excellence, the "fairness" within their own perverted system, that inoculated them against the moral poison coursing through their veins. They were too "smart" to be wicked or to be defeated; they were too "smart" to need to be good.

Knowledge does not prevent bright people from doing stupid things: Bill Clinton, QED; and Professor Joseph Ellis of Mount Holyoke College, a brilliant and applauded scholar brought low by a simple, stupid, and unnecessary lie.

In summing up, Professor Krimsky said:

> If there is no equation between education and virtue, this has implications for public decision-making. There is no reason to embrace a moral meritocracy on the basis of academic achievements.

In other words, if there is no connection between being smart and being good, you might as well save your parents' money and go home, or you should ask for a refund.

What does all of this have to do with us? Well, everything. We Christians cannot afford to forget that virtue, and not merely knowledge, is what our enterprise is in this place. We Christians must never forget, nor must we permit our College or our University ever to forget, that knowledge without virtue is a destructive danger that produces arrogant technocrats who are a danger to all that is holy, hopeful, lovely, and true, and who must be resisted. Our pious ancestors understood this, and thus they dedicated this small, fragile College in the wilderness to a truth that was seen in and for Christ and the Church. VERITAS—that is, true VERITAS, and not simply correct information—can never be separated from the one in whom it is most perfectly and fully seen: Jesus Christ. Not everyone may believe that, but those of us who do must not be intimidated by those who don't, and we must be emboldened to claim that truth not only as our own but as one that is essential to the definition of a University and College worthy of the name.

Now, who are we—a small, promiscuous, and subsidized band of Christians of varying sorts and shades of conviction—to presume to change the secular conceits of a University far too self-centered and self-satisfied, and with nearly twenty billion dollars pumping and pumping and pumping away every hour of every day? Who do we think we are? Well, last Wednesday I spoke to a conference of Harvard student leaders—a "summit," they called it—that we were pleased in this church to host for two days in the Pusey Room, although we didn't in any way run it. There were forty or so of our most able and committed young people from every religious persuasion, chiefly people in charge of significant secular and volunteer enterprises in the College. They were full of achievement, promise, and idealism, and I was honored to be among them; they made me proud to be in the same University with them. Toward the close of the proceedings, one of them asked a question that said, in essence, "Why does Harvard get in the way of everything we hope for and try to do?" That was both a sad and an encouraging question: sad because it suggested that Harvard was not only indifferent to, but actually hostile to, the moral ambitions of its students; and encouraging because it suggested that contemporary students, easily written off as self-indulgent little corporatists, actually believed that goodness was a part of the moral agenda of the University. They knew they belonged to a "great" institution, and that is why they were here and not elsewhere, but they also want to know why the great institution cannot also be good, and an encouragement to goodness. There must be more to education here than mere excellence and fairness.

Those of you who know me know that I do not favor the takeover of academic buildings: I think my views of over thirty years are well recorded on that subject. Nor do I endorse rioting in the streets of Seattle, or of Genoa, or of Washington, D.C., or of Cambridge. I applaud, however, with all the passion of a radical establishmentarian—which is what I am—the cry that says that mercy, kindness, and humility, the essence of justice and virtue, must be at the center and not at the side of our educational enterprise here. They have been at our foundation; they cannot be set aside in the name of modernity. I praise God that we have a strong church to make that proclamation known; that we have a free pulpit that no one can inhibit; and that we have a lively and contrarian gospel to proclaim from it, one that reminds us that our future ambition as a College cannot be divorced from the moral ambition of our founders. Although they themselves were tragically flawed and did not always practice what they preached, they understood—as we must never forget—that the moral dimension of greatness was goodness. There is no institutional greatness without personal goodness. Think of that as you make your way through the Latin hymn soon to come.

So, we shall struggle on, you and I and our successors, praying for clarity and boldness as we strive to be not only excellent and fair but virtuous and good. Let us begin, as always, with ourselves. The question is not, as so many would have it, even in the highest places in the land, "WWJD?"—"What Would Jesus Do?"—for Jesus isn't here and is not likely to come back in the short order of things. The question, rather, is "WWJHMD?"—"What Would Jesus Have Me Do?"—and the answer is clear and no secret, and you already know it. Remember what Micah said:

> He has showed you, O man [O woman, O professor, O graduate student, O undergraduate student, O special student, O President and Fellows, O Reverend and Honorable Overseers—he has shown you all], what is good; and what does the Lord require of you but to do justice, and to love kindness, and to walk humbly with your God?

Think about that as you think about both our pious origins and our hopeful future. Amen.

Elementary Glimpses of the Obvious

Text: The hearing ear and the seeing eye, the Lord has made them both.

—**PROVERBS 20:12**

By your presence here this morning I take it that you parents and students particularly, and others, are curious about the dimension beyond what you can see and hear with your eyes and ears; that you are curious enough about the spiritual dimension to your lives and your living to come to a place where we talk about such things. Perhaps you are smart enough to realize that this is the only place where they will pray for you while you are here, and you may be wise enough to know, right at the start, that you will need all of the praying that you can get.

Well, for whatever reason you have come, by whatever sight or insight that has brought you here, you are in the right place at the right time. If your parents have brought you, congratulations to them; and if you have brought your parents, which is very likely, given this generation, a double blessing on you.

Of all the duties that fall to me as Harvard's preacher, none gives me more pleasure than the task each year of preaching the first sermon to members of the incoming freshman class. There is something very nice about having the first word, and that first word being not my word but God's word. I have been doing this since 1972, before most of you were born, and in some cases I may have preached to your parents, and in other cases to older brothers and sisters. In any case, I have been at it for a long time, I have learned a lot, and I still find it an exciting pleasure, I still look forward to your arrival, rather than swallowing a yawn and saying, "Ho-hum; yet one more class of Harvard students." I enjoy the energy you bring to us, the variety and diversity of your gifts, which are so well and amply catalogued. I like the chemistry between the virtues of an ancient institution and youthful promise, I look forward to seeing how it all turns out, and I can't wait to see what happens to you—how you will fall, how you will pick yourselves up, how you will change, how you will become more of the same, how you will learn, how you will forget, and how, when all is said and done, by magic, by chemistry, by mystery, by prayer and a little work, you will be transformed. We must promise to talk about all these things when next we are together, on commencement morning in June 2004; and if we run into one another somewhere along the way between now and then, here or elsewhere, I hope you remember that the man who spoke to you on your first day at Harvard wishes you well, and will follow your career with keen interest.

Between now and then, however, there is much to be done, perhaps too much to be done, for you may be overwhelmed already by looking at the schedule of Freshman Week. I am relieved that I am no longer a freshman, for I could not keep up with all of the requirements, all of the expectations, all of the testings, all of the social maneuverings that will take place between now and even next Sunday. Much money will be spent both by you and by your parents, much time will be wasted—mostly by you—and there is much to be learned by all of us. Over the course of this week—in fact, beginning this very afternoon—you will be reminded over and over again of how clever you are, how much distinction you bring to us, and how much you have already achieved, for we have more class presidents, more valedictorians, more salutatorians, and more National Merit scholars than is decent for any one institution to hog for itself. Your parents will be congratulated on having raised wizards, your high school teachers will be congratulated for having produced such brilliance, your communities will be celebrated for having produced such sterling citizens; and, secretly perhaps, you will congratulate yourselves that it is still possible to fool a lot of the people a lot of the time.

After a while, however, perhaps by Wednesday, if I have my week right, when you will have been tested to death, made interesting conversation for the umpteenth time over breakfast in Annenberg, and been duly impressed, annoyed, or bored with your roommates, you will finally want to get on with the real business of living here. You will say, "Enough of this foreplay; let's get on with it! I am sick of being oriented and prepared and pointed in the right direction: is there no journey to this journey?" Even you will have had enough of the fantasy world of orientation, for you have come not to Disneyland, after all, but to Harvard, and you will want to begin to test and prove yourselves against life in the "real" world—if anything about Harvard can honestly be called real.

It is about life in that world, this world, our world—your world now— that I wish to speak to you briefly this morning, and I will offer a disclaimer right from the start, the only disclaimer of this sort that you're likely to hear in this University, and certainly not from my colleagues. I make no pretense at profundity. In the first place, one cannot speak about the profound: it is to be experienced, and not talked about. In the second place, you will know the profound when you encounter it. I wish for you many such encounters, but this does not pretend to be one of them. Nor am I going to be particularly original in what I have to say, or clever, for I am of the view that originality as a virtue is often overrated. Certainly there are new things to be discovered, new ways of doing, of thinking, and of being, but in most cases they really are not new; they are just new to you. You will discover things for the first time about yourselves, about others, about the world, and about God, but these things were never really lost; they were there waiting for you to discover them.

I am going to make several stabs at elementary glimpses of the obvious, but that won't prove interesting to most of you. Why? Because you have spent your life avoiding the obvious. That is why you are here. You have all discovered things and done things that no one has ever thought of, no one has ever done before; and certainly no one has ever done them as well as you. The obvious is not for you. Obvious people go to Brown, not to Harvard. So, I offer you something about which you know very little, which is the obvious; and I say something out of the experience of your predecessors, out of the experience of life in this place, out of the collected wisdom and happiness of people who have gone before you, who might be able to offer you something that may be useful for your journey while you are here.

With these flowers in the chancel I begin this morning. If you have read the notices you will see that they are in memory of a man named Sedgwick—The Reverend Canon Harold Bend Sedgwick, to be precise and correct—whom I buried on Thursday morning. Harold Sedgwick graduated from this College in the Class of 1930. That means, if you have done the math, that he attended his seventieth reunion this last June, and not only did he attend it but he was its chairman, and had been chairman of his five previous reunions. He was as lively, engaging, spry, wise, and happy a ninety-two-year-old man as you are likely to meet, although, alas, you will not have the privilege of meeting him now unless you have a pre-determined train to heaven, for that is where, I'm convinced, he now is. While he was here he was full of the joy of living, possessed of the two obvious characteristics that I want to propose for you this morning: wis-dom and happiness. He attributed much of these to his Harvard College experience in the Class of 1930.

When you cast up the numbers and consider it, from this point on an indelible mark has been placed upon you. Even more important than your fingerprints or your dental records is the fact that you will from this moment forever be a Harvard person, for good or for ill, for better or for worse. You cannot avoid it, you cannot evade it: it is part of your destiny, and what you do with that is what will determine how wise and how happy will be the years that remain to you. I speak of a ninety-two-year-old man, out of the College seventy years, just to put into perspective for you eighteen-, nineteen-, and twenty-year-old young people the scope and the span of life, to put things perhaps in perspective as we look at these rather obvious virtues of happiness and wisdom, wisdom and hap-piness.

Now, the problem in not trying to be original is that everybody at Harvard *is* an original by definition. Everybody is singular, unique, striving for a rampant individuality, not to be confused with anybody else, and that is why by Wednesday you will all look alike, dress alike, sound alike, like the same things and dislike the same things. That is the price of originality in a community such as this.

I know that I cut across the cultural grain when I invite you to work not quite so hard at being original. There are expectations of and about youth in college—that you are to be the first in everything and the first in anything—and I know that I am on the wrong side of well-regarded wis-dom and conventional knowledge from the past. The novelist Thomas Mann, who wrote in *Doctor Faustus* about originality, had this to say, which is often quoted on occasions like this:

To be young means to be original, to have remained nearer to the sources of life; it means to be able to stand up and shake off the fetters of an out-lived civilization, to dare—where others lack the courage—to plunge again into the elemental.

Now, that remains a worthy goal for you, but not quite yet for me, for I want to draw upon a wisdom larger than yours and mine, and available to us all, to provide some useful experience as you make your way here. That is why I call this sermon "Elementary Glimpses of the Obvious" and take as my text a verse from the wisdom literature of the Hebrew Bible, the Book of Proverbs, which reminds us that one of God's chief gifts to us is the gift of the power of observation. Notice the text: "The hearing ear and the see-ing eye, the Lord has made them both"—and for our wise help and use. In other words, you will learn a great deal by simply watching and listening, by observing, by taking in, and by not necessarily telling everybody what you have taken in. This text, indeed the whole Book of Proverbs, gives us a pretty clear indication that it is God's wish that we get all of the guidance we need for the living of a useful, happy life. Wisdom in the Bible is described not as a body of secret, esoteric, highly specialized technical knowledge, but as a gift of God for the use of the people of God. Wisdom is not something available only to the gifted few, but a gift freely available to all who want it, to all who seek it, to all who pursue it, and to all who recognize it in the variety of its subtle guises and forms—God's benefit for the bewildered. A wise person is one who accepts that benefit, and pro-ceeds to learn from it and to live by it.

Wisdom comes of observation—the hearing ear and the seeing eye, and God made them both that you might become wise in your own time, wise in your own place. Observation means seeing things not simply because they are there, but because they are as they are becoming and as they can be. Observation means looking beyond the obvious in order to see what is obviously meant for you to see. The ear allows you to discern, almost as a dog does, pitches that are far beyond ordinary perception. That hearing gift, that listening spirit, is one of the means to wisdom. You will become as wise by listening and observing as you will by studying and experimenting, for one of the keys to effective scholarship is to see and to listen with care. That is God's intention for you—that you be made wise by the use of these tools, these gifts, and these resources.

Let us say, then, that wisdom is God's gift to you, and that wisdom is not an end in itself but the means to God's end for us, which is happiness—the second obvious, elemental thing that I wish for you. I suspect that if we took a poll of your parents and asked them what they most dearly wished for their son or their daughter, they might say, in the intimate clarity of their hearts, "We wish for our son or our daughter to be happy." Now, that is a strange and difficult thing to communicate in a large, vast, learned place like this, for Harvard is "brains," Harvard is "pleasure," Harvard is "smarts," Harvard is "fun"; and thus it may seem strange to suggest that the objects of your career here, and of your life, as far as God is concerned, are wisdom and happiness. I suggest, however, the truth of that elementary observation: that when all is said and done, wealth, power, fame, reputation, and influence all yield and pale in comparison to the ideal of happiness, and it is that that we wish for you. It is that that God wishes for you.

How do I know? Because we read two lessons about it this very morning, which made the point very clearly. In Psalm 1 we read of the person who is blessèd because he does not walk in the company of the wicked, who is happy because she takes delight in the laws that God has made to help her, and who is secure—that is, planted and rooted like a tree—because she knows who she is and whose he is. "Blessèd is the man that walketh not in the counsel of the ungodly, nor standeth in the way of sinners, nor sitteth in the seat of the scornful. But his delight is in the law of the Lord; and in his law doth he meditate day and night." What kind of person is that? "And he shall be like a tree planted by the rivers of water, that bringeth forth his fruit in his season; his leaf also shall not wither; and whatsoever he doeth shall prosper." Happiness is the key to that identity.

In the second lesson this morning—the famous Beatitudes, which I read—blessèd is best translated as "happy." That's what it means. "Happy" people, whose wisdom in the way of the world has helped them not to be overcome by the world. Remember: Wisdom is the way to happiness, and Happiness is what God wishes for us.

Now, sad to tell, Harvard students are not famous for being happy. There is always something to complain about here, and our students are magnificent in complaint. A survey was published not too long ago, in the *Chronicle of Higher Education,* on undergraduate attitudes, and it said that the happiest undergraduates in America are at Duke. I bet you missed that edition of the *Chronicle of Higher Education.* They're very, very happy at Duke, and our stu-

dents are apparently among the least happy undergraduates. I congratulate
you in spite of that dubious distinction. In the same issue it also said that
Duke graduates are most stingy insofar as alumni giving, and Harvard graduates are the most generous alumni givers in the world. There must be a
correlation between unhappiness and generosity; I will leave that to the
Dean's office to determine. Happiness may even be a suspect virtue, for if
you are happy, or are too happy here, it may be because you are not bright
enough to see what is really wrong, or clever enough to realize that this is
all a mirage and all an illusion. Thus it is better to err on the side of cynicism than of joy, or so we think.

Happiness, however, as Jesus speaks and writes about it in our second
lesson, is not simply the absence of pain, or obliviousness to sorrow and difficulty. If you listen again to those Beatitudes, you will see that the happy—
the blessed—are those who are able to stand up in the midst of the real and
the worst that life has to offer, and are not destroyed or compromised or
overcome. "Happy are those who mourn," Jesus says; "happy are the meek;
happy are those who are persecuted; happy are those who have terrible
things said about them. . . ." If happiness of that sort is naive, then Jesus
himself was naive when he stood accused before Pilate and Herod; Dietrich
Bonhoeffer was naive when he faced a Nazi firing squad within days of the
end of World War II; and Nelson Mandela was naive when he sang hymns
in his imprisonment and refused to deal in the politics of revenge upon his
release from Robben Island in South Africa.

Wisdom is not a bad thing to seek while you are here. It can be found
in books, and we have read from one such book today, the Bible; it can be
found in conversation, in which you will engage a lot during this week and
in the coming years; it can be found in the encounters between your minds
and those of others, and even, occasionally, from the odd professor or two;
and it can be observed in the Fogg Museum, in Widener Library, in the lab-
oratories, on the athletic fields, in the dining halls, and on the streets of
Boston and Cambridge and Somerville. Wisdom is not just information
with a foreign accent: wisdom tells you what you have to know in order to
make a life and not just a living. You should be zealous and jealous for it.

Wisdom, however, is a means and not an end. The end is happiness, and
happiness—for the person of faith, for the spiritually minded, for the religious person—is contentment with self and with God. Not self-satisfaction,
but contentment with self and with God; and one has to work very hard to

discern that real happiness, for what passes for happiness is not always so. In our country the entertainment and diversion industries offer "happiness" as a commodity available to the highest bidder. The movies, the world of MTV, drugs, drink—the culture of self-indulgence—all promise happiness, and none of them provide it. My friends in the movie business—"the Industry," as they call it—tell me that Hollywood, capital of America's fantasy life, is one of the most miserable places on earth in which to live, especially if you mistake happiness for pleasure or pleasure for happiness. Recent alumni statistics here tell us that our students flock to Hollywood, New York, and Washington, and that no one expects to find happiness in any of those places—or at least, not yet.

One of the reasons, perhaps, that happiness is not to be found at the end of a rainbow or in a city, or even in a school or a career, is that happiness itself is not a destination but a journey, not a result but a process, not a content but a consequence. It comes from the accumulated experience of seeking to live the good life—that is, a life that is good, a process that begins anew each day, which one is never too young and never too old, never too bright and never too dull, to begin again.

Wisdom and happiness: pretty elementary, pretty obvious, pretty basic, the sort of stuff you see inscribed on the public-library wall, and just not the things to speak about in your college essay if you want to be taken seriously. How many of you said, "I want to go to Harvard College because I want to be wise and happy and good"? Your counselor would have said, "That will not do. That will not get you in. They will put that in the 'interesting' and 'slowly reject' piles. You must do something else." If you are true to yourself, however, I believe that most of you truly do want to be happy, wise, and good, and you have some naive conviction that we can help make you so here in Harvard College. I have a naive conviction too that we can. With a lot of help from yourselves, a little help from your friends, and all the help that you need from God, it can be so.

At the end of their College career, in the spring of the senior year, as I walk among the seniors of Harvard College, I hear them over and over again, in moments of wistful nostalgia, in beery/teary evening sessions, say, "I wish I knew something of true wisdom; I wish I knew something of true happiness; I wish somebody had told me in my beginnings here that these things were available to me," and I am too kind, too charitable, too Christian, to say to them, "Somebody *did* tell you those things." I am telling *you* now that I am telling you these things, and you must remember them and clutch them to your bosoms as your own, because no one will give them to you: you will have to seek them out for yourselves. This church stands here to remind you that they are accessible and available, and that there are people who will love you, and pray with you, and work with you in the pursuit of wisdom and of happiness.

A proverb, we are told, is defined as a "winged word, outliving the fleeting moment." Well, I have three winged words to outlive these now fleeting moments. What will you do with all of the time that is now ahead of you, the open book, the opportunities that await you as soon as you leave this church?

Let me suggest three things:

1. *Get over it.* If it is your past that is dragging you down, that you are lugging in all those suitcases, get over it. Get over your past failures and frustrations; get over also your past victories and glories. Put those trophies in the closet. Put those citations in the desk drawer. Forget all the things that have been so vital to you in the past, and get on with it. The past is both a blessing and a burden. You are no longer what you were. Put away your past triumphs and defeats. Do not try to re-create your old world here at Harvard. Be prepared, be exposed to encounter what God has in store for you here in this place, now. Listen, watch, wait for moments of revelation and discovery, and, as for the burden of your past, whatever it is, get over it.

2. *Get used to it.* This is where you are. This is the moment. The elbows, the ankles, the angularities, and the awkwardnesses of Harvard are now yours and you theirs. Cambridge now belongs to you. John Adams, Theodore Roosevelt, Ralph Waldo Emerson, Henry David Thoreau, Franklin Delano Roosevelt, John Fitzgerald Kennedy: they all went here, of course, but they are *dead* and you are *alive!* This place is yours; get used to it. Harvard, for better or for worse, is what you will now make of it. Get used to these new demands, these new opportunities, these new temptations, these new discoveries, and these new hopes.

3. *Get on with it.* There is work here that is waiting for you to do: don't just talk about it, do it. Walk through the doors that have been

opened to you; discover the things that are here waiting for you. Get on with it, for it is later than you think. You are older now than when I began preaching this sermon.

When God took the children of Israel out of slavery, out of Egypt, and through the Red Sea on their way to the promised land, for a short while they were very grateful and happy. Soon, however, they began to complain and to fuss, and some even wished that they were back in Egypt, where they had had regular meals. The wisdom of that transforming moment was this: God has not brought you this far to abandon you now. The essence of faith is that knowledge. You have been brought here for a great purpose; you have been given eyes and ears—as gifts of God—with which to observe and see, with which to seek wisdom and to gain happiness. Using those gifts, using these resources, and using God's abundant grace, which has saved you so far and will preserve you for a great day to come, you will find that the journey is worth all of the trouble.

The Consideration of Holy Things

**Text: . . . but as he who called you is holy, be holy yourselves in all
your conduct. . . .**

—1 Peter 1:15

This is a verse upon which to hang the next few minutes, the fifteenth
verse of the first chapter of the first letter of Peter. If you think about the
word *holy* throughout the next few moments, do not think of it in terms of
some alabaster form of protection but as it is actually translated in the
Greek: "whole," "complete," "without any disharmony." "Holy" is what it
means to be complete, and formed in the way we were meant to be: "but as
he who called you is holy"—that is, complete as you are meant to be—"be
holy yourselves"—that is, complete—"in all your conduct."

We've had quite a weekend here in Cambridge, and those of you not in
Cambridge may yet have heard a little bit about it. We have installed the
twenty-seventh president of Harvard University with great and fitting ceremony in the Tercentenary Theatre, just outside these windows, and that is
why the enormous tent still sits there and why you may still see a few of
the ruins of celebration outside along the grounds. I watched as many
people with tickets looked for a building that should have engraved over it
"Tercentenary Theatre" and were surprised to discover that they were in
fact in it. The weekend of celebration comes to a happy climax this morning here in this church, where we are delighted to celebrate with God's
ultimate gift, in God's ultimate language: the great gift of music, and the gift

of musicians, of sound, and of all of the things that work together to make music as good and holy a thing as it is.

As a member of the Installation Committee, I should confess to you that there was long and serious debate in recent weeks, in light of the events of September 11, as to whether we should proceed with the full course of celebrations that had been planned. Given our state of national and international crises, and the lowering of spirits, plus the sense of anxiety and fear that we all feel every hour of every day, would it be unseemly to proceed with what would generally be known as "These Festival Rites"? Should we revert to the simpler models of an earlier time? Perhaps nobody would come; perhaps something awful might happen. Yet we went on with the plans, and I think we were wise to decide to do so, for afterward, at the end of a near picture-perfect day and nearly flawless ceremonies, I heard person after person say, "God, we needed this." We needed this hint of promise of the future, we needed the sense of festivity, and, most important, we needed the symbolism, the metaphor, the ceremonial music that takes us out of our small mundane world and our private—and now altogether public—anxieties and translates us into another realm. We discover that symbols and ceremony are not luxuries or fripperies or add-ons to be dispensed with at the first sign of trouble, but quite the opposite: what in good and ordinary times might be considered merely ornamental or indulgent actually becomes essential.

So, while some might think that such ceremonies are delusions or diversions in a time of crushing reality, anyone who gives five seconds' worth of thought knows that these sorts of things are not diversions from reality, bur rather reality itself. Beauty, symbol, sign, and metaphor are not the opposite of gritty reality: they are reality, and the only things that truly endure. We can look at what we thought was reality, for nothing could have been more "real" in this world than those two proud towers of the World Trade Center seeking to breach the boundaries of heaven itself. We liked them, at least some of us did, because they were arrogant, human, material, "really real" assertions of the things we think are the most important things in the world. They seemed so permanent, so utter, so absolute; and so much in control of our imagination were they that every year thousands of our brightest and best young people here at Harvard went down to work in their shadow, because they were what was "really real." They are, however, no more. They are a pile of rubble, molten steel, broken glass, and broken hopes and lost bodies. Their power and their permanence were only an illusion, and, as we say in the Burial Office, they are "ashes to ashes, dust to dust." They are no longer real; but the song goes on. The spirit continues. The things that we take for granted in good times suddenly become our most precious commodity in bad times. I do not wish to make a cheap parable out of these circumstances, but one must now begin to ask what is "really real," what endures, what lasts, and what is subject to the fatality and deviousness of time and circumstance.

I have a feeling that those who spend their time in places such as this church, as so many of you have over these last several weeks, know what is "really real," what endures, and what lasts. You know that what endures is the spirit—that which animates human beings and gives us the breath of life that allows us the greatest privilege humans can know, which we call the "consideration of holy things": the consideration of things that, when put together, are greater than the sum of their parts. Although invisible, they last and prevail against the gates of hell itself. We call this the "consideration of holy things," the contemplation of that which endures when all around is decay and disaster; and at the heart of all of that which endures is not doctrine, nor is it explanation: it is music. It is the sound of the spirit breathing through and playing upon the instruments that we make and that God has made within us.

Now, you may think that this is a stretch, even for Gomes, and a pretty big stretch at that, but hear me out; let me tell you why I don't think it's a stretch. Have you noticed in the last six weeks the rediscovery of song as an element of both personal and national identity? You don't have to be a concentrator in music to have observed that the one thing that appears to have been generated out of all of the troubles of these latest weeks is the rediscovery of song as a binding and defining moment. Remember the old phrase "whistling in the dark"? Well, the reason you whistle in the dark is that you summon a force greater than your own to deal with a force greater than you. This rediscovery of song has attracted the attention of writers in the *New York Times* and all of the journals of thought and opinion: and by song, in this particular case, I don't mean the music that we usually hear, the music by which the rockers and the rappers and the crooners, and all those overcommercialized and overcompensated Muzak makers make, whose tunes usually fill the airwaves and the concert halls. It's not that sound that I am talking about. I mean those old-fashioned songs that evoke ideals and images, in which people can join when they can think or say or do nothing else.

As I look out over the congregation this morning, I recognize that there are many of you who will be able to say, with me—but you will not want to—"I remember Kate Smith singing 'God Bless America.'" It amazes me to see that song come back long after Lawrence Welk has gone on to his great reward, and come back as almost a second national anthem. It is extraordinary. Let me give you another instance: I saw a video recording of the service held in St. Paul's Cathedral in London on our National Day of Prayer and Mourning, a service which Her Majesty Queen Elizabeth attended, and which was an extraordinary outpouring of support and sympathy and affection on the part of our English cousins. I noted, as the commentator revealed it, the historical fact that this was the first time ever in the history of St. Paul's that "The Star-Spangled Banner" was sung in that place. They found it as difficult to sing as we do, but they sang it, and it was an extraordinary thing to watch; I only wish I could have been there, for it could not be repeated, and nothing but song could have achieved that moment. When we had our own vigil here on September 11 at five o'clock, just a few hours after the full devastation began to sink in, thousands of us out in the Tercentenary Theatre sang "We Shall Overcome," the generations melded and bound together by a song that transcends all time. In our own services here we have sung that old stalwart with which my generation was brought up in school, "My Country 'Tis of Thee." We closed the president's installation on Friday by singing our choirmaster's—Dr. Murray Forbes Somerville's—version of "America the Beautiful," and we have found ourselves moved in inexplicable ways by the power of music not simply to divert us—which, alas, is often its use—but in this case by its power to transform and inspire us.

In this church, of all places, we know that. It is obvious, but one of the reasons it is important to mention the obvious is that sometimes people don't see it. We recognize music's power, like that of worship, which it serves, to "allow the hidden splendor that is within to be released." Those are the words of Archbishop William Temple—that music like worship allows the release of the hidden power that is within. Music does not bring something to us: music releases what is already inside, and that is why it is magic, transforming, and empowering. Music in this place, as we know, happens in forms both great and small, from a thundering organ piece to the most exquisitely crafted simple "Amen" at the end of divine service.

Musicians themselves, if I may speak as an amateur musician, are often far too busy to fully know what it is that they are doing. At their best, musicians make music in spite of themselves, and if they spent too much time thinking about what they do they would never get around to doing it. Thus it is a poet, Walt Whitman, and not a musician, who gives us in words what it is that music does for us and what musicians do for music. Walt Whitman, in *Leaves of Grass*, says:

Music is what wakes within you when
you are reminded by the instruments.
It is not the violins and the horns, not
the oboe nor the pounding drums.
Nor the melody of the baritone who sings his sweet song.
Nor that of the men's chorus nor that of
the women's chorus.
Music is nearer and further than these.

Well, Walt Whitman may have said it, but our own John Ferris and Elliot Forbes, whom we celebrate today, know it, for they actually practiced it; and some of us here were privileged to have lived under their tutelage and to have heard it and been a part of it. John was here in The Memorial Church for thirty-two years, and El in Holden Chapel. They each created or re-created ensembles whose joint heirs, painfully young to the eyes of many of us, sing for us this morning, and they have left a high and exacting standard to their two successors who carry on among us today: Murray Forbes Somerville and Jameson Marvin.

What is most to be admired in Elliot Forbes and John Ferris, however, is not their musicianship, admirable and superb as it is, or even their friendship, genuine though that is—a friendship that I have always admired as a model of collegiality. What is to be admired, and is therefore instructive to us as believers who have been onlookers and beneficiaries of their work, is that they each and both were in service to something greater than themselves, their performance, or even their music. They were—dare I say it?—reverent in art; and they saw themselves, I believe, as doing God's work on our behalf, work that St. Paul in another place describes as a "ministry and stewardship of the mysteries of God." They were, not to put too fine a point on it, in the business of wholeness—in, as we read in the Old Testament lesson, the "beauty of holiness"; and they were in the business of the consideration of holy things. It was their daily work.

The title of my sermon, and the phrase that has appeared like a Wagnerian leitmotif throughout, if you've been listening, comes from a musician, Thomas Morely, in his practical treatise on how musicians should sing, entitled *Plain and Easy Introduction to Practical Music,* first published in 1597. In it Morely noted:

> Singers should learn how to vowel and sing clean, expressing their words with devotion and passion, whereby [—and this is the phrase to remember—] to draw the hearer, as it were, in chaines of gold by the ears to the consideration of holy things.

That passage of Morely's was a favorite passage of Archibald T. Davison and of G. Wallace Woodworth, and thus it has become, in some sense, a testimonial to the kind of work that music holds in this College, in this church, and in Holden Chapel. What a rich and suggestive image: that singers weave a "chaine" of gold by what they do, not so as to draw the listener to the music, but rather to take the listener by the ears and to allow the music to take the listener to the consideration of holy things—the things that make us whole, complete, and holy. The music is the means and not the end to that sublime purpose, and in my judgment musicians can be divided into those who understand that and are good musicians, and those who do not understand and are bad musicians.

What St. Paul writes, in the second lesson that we heard this morning, about the terrible time in which his people live, is that we should be reminded that we are not the only people nor are we the first people to live in terrible times and to have everything that we hold valuable called into question, held hostage, with the ground shaking beneath our feet. We must remember—we of all people, as Christian believers—that that is the world out of which we came and in which we are expected to live. That is the world that Paul knew, and so when he tells his people how to cope in terrible times, he tells them to redeem the times because the days are evil. He tells them, "Don't get drunk, and try to drown your sorrow," which is what drink does. Remember, drink doesn't drown your sorrows, it only irrigates them. He tells them, "Don't do that, but keep alert, and be filled with the spirit."

How is one to do this? Well, Paul is never at a loss for a practical application. This is what he says: "And be not drunk with wine, wherein is excess. Be filled with the spirit, speaking to yourselves in psalms, in hymns, in spiritual songs, singing and making melody in your heart to the Lord, giving thanks always for all things unto God and the Father in the name of the Lord Jesus Christ" (Ephesians 5:18–30). What does Paul say is the formula for coping with terrible times? Don't have a debate about it, don't write a letter to the editor, don't sit on your dunghill and scratch your sores, don't go write a book about it, don't even preach a sermon about it. Sing! Make melody in your heart! Recall the psalms, in which the history of redemption has been told. Use that extraordinary gift that transcends all loss. This is what people who are broken and dispirited, fearful and in despair are to do: they are to yearn for wholeness, the unity of body, mind, and spirit that is God's intention for us from the beginning, and it is worship, which music most perfectly allows, that makes that wholeness—and the consideration of holy things—possible.

Over these past few weeks my clerical colleagues here and across the country have been asked about the amazing crowds that have filled our churches since September 11. What is it, we are asked, that draws the most unlikely people in such unprecedented numbers to these unlikely places? Is it sheer superstition? Is it terror? Is it fear? Is it the resurrection of some primordial, primitive urge to spiritual renewal, like the swallows returning to Capistrano? Is it just a cheap insurance policy like "foxhole" religion? It may not be true, people think, but if it is I want to be there. If there is a God, they think, I hope he will do what he is supposed to do. Is it that? Who really knows? I don't. I'm grateful, but I don't know, and I am suspicious of those who claim that they do. I have a hunch, a sense, an intimation that part of what has driven so many to their knees and to church is the profound self-awareness that we have been and are now deeply wounded, deeply broken, deeply fractured—and by that I don't mean the brutal physical facts of Ground Zero, vivid as they are. Something else I mean by this: that something within each of us personally, existentially, had been fractured; or, even more, that we are reminded that we have always been broken and less than whole. Our prosperity and our security could protect us from thinking about those things heretofore, but now we have been forced to pay attention to the crisis outside. We are also compelled now to pay attention to the crisis within, and the only place where that brokenness, that fractured state, is attended to is here in this church and in places like this church. It is as the old hymn puts it:

Father, in thy mysterious presence kneeling,
Fain would our souls feel all thy kindling love;

For we are weak, and need some deep revealing
Of trust and strength, and calmness from above.

I think that's why you're here. I think that's why you have been here, and at the risk of making a prophecy I can't fulfill, I think that's why you will continue to be here. For we are weak and broken and wounded, and need some deep revealing of trust and strength and calmness from above. You will not get that from CNN or the Fox Network of all-day-all-live-all-world news. We need to hear and to know the news, but that is not where healing comes from.

We are drawn by instinct and by disaster to the consideration of holy things, and we long to be whole again, to be recompleted, to be holy even as the one who has called us is holy. We long to believe that what God meant for us at creation is what we can aspire to be now: at one with ourselves, at one with our neighbors, and at one with God. We are today in the very busy and significant work of reconstruction, and by "reconstruction" I certainly refer to the reconstruction, the rebuilding, of the devastations in New York City and in Washington, D.C. Of course I mean reconstruction in that sense; but I also mean a reconstruction, a rebuilding, of a world that Woodrow Wilson—someone I do not frequently quote—once said would be made "safe for democracy." Certainly we are interested in the physical kind of reconstruction; but the most fundamental kind of reconstruction, the one in which everyone here or within the sound of my voice is dying to be engaged, is the reconstruction of, the rebuilding of—that is, the interior work of reconstructing—who we are, whose we are, and who we hope to be. That interior work is as old as the prophets and as new as tomorrow's scary head-lines. We desire, we need, we wish to be rebuilt from within, to be made whole and complete, at one with ourselves, at one with our neighbors, and at one with our God. That, my friends, is holy work, and it begins with what music best helps us to do. It begins with the consideration of holy things, the things that make a difference not only in this life, but in the life to come.

So hum the tune, sing the song, mouth the words, take the signs, the symbols, the metaphors, the analogy, the ceremonial—take it all to your hearts and bosoms, for when all has been said and done that is the only reality we have, the only reality we can depend on; and it is that which will help to make us whole and holy again.

Who Do You Think You Are?

Text: Do not be conceited or think too highly of yourself. . . .
—ROMANS 12:3

The apostle Paul is usually thought of as having been possessed of an enormous ego, a huge sense of who he was and of what was expected of him, and certainly of a huge sense of what he expected of others; and in his letters he is constantly concerned with the question of identity. Who are we? Whose are we? How do we know in the world who we are? So, in the twelfth chapter of Romans, which I would argue is the greatest chapter in his greatest letter, he offers some significant pastoral advice on who we are and on how we are to behave. Now, not all of the advice is summarized in the words of my text this morning, but a very good place at which to begin, particularly in this place, is where he says, in the third verse of Romans 12, "Do not be conceited or think too highly of yourself."

For a few minutes last Friday afternoon the eyes of the world literally were upon us in the Tercentenary Theatre, and for a minute or so—I hope you rejoiced as I did—it was wonderful to be able to escape the tawdry scandals in Washington and the tiresome malice of our public life, and for a moment to rise above it all, to be inspired, to be cleansed, to be moved in a direction in which we have not been moved in a very long time. The visit of President Mandela to Harvard will go down as one of the great moments in our history, not simply because he joins George Washington and Winston Churchill in having received honorary doctorate degrees from this University, but because for a moment one man was able to transform thousands in this place as he has been able to transform millions in his own country. The "angels of our better nature," to whom President Rudenstine alluded in his citation, were summoned, and were present. I watched all of us transformed: noisy, pushy, self-centered, conceited undergraduates and graduate students became quiet and calm, thinking absolutely about somebody else for a change; and my pompous, pushy, arrogant colleagues, all of whom are always fighting for every square inch of turf on that platform and elsewhere, were overwhelmed by the magnitude of the person in our midst; and for a moment we were all changed. We all went back to what we were by six o'clock; that can't be helped, but for an instant all reality was suspended in this wonderful kind of new reality, and for an instant we were able to associate ourselves with a man of such magnificent moral stature that the association elevated us all. It pleased me to realize that the young, raised on a diet of cheap and promiscuous celebrity, could at last recognize a hero when they were privileged to see one; and, unlike at commencement, when the unrestrained and competitive egos of the candidates for degrees turn the Yard into a barnyard, on Friday we were all as one, and our only thought and care was to share something of this great man. If you want to know the difference between Friday and commencement, it was that this was not about *us,* it was about *him,* and for that for which he stands. It was extraordinary, and those of us who were there will never forget it.

So, what is the secret? If you were the *People* magazine reporter observing this phenomenon on Friday, you'd ask, "What is it that distinguishes Nelson Mandela from the rest of us?" Well, twenty-seven years in prison and a Nobel Peace Prize is a good place to begin. That distinguishes him from nearly everybody else in this room and in that vast audience, but my chief impression of what distinguishes Nelson Mandela and allows him to stand above and beyond so many of us, from having observed him from afar for many years and up close for a few precious minutes on Friday, is the very simple, unsophisticated fact that this is a man who knows who he is. This is a man whose ideals are intact, but who does not necessarily live with the demons of his delusions. He has been neither seduced nor intimidated by what others think; rather, his authority—gravitas combined with grace—comes from that sense of knowing who he is and from being secure, stable, in his sense of worth and of being. As one of the old collects from the Book of Common Prayer tells us, "He does not stagger at the uneven motions of this world"—so much so that he can laugh at himself and allow us to laugh at him and with him, and he can sustain himself and his moral purpose under the most dire of circumstances. It is his sense of secure self, I believe, that impressed and sustained his fellow prisoners on that bleak and barbarous Robben Island, the place of his imprisonment for so many years, and it was that same sense of self that charmed and inspired all of us who sat or stood within his presence on Friday afternoon. He knows who he is; and it is God's greatest gift: to allow us to know who we are.

Well, that's all well and good for Nelson Mandela, but how do you and how do I answer the question of who you think you are? Who do we think we are?

Our text from St. Paul's letter to the Romans warns Paul's hearers not to think too highly of themselves, not to be conceited, and at the start of another academic year here in Cambridge that is not a bad thought to keep in mind. If we Harvard people have one reputation with which we must contend in this world, it is that we think too highly of ourselves; at least, people think we think too highly of ourselves. However, as with so much conventional wisdom, I think there is something wrong with that analysis. It is not that we who are at Harvard think too highly of ourselves, for we are too smart for that; it is that others think too highly of us, and why should we be blamed for the misperceptions of others? We know one another well enough to know that we really aren't as great as everybody else thinks we are; but because they think we are, we have to take on the burden of greatness.

We are not the first people to find that knowledge and arrogance are intimately related. Our ancestors Adam and Eve discovered that, alas, in the garden, along with a host of other disagreeable facts that have since not gone away. The Jewish storytellers who gave us the story of Adam and Eve would have us believe that all was well when those two were barefoot and ignorant in the garden, and that their trouble came when they learned more than they could handle. They thought that they could become as gods, the creation story tells us, for that is what the tempter offered them in the apple, and yet when they ate they discovered that they were naked; in other words, they discovered that they really didn't know very much at all. In theory they, with that knowledge, then should have lived in a state of perpetual modesty and self-abnegation, with a certain amount of regret at having been so adventurous—but, as we know, they went off to rule the world, and we, their children, are still trying to do so.

When St. Paul tells us not to think too highly of ourselves, he is asking us to remember that record, to remember that inheritance, which we bear with us every day. When he wants us not to be conceited, he wants us to know that we are *not* our identity.

Who do you think you are? Do you really believe in your heart of hearts, when the lights go down low, that you are in charge and have control, and that you are masters and mistresses of your destiny and of the universe? Do we really believe that we know much more than our ancestors? King Canute, you remember, thought he was so powerful that he could bid the tide not to come in. It did, of course, and the hem of his garment got wet. Hitler thought he was so clever, so smart, and so powerful that he could conquer and rule the world, and we see him in reruns on the History Channel. There are young men and women, many of whom are our own graduates, who think they can actually control the destinies of the world and rule the world and themselves through the power of Wall Street or of Washington. There are movie stars, moguls, and celebrities aplenty who actually believe that they are what their press agents say they are, and we know the folly of them because we know our own folly.

Conceit, however, is an easy target to hit—for we can always get a few cheap laughs and a few good rounds of applause in talking about the conceits of others—and a rather cheap shot at our question. You and I know that the posture of arrogance and conceit is usually a cover for a sense of insecurity, inferiority, and anxiety, and the posturing rather like whistling "Dixie" out loud while passing through a graveyard at night. We are dealing with issues of identity, and ever since Adam and Eve we have been a little uncertain about what identity means.

I recall hearing my old friend and colleague Dennis Campbell, then dean of the Duke University Divinity School, tell a story from this very pulpit of the funeral service of the last empress of Austria. The scene is wonderfully painted. Her splendid cortege arrived at the great west doors of St. Stephan's Cathedral in Vienna, with thousands in the streets watching its progress and thousands in the cathedral awaiting its arrival. When it did arrive, her majordomo took his great cane of office and banged on the cathedral door three times, demanding entrance for Zita, Empress of Austria, Princess of the House of Hapsburg, Mother of Sovereigns. There was a great silence, and the doors remained shut. He banged a second time, and repeated his words with even more force and fury in case those on the inside hadn't heard him. Again, a great silence. Finally, a third time, he knocked with his open palm on the great door, and said, "Please admit the earthly remains of Zita, a poor sinner who desires the mercy of God." Immediately the doors were flung open, and the service proceeded. Knowing who you are makes all the difference.

What, though, of that sense of identity that works in the other way, that moves in the opposite direction, which is not tearing down a false sense of ego and pride but is affirming a legitimate and justified sense of ego and pride? What about that sense of who we are? In 1896 a black man in Louisiana paid his fare and sat himself down in a railway car. He was asked to move because that particular car was reserved for white people and there was a perfectly adequate, perhaps even comparable, car elsewhere reserved for colored people, and all colored people were expected to sit in that car on the train. He refused to leave his place, and what is more, he sued. In answer to the surely asked question, "Who do you think you are?" he doubtless replied, "I am equal to anyone and everyone else on this train, and I insist upon being treated the same." He was of course to be denied and disappointed, and the famous case, *Plessy v. Ferguson,* decided by the Supreme Court in 1896, provided the basis for legal segregation until *Brown v. Board of Education* and the modern civil rights movement.

Surely, in the increasingly segregated world of the mid–twentieth century in South Africa, the young black Nelson Mandela must have been asked many times, "Who do you think you are?"

St. Paul tells us that we ought not to be conceited, and that is wise counsel, but we also ought to know who we are, and that is the essential counsel of our first lesson this morning. In the whole summary of the creation story the most important event in terms of you and of me occurs at the end of the sixth day, where Genesis 1:27 reads, "God created human beings in his own image; in the image of God he created them; male and female he created them."

This verse, Genesis 1:27, is the fundamental basis for our identity as human beings, and the particular basis for our identity as Christians. We are made in the image of God, and everything that we believe or do or that is done to us has to be understood in the light of that affirmation. We are made in the image of God, which means that there is that of God in every one of us, that every one of us bears the maker's mark, the maker's image; and it also means that there is that of every one of us in God. Now, just think of the radical implications of that. If you would see who God is, first look in the mirror; but that's only a partial image. Then look around: it is the totality of what you see that gives you a clue of what it is that the Creator had in mind in the first place. Any person who rejects another person rejects a part of God; that is the basis of the moral law. Any person who rejects any other person rejects not just that person but a part of God, and anyone who rejects God rejects the image of God to be found in brother or in sister, or even in nature. Because we are created in God's image as human beings, we are able to have fellowship both with one another and with God. Our identity stems not from what we do, or from whence we come, or from what we have, but from that and from whom we come. Our identity is not ourselves; our identity derives from the one from whom we come, and the beginning of all of that is God.

Perhaps you read, as I did, a marvelous short account in the *New Yorker* of a young boy who met his ancient grandfather and sat on the porch with the old man in darkest Appalachia, not surrounded by any of the sophisticated media of communication. It was clear through the story that the boy somehow wanted to communicate with his ancient grandfather and that the grandfather was more or less interested in communicating with the boy, and this is the exchange recorded. The grandfather said to the little boy, "Who are you?" and the little boy replied, "I'm so-and-so's son, so-and-so's grandson," and he made the obvious point that his identity was not in himself but in his relationship to these other people who in turn were related to this grand old patriarch; and he goes on to say, "I did not answer for myself, I answered for my people." We are related to all whom God has made, and thus, while there are people we do not know, there are no strangers; while there may be people we do not like, there are no foreigners; while there may be people who live in other places, there are no exiles; and there is no one beneath contempt, no one beyond concern.

Such an obvious fact has always posed difficulties for thoughtful Christians, because once a thoughtful Christian has concluded that he or she is made in the image of God, he or she comes to almost the opposite rational conclusion that nobody else could possibly be; and hence our identity and our ego, instead of allowing us to share our relationships with other people, force us to become exclusive of other people, and somehow we become God's "chosen" people—or, in this community, perhaps God's "frozen" people. Whatever we are, we have no truck with others who do not share our race or our class or our ethnicity or our language or our sexuality, or any other of the distinguishing marks that make us so interesting. Even the white Christian slave owners in America in the nineteenth century understood this essential fact—that we are all created in the image of God and are therefore equal—and so they had to define their slaves as less than human beings, for if they were human beings they would have to be treated as spiritual equals, and if spiritual equals then the whole sordid system would begin to fall apart, as surely it did. We demonize and dehumanize others in order not to have to accept them as the same creatures of a Creator God, and we learn our lessons only when we recognize in that diversity of human experience the presence and the image of that same God. God is not just *nice* to people other than ourselves, God *consists* of people other than ourselves, and so if you occupy a singularly unique place in the world you ought to recognize not only that God is there but that God is elsewhere as well. God is as foreign as the foreigner, as exiled as the exile, as different as the most different person can be. That is where the doctrine of God and the doctrine of human identity come together.

If you know this, if you understand this, if you realize in some moment of insight, of inspiration, that you are indeed a child of God, that you as you are now—with your thick lips, your yellow skin, your hooked nose, your life-giving breasts, your aging body, your youthful, vigorous body—are a part of the image of God that God intended, then you are empowered, you are liberated; you are not merely born again, you are created again anew, bearing the image and the mark of the maker. It is that which gives you power, it is that which gives you security and stability, it is that which allows you not to stagger at the uneven motions of this world. When you know this, when you realize this, no harm can come to you. Now, that doesn't mean that you are immune from all of the terrible things of this life and this world; it means that no *harm* can come to you, because the only harm we need fear is the loss of the knowledge of who we are, and if we know that we are a child of God, then nothing that this world can give or take away can harm us. We are secure in that knowledge. Nothing, nobody, can destroy you. They can lock you up for twenty-seven years, they can force you to hard labor, they can deprive you of music, they can humiliate you in a thousand countless artful ways, and yet you rule in the prison house and you walk out a prince, free on the outside because you have always been free on the inside. That is security, that is stability, and it comes from knowing that you are a child of God, that you are created in the image of God, and that it is God's intention for you that you should represent God in the world.

Well, what an extraordinary week last week was, when you really sit down and think about it. I didn't know, for example, that George Corley Wallace had died until Tuesday, when I saw the picture in the paper of his funeral in Montgomery, the birthplace of the Confederacy, the capital of Alabama. I knew that place very well indeed, for thirty years ago this month I began to teach at Tuskegee Institute in an Alabama that had been ruled ruthlessly by George C. Wallace. When I arrived there his wife was serving as governor while he waited to return to overt power, and his malevolent spirit still brooded over the land even as I took my students to see the state capitol and the birthplace of the Confederacy. So, on Tuesday I looked at that photograph with keen interest. Did you notice what I noticed? Did you notice the sweet and delicious irony of Governor Wallace's coffin being borne up the capitol steps by white-gloved black state troopers who were hardly born when he was at his awful power? Here was a man who had done so much harm out of both ignorance and fear, but whose last years were marked by the growing sense that reconciliation of all of God's children, black and white, finally was what it was all about. He spent the last ten years of his life getting ready for last Tuesday morning. While he was free he was imprisoned by his own demon and his denial of God's creative power in other people; and while our Friday guest, Nelson Mandela, was in prison in almost exactly the same period of time, *his* spirit soared because he knew that he was God's child.

In the Book of Proverbs there is a verse that reads, "For as [a man] thinketh in his heart, so is he" (Proverbs 23:7). The context is unhelpful, but the point is that it is from within that we form our sense of who we are. That, alas, is where the self-esteem people start out well but get it wrong: they think that we should think well of ourselves in order to protect ourselves from criticism and difficulty, while the Bible's point is that we must think well of ourselves because we reflect the goodness of our Creator, and that imposes a burden and not a liberty. Low self-esteem is not the issue but, rather, high expectations. We treat others well not because we are good but because they are created in the image of God, even as are we. We expect to be treated well not because we deserve it but because the God who created us all requires it. As Jesse Jackson might put it, "If you *think* you are some-

body, you will *act* like somebody, and you will *treat* everybody like somebody"—somebody created in the very image of God.

Relationship and identity go hand in hand. We have no solitary identity,
no being that is solely our own. The whole context of Romans 12 is corporate, cooperative, the parts of the body united in their specific duties for
the well-being of the whole. Our image in Christ is a corporeal one, as St.
Paul said, a unity in purpose—a difference in function, but an ultimate re-
creation of the unity of our original creation. We forget that at our peril.

Who do you think you are? What Nelson Mandela knows, what
George Corley Wallace found out, you too can know, for when you know
yourself to be a child of God made in the image of the divine, and that
everybody else is made in that same image, you will not be content with
anything less than that truth. If you understand and accept yourself as the
image, the creation, of God, then everything else will take care of itself.
You can bank on that.

Ignorant Worship

Text: Whom therefore ye ignorantly worship, him declare I unto you.

—ACTS 17:23

My text this morning is the twenty-third verse of the seventeenth chapter of the Acts of the Apostles, where, in the midst of a very subtle, very soft sermon that Paul offers to very subtle and very sophisticated Athenians, there is found a little twist of irony, a little sharp word stuck in the middle of an otherwise pleasing, euphonious, and sensitive speech. I have given it to you in the King James version so that its sharpness is not lost: "Whom therefore ye *ignorantly* worship, him declare I unto you."

This is a sermon with two images.

The first image is that wonderfully vivid account of the golden calf idol set up by Moses's brother Aaron for not a bad motive—the calf was fashioned because the people wanted something tangible to worship and adore—although the motive, good as it was, was not good enough. I hope you noticed that the gold that was melted down to make the golden calf came from the ears and noses of men, women, wives, sons, and daughters who were all decked out. Earrings and nose jewelry are nothing new, and the people's jewelry in this case was used to provide available golden metal to produce the golden calf. We know how the story turned out: first God was angry and Moses calmed God down; then Moses became very angry because the people he had led out of Egypt and through the wilderness had forgotten what it was that saved them, and God had to calm down Moses. It was an extraordinary enterprise.

The problem was that their worship was misdirected. The golden calf did not deliver them, God did; and the least they could do was to remember that. When the reissued commandment began "Thou shalt have no other gods before me," it was not simply to assert God's priority in abstraction or in principle, but to remind the people that God deserved priority because it was this God and no other who had delivered and preserved them. It was a matter of giving credit where credit was due; and remembering is the corrective to ignorant, uninformed worship.

That is one image and one confrontation.

The second image is set on that marvelous Areopagus in Athens, that hill where the great council met, the hill dedicated to the Greek war god whose Roman counterpart, Mars, now lends his name: Mars Hill. There is Paul, describing subtly the subtleties of Athenian religion and the altars and temples that he saw, taking particular notice of the one to the "unknown god." It is of that that he speaks when he says, in essence, "That which you in ignorance worship, let me now tell you what it is all about . . ."

These are fair questions about false gods, and it is at this point that most preachers of either of these two texts will usually, and quite wisely, say to their congregations, "Now, I want you to think of the false gods that you have erected in your own lives, the false images to which you bow down and pay obeisance, the unknown gods to which in ignorance or in fear or terror you pay tribute, to whom or to what you give more attention, devotion, and priority than you give to the God who created you, sustains you, and redeems you." This is a fair request, and this is the right moment to put it forth.

When I was an undergraduate at Bates College we had required chapel three days a week, with some of the most miserable preaching I have ever sat through in my entire life. Strangely enough, though, miserable as it was, there are bits of it that I still retain, that I can't get rid of; and one sermon I remember was when an assistant professor of religion—a Harvard graduate, needless to say—was giving a morning chapel talk to us and reached inside of his gown and took out what seemed to be an unmentionable representation in wood from some country in Africa. It was erotic and suggestive and quite visible in the chapel, and he left the pulpit and went down to the altar and placed it in the middle of the table. He said, "Well, now, this is the god that I worship," and he described the qualities of this rather priapic deity, and how effective it was, and what it did for him, and what it did for others, and what it doubtless had done for many people; and he asked us to ponder what we would put up in its place. Well, this was a small, provincial Baptist college, and that was forty years ago, so, needless to say, he got our attention. He also got the attention of the dean, and he never preached in Bates College Chapel again, I hasten to say. Perhaps, though, he asked a fair question. What is it—if *you* were invited to build a place, and endow and invest it—that you would place as the centerpiece of your devotion, the centerpiece of your worship?

Perhaps you will recall that our commencement speaker last June was Alan Greenspan, the oracular chairman of the Federal Reserve. There was a time, in the more recent history of Harvard commencements, when Harvard students enjoyed being rude to commencement speakers, or at least showing them that they didn't take them all that seriously, but not this year. No one dared be rude to Chairman Greenspan. Why? Because most of them wanted a job, and others feared that an annoyed Chairman Greenspan might wreak havoc on the money machine that is this so-called boom economy of ours and that one wink of his eye would send the whole market tumbling to an endless bottom.

So there was a great deal of bowing, scraping, and sucking up to the chairman—postures, I hasten to say, by no means restricted to needy students. My colleagues were shameless. The golden bull of Wall Street is a very attractive god: once upon a time students were embarrassed to say that they wanted to use their Harvard degrees to make money, and lots of it, as fast as possible, but they blush no more. Fortunes are made and lost and made again by the age of thirty. Money, however, is only a symptom of some of our other gods of human construction and devotion and ambition.

Success, for example, is one of those gods frequently seen and heard about in this place. Literature and life are full of accounts of those who courted and won success in whatever it was they desired, and who rarely, rarely lived happily ever after—for, if they did, there would be no occasion for poetry or drama, tragedy or comedy: "Be careful what you ask for," the brothers Grimm tell us in their Gothic fairy tales, "for you just might get it." Can this god-of-convenience, therefore, deliver the goods for you? Not if history is to be believed.

Money, success; now, how about power? How many times have we heard of the man or the woman who has said, "I aspire to power, and with it I will do good"? This I hear often in the corridors of the Kennedy

School. "If I could only have power," a man or a woman will say, "or get back the power I have lost, which is why I am here, then I will use it for good." Along the way toward the good, however, one must invariably do what is expedient, what is necessary: "You must break eggs to make an omelette," we are told. Think of the agony of a president of the United States—you fill in the name you wish—who wanted to use his power to do good, and found that he had to use his power to send young military people to their deaths; and he never got over it.

Money. Success. Power. Why do I invoke these tired old clichés like some Greek Cassandra? Well, remember, Cassandra was right. She was annoying, but she was right. I invoke these three clichés—money, success, and power—not because I am against money, for I'm all for it, and as much of it as possible, to do good; I am not against success, for it would be nice to be able to do what one aspires to do, what one is called to do and talented in, and we should encourage success; and I'm not against power, because power is better than weakness in doing good. All of those things are good things, and that is what I see and hear about all the time, not just in the College but in the professional and graduate schools as well; but, like the golden calf, they are not good enough, and the only way that you will really know just how inadequate and unsatisfactory they are is to have a whiff, a taste, a sample of any or all of them. Certainly there are happy and noble exceptions—and some of them are perhaps here today, or just tuning in—but it is so very easy in a rational community, a self-justifying community such as this one, to forget who it is that creates, sustains, and redeems; so easy to forget who it is who is our "Maker, Defender, Redeemer, and Friend," as we sang in our hymn this morning; so easy to forget who it is who brought us out of the land of slavery and into the freedom and glorious light that we now enjoy. It is so easy to forget all of that, and in the interim, like those people who so annoyed Moses, to create for ourselves handy-dandy, portable, manageable, manipulable little gods of our own, domestic deities that, instead of being the real God, become real demons.

The governor of Minnesota is right. Jesse "the Body"—now "the Brain"—Ventura is right: weak-minded people do tend to worship the first thing that appears to be bigger than they are; and sometimes they even vote for them, and elect them to high office. Religious people, however, the people of God, faithful people, are meant to worship only the one who can deliver, who has delivered, and who will deliver the ultimate goods.

Religious people are not invited to worship out of ignorance or fear, or out of the terror of the unknown. Religious people in general, and Christians in particular, are invited to worship on the basis of the record. You are not invited, you do not come into the house of God, because you don't know what else to do, or because there is a great vacuum in the churches that must be filled by wild speculation; you worship because you have something worth worshiping. You have evidence—demonstration and experience in your lives and in the lives of our people—that gives affirmation, knowledge, and content to the God who creates, sustains, and redeems. So, we worship not out of ignorance but on the basis of the record.

Who, for example, created you out of nothing? Who gave you the breath of life from his own mouth, and blew into your nostrils? Who protected you in a venial and vulnerable world, and gave you a name that is above every name? Who gave his own life for you, a ransom for many? Who comes to you and calls you by your very name in your moments of deepest anxiety and fear and frustration? Who is capable of giving you the only joy so utterly inexpressible—a joy that this world can neither give you nor take away from you—that you have to cry out, "Hallelujah!" "Praise the Lord!" "Amen!"? Who does that? Who is it who destroys the last enemy, old death itself and the fear of death, and gives you the promise of new and everlasting life? Tell me who does that, and we will build a temple to him or to her and fall down on our knees and worship him or her. Anybody else is not worth the time of day.

Do you remember—we didn't read it, but perhaps you will remember—what Moses did in his fury over the golden calf? He had it melted down and mixed up with dust, and he forced the people to drink it. Now, he was a little ticked-off, I would say; that is a little excessive, but here is the point: a god you can create like that so easily, out of material, is a god you can consume and destroy, and that god is not worth our time or our trouble.

Money, power, and success can do none of these things that we have just invoked. They can do nothing in the face of death; they can do nothing in the face of fear or terror; they can do nothing to change you from nobody to somebody and give you title to eternity: they can't do that. Money, power, and success, like drugs, can give you a high, a kick, a thrill, a sensation; and even if you can get all you want from that kind of kick or sensation, as with drugs, you need more and more. Drug taking is the satisfaction that never satisfies; and even if you can get all that you want or need, the sum total is death, not just for you but for all who love you and all who care for you and all for whom you care. We know that; there is no denying it. All of the money on Wall Street, all of the power of Washington, all of the intelligence of Harvard, all of the fantasy of Hollywood cannot deny that fundamental fact.

To worship these things—money, success, and power—to be seduced by these things, tempted and enraptured by these things, is to be deceived: it is ignorant worship. It is self-deception of the worst order. We believers, we Christians, celebrate the fact that only God can supply the fundamental needs of our soul, and we know this to be true not as an instance of mere speculation, but because it has already happened. We have heard with our ears and we can tell with our own tongues the experiences of our creation, preservation, and redemption. This is Paul's point in his sermon from Acts 17; and when he says, "What you in ignorance worship . . . ," he is saying that, concerning what you worship and do not know about, let me fill in the blanks, let me tell you what it is all about, let me give you chapter and verse, let me give you a personality, a profile, a place; let me give you some information.

Now, these Athenians to whom Paul preached were far too sophisticated to worship a mere golden calf. Athens was an intellectual city, a university town very much like Cambridge, with every possible opinion and two or three people to expound upon it brilliantly, and three or four people to argue with those brilliant exponents, and to move around from place to place. It was also a religious town, we are told in the commentary, filled with temples, places of devotion, places of worship, and Paul observes this straightaway. I thought of Athens when I visited Atlanta, Georgia, a few years ago on a book tour. On every other corner of Peachtree Street, that great central boulevard of many miles that runs through the city—the Atlanta version of our Massachusetts Avenue—there stands a large and impressive, well-patronized church. If you've ever been to Atlanta you know that this is true. Methodist, Baptist, Presbyterian, or Episcopalian— you name it, they have it, and in several versions and varieties. Such a plethora of churches leads one to the conclusion that Atlanta is either the holiest city on earth or the most wicked: it is hard to tell which.

This is the sort of thing that Paul discovered upon his first visit to Athens, a place equally filled with temples and places of worship, and with people who liked religious and philosophical debate. Every religious taste and deity was catered to in Athens, a monument to pluralism and religious multiculturalism; and even Professor Diana Eck, who runs the Religious Pluralism Project, would be exhausted trying to catalogue the varieties of religious experience in Athens. They had a temple in case they missed one, to a god they didn't know, just in case that unknown god had done something good for them for which they should be thankful, or could do something bad to them of which they should be afraid. This was the altar inscribed "To the unknown god" that caught Paul's eye, and describes the text for his sermon and mine: "Whom therefore ye ignorantly worship, him declare I unto you."

When he said that, he got their attention; but he had also elicited their attention earlier, because Paul, never backward about coming forward, had been invited to dispute before them on his strange religious ideas, this content-filled religion that was strange and new to them. They called him a charlatan, a fake, a quack, a babbler, a Harvard Square oddity, but nevertheless he had aroused their curiosity, and they invited him before their high council in the Areopagus to examine him like a specimen in the Peabody Museum.

What does he do? He gives them a stump speech or a stump sermon, versions of which he had used many times previously, but this is a stump speech or a stump sermon with a sting in the tail. He cleverly adapts his agenda to the interests and vanities of his listeners. He honors their religiosity: "I perceive that in every way you are very religious." He appeals to their sense of argument and debate, and by proceeding from what they could agree on together from a shared proposition, the existence of God—for them, many gods—he leads them up to the critical moment, he gives a particularity and content to their "unknown god," and says, "What therefore you worship as unknown, this I proclaim to you . . ."—which is to say that he will tell them what their unknown god has done, and who he is. He speaks, as their gods cannot and do not, of the resurrection; for what good is a god that cannot deliver on the ultimate need, alleviate the ultimate terror, and promise the ultimate reward? What good is a god that cannot do this? Paul speaks of the God who raised Jesus from the dead, and who not only raised Jesus but will raise all those who believe in him. Only at the close does he clinch his bait and switch, by asserting the one thing that his God did and does that theirs did not, do not, and cannot: he speaks of the resurrection. According to Acts, "Now when they heard of the resurrection of the dead, some mocked; but others said, 'We will hear you again about this.'" Doubtless they had to run off to lunch, somebody was meeting them at the restaurant, the family was anxious, there were other things to do: whatever their reasons, they said, "We will hear you again about this."

How did that go down? Well, this sermon was not an overwhelming success as numbers go, but Acts tells us that "some men joined him and believed, among them Dionysius the Areopagite and a woman named Damaris and others with them." When Paul here speaks of "ignorant worship" he is not calling his hearers stupid, for they certainly were not; nor is he saying that they worship ignorance, for they certainly did not. He is saying, simply, that he wants to give them a name for the one who has no name, a face to the one who has no face, a content for their empty vessel, a picture for their empty frame.

To worship the unknown, the vast unknowable, is what makes a Christian—so it may seem; this, however, may describe nature worship or mystery worship, but it does not describe Christian worship. We do not worship the unknown; we do not worship the vast imponderables of sea and mountain, lake and shore; we do not worship mystery, although mystery is involved in our worship. We worship what we know, what we have experienced, what we expect. We worship the living God because we know what he has done for us, and we say that every Sunday in the General Thanksgiving when we thank God for our "creation, preservation, and all the blessings of this life"; and also for that "inestimable love" that is expressed in Jesus Christ, who is understood to be the "means of grace" and the "hope of glory." We worship a God known to us by name, by place, by his deeds in history in our own life, by his present mercies, and by the promise that even death will have no final dominion over us.

We worship what and whom we know, and that is why we know what and whom we worship. There is a content to Christian faith, there is an experience of Christian faith that is not just wishful thinking or abstract terror or elegant theory. In the words of our text of three Sundays ago, "For I know whom I have believed, and I am sure that he is able to guard until that Day what has been entrusted to me" (2 Timothy 1:12). It is that astonishing knowledge and the affirmation of that commitment that stunned the ancient Athenians, and continues to stun the world today.

Last week I was interviewed by a chirpy young reporter for *Life* magazine, for what I am sure will be one of many tedious "millennial" magazine issues. I told him that he was a year too early but that I'd talk to him any-way, and he didn't quite get it, but that's all right; he was on assignment. The question he was told to put to me was: "What was Christianity's most sig-nificant achievement of the past hundred years?" My answer was easy: "Its survival; it's still here." He wasn't at all happy with that answer. "Tell me, what things has it done? What institutions has it erected? In what causes has it triumphed?" My answer remained that the fact that these astonishing claims of conviction can still be made and are made by more and more rather than by fewer and fewer people is an astonishing fact not only of the last century but of the last millennium.

Think of it: the Christian religion is a religion inspired by the life of an unpublished and executed preacher; sustained by crude and unlettered fol-lowers; contending against the greatest secular forces the world has ever known; surviving both good times and bad times; surrounded by such rival gods as science, economics, pleasure, profit, and power; adhered to by those who have nothing else; aspired to by those who have everything else. The Christian faith survives because it points to the incarnate God, the content of our faith who from another dimension invaded ours and allows us to put a name both to providence and to promise. The Christian faith allows us to say that we do not worship an unknown god, we do not worship in igno-rance; we worship the one who made us, who preserves us, who sustains us, who redeems us, and who comes to us in the person of Jesus. That is who we worship. We know who this God is, and that is why our God continues to be worshiped in spirit and in truth.

Innocence and Experience

Text: Behold, I send you out as sheep in the midst of wolves; so be wise as serpents and innocent as doves.

—MATTHEW 10:16

My text is the sixteenth verse of the tenth chapter of St. Matthew, the Gospel that Dr. Mullins read for us this morning: ". . . be wise as serpents and innocent as doves."

Two weeks ago, on the Solemnity of All Saints and All Souls, we had a wonderful celebration of baptisms at Evensong in Appleton Chapel. Janet— The Reverend Janet Hatfield Legro—and I love this sacrament for its ability to unite the whole church into one glorious moment, and she spent weeks preparing the candidates, one adult and two well-named babies and their parents, and we welcomed them into the family of God. The experience was great: just ask anyone who was there. It was so great, in fact, that it was easy to overlook the fact that baptism into the Christian life is not inoculation but initiation, and instead of hugging and kissing the newly baptized, perhaps we should have warned them, and said, "Now your troubles are just beginning." To symbolize this in the Orthodox Church, just before the priest admits someone to the sacrament he hits them hard on the chest, whacking them with his pectoral cross to remind them that the cross hurts and that there is a price to be paid in taking it up. Christians are not protected from the world, but rather are sent out as sheep into a warring world.

Perhaps we should have warning labels from a spiritual Surgeon General, which would advise would-be Christians that following Christ and sharing his faith could be dangerous to their health; perhaps I should warn each of you this morning that if you really want to hear the gospel and to take it to heart, and to take up the cross, and if you want to continue coming here to this church or going to another, you could be at serious risk.

The warning label is our text this morning, and it is given not by the Surgeon General, nor even by me, but by Jesus himself: "Behold, I send you out as sheep in the midst of wolves; so be wise as serpents and innocent as doves." Doesn't that sound a little paranoid? What's the matter with Jesus, anyway? Doesn't he believe his own press clippings? Doesn't he know that if you become a Christian all will be well, no troubles will assail, hassles will be over, and you will enjoy peace, prosperity, and honor? With such a warning as this, such a pessimistic view, Jesus would make a terrible American evangelist, for who would accept an invitation that almost guarantees personal discomfort? No one would watch his television shows; no one would buy his books. Remember what the lesson says? It says that Christians will be investigated by church councils, flogged, indicted before congressional committees, betrayed by their families; that children will rise up against their parents and have them put them to death—remember Nazi Germany, when children turned their parents in?—and that they will be hated by all because they bear the name of Christ. That's a rough translation of Matthew 10, but that is what it says: there are no promises of sweetness and light, no postbaptismal bliss, but trials and annoyances with plenty to spare. That is the warning on the label of the Christian faith, and you are foolish, stupid, and naive if you do not take it seriously and know that it applies to you. Oh, how I wish I had said to the newly baptized, "Now your troubles are just beginning."

It is not difficult to identify the wolves among whom we are sent, but of course it would be easier to identify them if they looked like the satanic wolves of our imagination: seven-headed beasts, dragons, tempters and temptresses . . . "lions and tigers and bears!" To a very real extent we are all Dorothy and her helpless friends, wandering through a frightening wood and hoping to make it home to safety.

Our wolves, our lions and tigers and bears, I suggest, however, are much more subtle and much more elusive, much more chameleonlike, and much more dangerous. Few of us will be tortured or persecuted for Christ's sake, but many of us will be in the great company of the bored, the tolerated, or the seduced, because of Christ.

If we hold to a gospel of love and an ethic of responsibility, if we crave decency and order, and if we seek to live by the standards of the prophet Micah—remember where he tells us that what is required is to *do* justice, to *love* kindness, and to walk *humbly* with God? a creed, I might add, sufficient for anyone and everyone—then at the least we will be ignored by the world, and at the worst, destroyed.

We are not programmed to win; we are not designed to win. You don't believe me, I can feel it, but remember Jimmy Carter? He actually thought that being a Christian in this most Christian of nations would be enough to help him in the White House. Did we admire his faith, his piety, his charity? We laughed at him, and we sent him packing home to Plains. That we have now made a saint of him, and he is indeed admired and revered as much for his work with Habitat for Humanity as for his presidency, in no way mitigates the fact that we thought him a sheep, we sent him among wolves, and we ate him up.

You will recall perhaps an old pre-perestroika Russian story of the Russian exhibition at a world's fair. The title of the Russian exhibition was "World Peace," and it featured a large cage in which a lamb and a Russian wolf were living peacefully together, a living witness to Isaiah's vision where the wolf and the lamb lie down together in the peaceable kingdom. The exhibit was impressive, needless to say, attracting great curiosity, and somebody ultimately asked the Russian curator, "However do you do it?" To which the curator replied, "Oh, it is really very simple: we replace the lamb every morning."

Parents know all about sending their lambs out to live among the wolves: parents want their children to grow up to be decent adults who care about fair play, who act honorably, who abhor violence, and who will not lie, cheat, or steal, but parents know that they are fighting a losing battle. The schools barely have time for education, let alone for virtue, and the television is filled either with invincible mediocrity daytime, nighttime, prime time, all the time, or with more murder and mayhem than in all of the novels of the nineteenth century. Is it any wonder that we appear to be raising up a generation of hoodlums, thugs, and witless victims?

Nowhere seems "safe" anymore, nowhere immune. Yesterday's papers alone told of a respected Mormon elder in Utah indicted for child molestation, sex scandals in the United States Army, cheating scandals at West Point, gambling at Boston College, and racism at Texaco—and that was only on page one. It is a jungle out there, and the temptation is great to withdraw, which explains why home-schooling is popular, for example. I can see why angry white males head for the hills of Montana eager to pull the road up after them; I know why many African Americans harbor romantic notions about a return to Africa or even to the now sanitized rural South; and I can see why Christians huddle in self-protection in their little Bible study and prayer groups, and live defensively in an antagonistic world—but whoever promised us otherwise? "Behold," says Jesus—and *behold* always means "slow down, pay attention, listen up, here comes a flashing yellow light," even though in Massachusetts we accelerate on flashing yellow lights, going even faster in a dangerous contact sport. "Behold, I send you out as sheep in the midst of wolves; so be wise as serpents and innocent as doves."

Must Christianity be so heavenly pure that it is of no earthly good? Is the Christian faith a battle plan for losers? Are we meant to die heroically so that those who hate and mock us may live profitably? Jesus is a practical man, and while he warns against the wolves, the wolf culture into which we are sent, he also tells us how to defend ourselves against it: we are to be as wise as serpents and as innocent as doves. In short, we are to share equally in innocence and experience. We cannot beat the wolves at their own game, but we ought to know what that game is, and be guided by a better one.

Now, this being a university congregation, there are those here of a literary bent. I know that you read—and that there are many of you who will recognize my title this morning as derived from a set of poems by that crazed seer William Blake, he who gave us the hymn "Jerusalem"— "And did those feet, in ancient time . . ."—which we sing and do not understand. He also wrote two sets of poems, together called *Songs of Innocence and Songs of Experience,* the one a childlike vision of the world as it is meant to be, the other a more realistic assessment of the world as it sadly is. They are rewarding to read and easy to get, and if you want to know more you should take an English course from one of my colleagues in the English department, if you can find one on Blake . . . and you will know that I am a well-read preacher.

Blake's point is the same as Jesus' point: you need both innocence and experience, both the dove and the serpent, if you have any chance of making it as a Christian in this world. Innocence without experience eventually becomes a state of pure illusion, and experience without vision deteriorates into cynical despair. Blake invites us into a creative dialectic between the two.

That is easier said than done. In my home town of Plymouth I knew a man called Innocence, named by his devout Cape Verdean parents in honor of that virtue that gave its name to at least three popes, but our poor old Innocence was better known in the town as the town drunk: so much for innocence. Also in Plymouth there is one of my favorite gravestones in the Pilgrim burial ground just adjacent to my house, a stone marking an eighteenth-century woman with the name Experience Mayhew. Now, today you wouldn't name a daughter Experience, I suggest, but then it meant somebody who would experience and know the joy and love of Christ, and because of that knowledge would be safe against the troubles of this world: our Experience died quite young.

When Jesus speaks of the wisdom of the serpent he is not giving us an invitation to cynicism; he wants us, like the serpent, always to know what is going on. Of all creatures, the serpent is the one most aware of his environment, most sensitive to his surroundings, most in touch with his circumstances, for his entire body is a live wire of sensation. We are meant to be aware, heads up, eyes open, mind on full throttle, not easily fooled or seduced by the blandishments of this life. Dr. George Buttrick, my predecessor, was once asked what he thought of fraternal organizations. He replied, "I am not an Elk, I am not a Lion, I am not a Moose, I am not a fool." We are not meant to be fools in a world where reality is determined by the manipulative illusionists of the Disney company: we are meant to be wise as serpents.

In our worldly-wise ways we are also meant to be as innocent as doves, and to some that sounds like an invitation to pious ignorance. Innocence and ignorance are not the same, however, and those Texaco executives whose racist remarks were recently captured on tape were ignorant, not knowing that the tape was running; but they were hardly innocent.

To be innocent as a dove is an exercise neither in naïveté nor in deception. The dove is the symbol of the spirit of God, and where the dove is, there is to be found serenity, reconciliation, and peace. When Noah wanted to know if it was all right to go back into the world, he didn't ask for a weather report; he sent out for the dove. When Jesus was baptized, God's favor was shown in the descent of the dove; and the Holy Spirit, the present tense of God, is represented in Christian art by the dove. Give me the dove any day; the dove is no dumb bird. In this church the eagle may be bigger than life, but it is the dove in that chancel screen that represents the spirit of

God in a shaky world, and if I had to bet on a bird, I'd put my money on the dove anytime, and not on the eagle.

In other words, Jesus tells us that to survive in this world in order to get to the next—and that, after all, is the whole point—we need to know what is going on and not be overwhelmed by it; and to do that we need to live all of the time in a divine and creative dialogue between innocence, the first and last love of our faith, and experience, by which we learn what we need to know.

Innocence and experience. Well, you're all practical, experienced consumers pinching the divine fruit, and you want to know, "Will it work? Is there a warranty?" Jesus says, "When they persecute you in one town, flee to the next. . . . ," and it doesn't sound as if he expects success. He also says, "He that shall endure to the end will be saved." In other words, in the words of the old aphorism, we are not meant to be successful but we are meant to be faithful, and the faithful will be saved. The experience of the love and the knowledge of God, the sure and certain knowledge that we are loved and known by God, is at the heart of our innocence; and against that in the long run—the only run that counts—neither the gates of hell, nor all of the subtle wolves of this tedious world, can prevail.

So, when you leave The Memorial Church to go out to brunch or out to lunch, and on out into the world, remember that you are sent as sheep in the midst of wolves, and be wise as serpents and innocent as doves, for Christ's sake.

Profit and Loss

Text: **For what does it profit a man, to gain the whole world and forfeit his life?**

—MARK 8:36, RSV

For what shall it profit a man, if he shall gain the whole world, and lose his own soul?

—MARK 8:36, KJV

What does anyone gain by winning the whole world at the cost of his life?

—MARK 8:36, REB

"If any man would come after me, let him deny himself and take up his cross and follow me. For whoever would save his life will lose it; and whoever loses his life for my sake and the gospel's will save it. For what does it profit a man, to gain the whole world and forfeit his life?"

Jesus needs a very good public-relations expert, I think, because these words are hardly a gilded or a charming invitation to the Christian life. They talk about profit and loss, risk and misadventure, danger and sacrifice, self-lessness and selfishness; and given what Jesus says about himself and about those who would follow him, it is amazing that there are any Christians around at all. Maybe it is that Christians simply don't believe what Jesus says; maybe it is a kind of wishful thinking, that perhaps these words were interpolated into the text by a later tenacious, overzealous editor, somebody who had a bad morning and decided just to stick these words in. It would be nice to imagine that these so-called hard sayings of Jesus are really not the words of Jesus but of some editor. Perhaps the Jesus Seminar can relieve Jesus of the burden of his own words, and us too, for that matter, and we don't have to take them seriously.

The selling of the gospel—its promoting and marketing, I suppose we should say—could use a little help, for it ought to be an easier enterprise, don't you think? It ought to say, "Look, if you follow me, all will be well. I will satisfy all your desires, I will comfort all your needs, I will take care of all your anxieties. The job, the concentration, the spouse, the pension plan you so desire—I will provide these for you. All you have to do is on occasion do me the favor of coming to church or of asking someone else to go to church; that's all you have to do." Anybody but the evangelists could sell the gospel in a better way than the gospel sells itself; but Jesus says, "If anybody would follow me . . ."—that is, if anybody would take my name—he or she must give himself or herself up, take on the cross daily, and follow me. That is hardly the kind of invitation people are ready and willing to accept, and that is why that invitation is not always the one that is offered, but rather what is offered is the one that I earlier described as a way to an anxiety-free, trouble-free, stress-free, loss-free, risk-free life: "Do this and all these things will be yours, and then some." Jesus, however, says, "What does it profit a man if he should he gain all of this and forfeit his life?" That's what he says, and that, I believe, is what he means.

Instead of a gilded invitation, then, Jesus issues a warning: "If anyone would come after me, let him deny himself and take up his cross and follow me."

So, it seems to me that at the beginning of our three hundred sixty-first academic year we should be warned not of the delights and seductions of the Christian faith but of the dangers of the Christian *life*, of the risk of following Christ, of the cost we are expected to bear, and of the loss we are required to endure. We are meant to consider what Dietrich Bonhoeffer once called "the cost of discipleship," and if anyone would know what that was, Bonhoeffer, from his prison cell, would, who paid for it with his life.

Now, this admittedly is, as they say across the river in the Business School, a "high-risk strategy." If people really knew the cost of discipleship, of what it takes to follow Jesus and to take up one's own cross, they very well might not want to take up the offer. We should accentuate the positive, look on the bright side, and seduce people into faith and belief: feed them and flatter them is the formula of Protestant Christianity, by and large; feed you lots of food—coffee at the coffee hour, spaghetti at the ecumenical forum, potluck at the potluck supper—and flatter you by saying how fortunate it is for *God* that you consider following him. That's the formula, but that is not what the gospel says. That is the Madison Avenue approach to evangelism, and too often it is the way of the church. I even thought about it myself, for at the start of the academic year, with so many of you at a teachable and vulnerable moment, I should be selling you the goods about Jesus and the Christian faith, and suckering you into coming to church. I should seize this opportunity to get you while you are paying attention, and reel you in on the hook of the good news at no cost and on easy terms.

We certainly want you to come back, we certainly want you for Christ, and we certainly want you to want Christ for yourselves, but we most of all want you to want all of this on Christ's terms and not on your own, and those terms are clearly stated in the lesson from St. Mark. There is a cost to Christ; there is risk—that is, the risk of losing your investment; and there is also the risk that you might gain less than the real thing, thinking that you have made a profit when in fact you have sustained a loss.

So many people are "won" to the gospel on the basis of a quick and surefire investment that will always pay off dividends: "If I follow Jesus, all will be well," they think. "I will do well in school, I will meet a nice life partner, my doubts will be diminished, and I will discover that ultimate truth of modern society—that God, like life, is 'nice.'" If all that were so, then my text for today would be no problem. I know many Christians, in fact, who bought the gospel on easy terms. Perhaps they were discouraged at a vital moment in school or in life, and the gospel sounded like a quick loan with low, easy payments. It seemed to work for a while, and then when the going got really rough those terms weren't so easy anymore and there was more suffering than satisfaction, more pain than gain. "Where is God when I need God?" goes the cry. "I have more trouble now than I had before I became a Christian."

That is usually true, and I am sure that many of you will agree. At least when you are not a Christian you don't have expectations that the Christian faith is supposed to meet. Many, however, when they become Christian, imagine that their problems are over, their troubles solved, and that Jesus, who saved Peter from getting in over his head, will do the same for them—and for me—every time. What else explains the marked increase

in attendance at daily Morning Prayers during the winter and spring reading and examination periods?

The American humorist Josh Billings once said that ignorance is not
what a man doesn't know, ignorance is what a man "knows" that isn't true.
That, we might add, is a special kind of ignorance reserved for people like
ourselves who think that we know it all: when the going gets rough and we
are messed up and tossed about, we discover how very little we know that
is really true.

One of the things that we think we know, in a community such as this,
is that our learning will make us free, even happy, and possibly rich as well.
There are many, and perhaps some of you, who in hearing the famous verse
of our text this morning—"For what does it profit a man [/ woman] if he
[/she] shall gain the whole world and lose his [/ her] soul?"—would reply
with some worldly analysis such as this: "I don't know much about the
soul, I'll leave that to later. I do know quite a bit about the world, and I
know that to win in this world is the only game in town." For many there
is that sense that once they have gained the world, *then* they can worry
about whether or not it is worth having. The argument here is very simple:
if I don't have it I can't give it away, so let me get as much of it as possible as
quickly as possible, and *then* I can give it away. *Then* we can consider the
implications of this text.

We are not the only college or university at the start of a new academic
year in this season, and last week I went off to speak at the opening convo-
cation of a small Christian college in South Carolina, Wofford College,
founded in 1855 by pious Methodists who wanted to produce godly citizens, and set about doing so with a will. They were quite successful, and
had the largest endowment of any new college in the nation until in a fit of
misplaced political idealism, and just about six weeks before Appomattox,
the trustees of the college invested its entire endowment in Confederate
war bonds. One of the professors said to me last week, "We have always
been a little cautious about misplaced enthusiasms, ever since then."
Rightly so, but the virtue of that small college is that it has tried, against
great odds, to instill in its young an enthusiasm for the life of the mind and
the heart that is not directly related to vocational success; and this has
proven to be a difficult but worthwhile continuing struggle. "We want," say
the teachers, "to introduce our students to art, music, and literature, the glories of the classical world and the critical mind, the place where the heart

meets the head, while they—the students today—want to know how useful all of this is in getting a job."

Now, I have nothing against vocation; I am not antivocational; I hope that everyone has a job. I am certainly glad that I have a job, and a wonderful job; but a job, my dear friends, is not a *life*.

One of my freshman advisees about fifteen years ago came into my office to have his first study card signed, and he showed me in charts and graphs on beautifully unspoiled paper how he had orchestrated the remaining three and a half years of his college life: all twenty-eight remaining courses had been chosen, and an ironclad program of useful study undertaken and mapped out. He was so pleased with himself, that he had covered all his bases and would never again have to think about what to do while he was here at Harvard. I asked him if he had considered the possibility that either he or the catalog might change during the years, as both often do, and that perhaps some of his chosen courses would not be on offer, that perhaps the professors might retire or go on leave or change their minds, or die. He hadn't. Then I noticed that among all of the courses available to him he had chosen no humanities courses apart from those required—no music, no fine arts, no literature. Wistfully he said, "Oh, I wish I had time for those, but my parents and I regard them as luxuries. I want to be practical with my life; I can do all of that later."

The nice thing about being a freshman is that you can actually learn from your ignorance, and this student in later college years discovered worlds he could not have imagined; and within the limits permitted by our curriculum he actually began to learn how to make a life and not just a living.

We have been speaking in terms of risk and cost, about the risk of losing something and the cost of gaining something. Our venture capitalists understand this: if they risk nothing they gain nothing and they could lose everything. In the gospel we are told that if we are not prepared to risk everything we risk gaining nothing and in fact losing everything. "To save all we must risk all," as Schiller wrote.

How do we apply this, especially at the beginning of a new year, especially in the context of the Christian gospel?

First, we must recognize that our ambitions are in conflict: we desire the safety of the material, consumerist world *and* we want to know the meaning and joy of life. We must recognize that our temptation is always to choose the easier and more accessible of two difficult and opposite ways: we live in conflict.

Second, we must recognize that we are all too often prepared to accept second best, and to live with mediocrity and with quiet desperation. We are too lazy to do otherwise. We think that we know what we must accept, and we put our aspirations on hold. How often do I hear from alumni at reunion time: "How I wish I had done 'A' rather than 'B'! How I wish I had asserted my true desires and taken the risk: my present state has been bought at a very high price."

Third, we must accept the fact that what the world has to offer is not enough. Cardinal Newman once wrote that to the unbeliever the world seems permanent and secure and invincible, and the individual solitary, fleeting, and insignificant; but to the believer the world is a temporary illusion, and the more glittery and powerful it seems the more illusive and elusive it really is. For the believer eternity is the goal in the mind and heart of Christians. This earth, with its demands and opportunities, is merely where we happen to be for the time being.

I have promised both you and myself no glib reflections on the deaths of the past two weekends, those of Mother Teresa and of Diana, Princess of Wales, but I can only observe, in the context of Cardinal Newman's observation and of this third point, that the outpouring of therapeutic grief at the death of the Princess of Wales was a mourning not so much for her as for the ultimately unsatisfying investment in this life, where even beauty and glamour and virtue all fade away and all end up the same. It is the death of an illusion that most distresses those of us who live in a world of illusion.

Thus, only the impossible becomes even remotely possible, for ". . . whoever would save his life will lose it; and whoever loses his life for my sake and the gospel's will save it. For what does it profit a man [or a woman] to gain the whole world and forfeit his life?"

Life here is not just existence but purpose and meaning that goes beyond where we are, what we do, and what we have. It is into that life, with its risks of profit and loss, with all of its threats, ambiguities, and opportunities, that Jesus invites us; and I reiterate his invitation at the beginning of our three hundred sixty-first year together here in Cambridge.

Let this be the year in which you aspire to make a life, and not just a living. Amen.

Secondhand Religion

Text: And when he saw their faith he said, "Man, your sins are forgiven you."

—LUKE 5:20

The New Testament is full of healing and miracle stories, but I suggest that with the possible exception of the raising of Lazarus from the dead—and we all have to admit that that's a pretty amazing story—this one in the early chapters of Luke's Gospel is perhaps the most vivid of all. Anyone who has ever been to Sunday school can still see in the mind's eye the image of those men carrying their crippled friend on his pallet, his litter, his bed, to be healed by Jesus. Word had spread that a healer was here, that Jesus could make the lame walk, the dumb speak, the blind see, and even those with sciatica cured. He could heal, the men had heard, and they were eager for their friend to have a chance at a new life. They had heard that the healer was in the neighborhood, and so, as the gospel tells us, they took their friend, litter and all, to the house where Jesus was teaching. Everyone else, however, in the neighborhood had had the same idea, and everyone in the neighborhood was present. You cannot keep a good thing secret, everyone wants to be a part of it, and as we heard in the lesson, there was no room in the house and no way in, for like any good free show, the place was oversubscribed.

Here comes the good part: the friends, not to be deterred on behalf of their friend, climbed up onto the roof, broke open the tiles, and lowered the litter down into the midst of the room. The inaccessible was made accessible, and he who had been excluded was now the center of attention and on the inside—sort of a *deus ex machina*—and, lowered like an angel, he lay literally at Jesus' feet in the midst of the crowd, and beneath the ruined roof. This is a wonderful story, a miracle, and we could stop right here, for what more is there to say? What more is there to do? What more is there to know?

Here, however, the story goes off the rails. The narrative does not work according to plan or expectation; it doesn't follow a pattern. Presumably the man was brought to be healed of his paralysis, the disease that had kept him on his back and out of work, and that had made him dependent upon the consideration of his friends and on the kindness of strangers, and we all know that it is not a good thing to have to be dependent upon one's friends or on the kindness of strangers. What happens next? Jesus does not "heal" him, at least not in the conventional sense, or at least not yet. Rather, he forgives the man his sins, saying, "Man, your sins are forgiven you." Instead of a healing, the man gets a pardon. Only after some theological wrangling and toward the close of the story does Jesus utter those famous words, "Rise, take up your bed and go home"; and, wonder of wonder, the man does: "And immediately he rose before them, and took up that on which he lay, and went home, glorifying God" (Luke 5:25). Luke says that the crowd was impressed: who wouldn't be? "And amazement seized them all, and they glorified God and were filled with awe, saying, 'We have seen strange things today'" (Luke 5:26).

When the blind are given their sight, when the deaf hear, when the lame walk and the dumb speak, these are miracles we understand and appreciate; we are impressed. When the Elmer Gantrys of this world, the television faith healers, and the tent-revival wonder-workers do their thing, it is not to forgive sin or to give out blessings; it is to overcome the frailties of the flesh, to impress us, to turn the crippled into leapers and walkers.

Now, I do not wish to take anything away from the power of the healing; I am not trying to deconstruct the scripture: the man was grateful, the crowd impressed, and I with you remain amazed.

When I went to a chiropractor early this summer in a desperate effort to find a cure for my aching back, and when after some cracking and crunching my pain was gone, I forgot all of the horror tales that I had heard in my youth about chiropractors and I rejoiced; and, for a fee, I continue to rejoice in my new and improved state. I am not against healing or miracles, and I don't want to take any of the wonder away from this passage, but this story is not about *healing,* it is about *faith,* and secondhand faith at that, or secondhand religion. If you look carefully at the passage and do not fast-forward through the Bible to get to the interesting bits, you will discover the strange words of Jesus at the heart of the story. Luke says, "When he saw their *faith* he said, 'Man, your sins are forgiven you.'" The man is first forgiven and then healed because Jesus is impressed with the faith of those who had brought the man to his feet. It was not the faith of the man forgiven and healed that mattered here, for we know nothing of it. We know nothing of the man: he doesn't say, "Heal me!" or "Forgive me," or "I'm sorry," or "I repent," or "I believe." He is the silent witness. What speaks volumes, loud enough to get the attention of Jesus, and his forgiveness and healing as well, is the faith of his friends: and this is where you and I come in.

We should linger just a bit to say a good word for secondhand religion, for secondhand faith, and for what the gospel is saying and doing. We could speculate, wonder, imagine what it was that moved those friends to go to such lengths to get their friend to Jesus, for surely they cared for and per- haps even loved their friend, and wanted to see him well. Perhaps they had heard of the great healer and saw this one chance to do a great thing in friendship's name: "He's not heavy, he's my friend . . ." sort of thing.

Perhaps too they were sick and tired of having to carry their friend around everywhere they went. Perhaps they were sick and tired of their friend, for, after all, they had to drag him *everywhere*. Our friends can often be a burden, a chore, a task to be endured, and we often drag our friends through life even as they drag us, and no matter how noble it is, there are times when it is downright tiring. "The difference," one cynic has said, "between a friend and an enemy is that a friend never goes away." Thus, per- haps they were tired, tired of their friend and tired of each other, and in this healing everybody, crippled as well as whole, would be liberated and relieved.

They may or may not have had all the faith they required in their friend, but Luke wants us to know that Jesus was impressed by their faith in him, their faith perhaps not great enough to remove mountains, but cer- tainly their testimony to the persistence of friendship and to benefits accrued—faith enough to raise the roof in order to get their friend as near to Jesus as possible.

In the preaching business this is what we call a small point upon which to hang a great truth, for most of us—indeed, all of us—are brought to our faith as a result of the faith of others. We are not the self-achieving self- starters that you think: we did not get here on our own; we got here because somebody brought us here, somebody carried us along, somebody took the trouble to remove the obstacles and to place us at a critical time in proximity to Jesus. We are all the result of somebody else's initiative. It was Oscar Wilde who said that his life was never the same again when he realized that his first postnatal memory was that of being born, and of waking up in the arms of a strange woman. We are all the result of somebody else's initiative, and that which we know of good and of God is usually dispensed to us at the first and formative instance at the hands of others—parents, teachers, friends, churches, even schools and universities.

This is the point of the first lesson from the Epistle to Timothy that President Rudenstine read for us this morning. The writer, thought to be Paul, offers encouragement to his young apprentice disciple Timothy, who appears to be a little shaky in the apostle business. What form does this encouragement take? Paul reminds the younger man that he has what it takes because he has received it, as it were, in the bloodstream, and, literally, in his mother's milk. "I am reminded of your sincere faith, a faith that dwelt first in your grandmother Lois and your mother Eunice and now, I am sure, dwells in you." In other words, because of what they had and gave to you, you now have what it takes: they brought you to faith; now take up your faith and walk, no, run with it. ". . . Rekindle the gift of God that is within you. . . ." Secondhand religion is not a bad thing to have.

Now, I am a Cambridge man—the other Cambridge, not this one— while President Rudenstine and Murray Forbes Somerville are Oxford men, and so I know that they have doubtless seen the source of my sermon title, in Blackwell's Books. In the Norrington building there is a section of used religion books with a great hanging sign that says, "Secondhand Theology." We all know what it means: clergy widows and children have sold off their husbands' and fathers' old books, and they form a sort of theological compost heap. There is nothing more daunting for one who aspires to original thought in religion or theology—and who doesn't?—than to pore through books that were once on the cutting edge, once thought to be current and up-to-date, and are now merely "secondhand": the greatest fate in the life of a scholar is to be remaindered too soon!

In a world where a bad "original" thought is regarded as superior to a "good" secondhand one, all of us are always tempted to try to think up something new, always dreaming up something new, and always on our own: the notion that we are dependent upon someone else, or someplace else, or some other time is anathema to our arrogant sense of autonomy and independence.

Religion, however, by its very nature is *not* original, but rather derived, inherited, passed on and received, and passed on again. We are where we are because of others, and by God's grace others, because of us, will be where they are to be. That is reassuring, is it not? It doesn't all depend upon me alone: someone was here before me and cared for me! You don't have to crank up the universe every day to make it go: someone was here before you to make it so. Isn't that reassuring?

We sang of that inheritance in the hymn version of Psalm 78 before the sermon:

> *Let children learn the mighty deeds*
> *Which God performed of old,*
> *Which, in our younger years we saw,*
> *And which our fathers told.*

We will recall that lively sense of inheritance in the "Harvard Hymn," which we are about to sing. Make no mistake: this is not about the worship of Harvard; it is rather the affirmation that we are heirs, like Timothy, of a faith that was manifest in our predecessors; and that, like the crippled man, we are brought to our present place of witness in that faith by the hands, the perseverance, and the persistent love of others.

At the beginning of our three hundred sixty-first year as a community of memory and of hope, and of faith and learning, it is no small thing to remember that we didn't get here on our own, and that it is not for ourselves alone that we are here: we are the happy heirs of secondhand religion.

Now, where are we in the narrative? We'd like to be those brave and persevering, sacrificing souls, those litter-bearers for Jesus who risked all for their friend and literally raised the roof on his behalf, but no! You and I are the crippled people who have been brought to a place of healing—to the "House of the Interpreter," as John Bunyan called it in *Pilgrim's Progress*—by our mothers, our grandmothers, our friends, and our colleagues. As generations before us have done, we are to rise up from where we are, take up our faith, and run, not walk, with it, for the sake of the truth, for the Church, and for Christ: "Veritas: Christo et Ecclesiae"—Harvard's ancient motto. As the old Sunday grace before dinner goes, "For what we are about to receive, may the Lord make us truly thankful, and mindful of the needs of others." You are never too old, never too young, never too dull, and never too clever to be reminded of this astonishing fact.

Patriotism Is Not Enough

Text: Thus says the Lord: "Let not the wise man glory in his wisdom, let not the mighty man glory in his might, let not the rich man glory in his riches; but let him who glories glory in this, that he understands and knows me, that I am the Lord who practices steadfast love, justice, and righteousness in the earth; for in these things I delight, says the Lord."

—JEREMIAH 9:23–24

Once again I have taken as my text a passage from Scripture drawn from neither of the lessons that have been appointed for today, but one that links the two together and highlights the substance of the messages of the prophet Joshua and of the apostle Paul. I ask you to listen to this text from the book of the prophet Jeremiah as a hinge between these important lessons that we have had this morning: "'Let not the wise man glory in his wisdom, let not the mighty man glory in his might, let not the rich man glory in his riches; but let him who glories glory in this, that he understands and knows me, that I am the Lord who practices steadfast love, justice, and righteousness in the earth; for in these things I delight,' says the Lord." Those are the twenty-third and twenty-fourth verses from the ninth chapter of the book of the prophet Jeremiah.

I must begin with a confession. For the first time in more years than I can remember, my text this morning is not derived from the tranquil meditations of a summer's day in Plymouth, when I usually give final thought to the sermons that I will preach to you in the coming year—those texts and sermon titles that you have become accustomed to seeing in bold print in the *Term Book* late in August or early in September. The sermon that I had planned to preach today, entitled "The Power of Little Things," bit the dust on Wednesday morning, and in its place has come this sermon, conceived, quite frankly, in the rising anxiety of a country surprised to find itself on the brink of war, and on the eve of the evening in which the president of the United States will attempt to justify his policies to us.

In a few weeks we will commemorate the seventieth anniversary of the building of this church, dedicated both to the war dead and to a great mission for peace. It was not just because of the remembrance of war but to ford a great hope of peace that in 1932 this church was built. Here, then, of all places on earth, and now, of all times, I, of all people, must speak of the dangers of war and of our Christian mission for peace.

Last Monday I was in Kansas City, Missouri, where, as you know, everything is up-to-date. I was there giving yet another book talk, this time in a large suburban Presbyterian church, and, happily for me, for my book, and for my publisher, hundreds turned out for the evening talk on *The Good Life: Truths That Last in Times of Need*. Afterward, as I signed books, I found that almost everyone in that large congregation had our present war fever on his heart and mind, and each was asking himself, and me, "How did we get here? What ought I to do? I feel so powerless, so helpless, and without a voice." Person after person said that, and I was compelled to think about it. These were not by any means your garden-variety leftists or pacifists, who form the usual list of suspects, and these were not Cambridge liberals, by any means. This was Kansas, for heaven's sake—Alf Landon and Bob Dole country—and these were Presbyterians. They love their country, and they love their God; and what do you do when your country is headed where you think your faith and your God don't want you to go?

In another instance, one of my colleagues here on the staff recently told me of a telephone call he had made to an artisan doing some work for us; in fact, he was the very man whose skills fashioned the tablet to the Radcliffe women of World War I on the north wall, which we dedicated last Armistice Day. We have a small job for him, and apparently after sorting out the details he said something of the following to my colleague, in a rough paraphrase that I now make: "What kind of place is Harvard? Is it liberal or conservative?" Now, that's a hard question, to which there really is no answer, as you know, except in the perception of the beholder. "Why do you ask?" inquired my colleague.

Replied the artisan, "Because I don't hear anybody there or anywhere else talking much about this war, except those who want it; and I'm scared."

In yet another instance, let me mention that it might not surprise you to learn that over my transom passes a vast number of unsolicited church newsletters, bulletins, and pastoral communications from all over the country, and that it might surprise you to know that I read them all. Last week I was reading one from the First Parish Church in Plymouth—not from my church, but from my hometown. In his column, the minister of that old congregation remarked upon the phenomenon, new to him in Plymouth, of perfect strangers coming up to him in the street, in the supermarket, and at the gas pump, knowing him to be the minister of the First Church, and asking him what to do about this war fever. How, they ask, can we have an intelligent conversation on the most dangerous policy topic of the day without being branded traitors, self-loathing Americans, antipatriotic, or soft on democracy?

That's a good question, especially when even the president of the United States questions the patriotism of those few in the U.S. Senate who question his policy or challenge his authority to wage war at will. Must the first casualty of patriotism always be dissent, debate, and discussion? I confess to you that this is a frightening time, more so than anytime in my memory; and if one cannot speak out of Christian conscience and conviction now, come what may, then we are forever consigned to moral silence. We hear much talk of "moral clarity," but it sounds more to me like moral arrogance, and it must *not* be met with moral silence. At the service of Morning Prayers on Wednesday morning last, Anthony Lewis, formerly of the *New York Times,* said in his address to a very startled congregation that if the purpose of the terrorists of September 11, 2001, was to destroy our confidence in our own American values, then, he feared, they had succeeded. In the name of fighting terror both abroad and at home, our government—particularly through the Attorney General, together with a culture of patriotic intimidation—has suspended our constitutional liberties, stifled dissent, and defined a good American as one who goes along with the powers that be, in a "My way or the highway" mentality. When patriotism is defined in this narrow, partisan, opportunistic, jingoistic way, then perhaps that old cynic, Dr. Samuel Johnson, was right when he defined patriotism as the "last refuge of a scoundrel."

Frankly, I prefer his contemporary, Edmund Burke, who said, "To make us love our country, our country ought to be lovely." Our country *is* lovely, which is why we love it and are willing to serve it and, if necessary, to die for it. It is because we love it, and want others to love it as well, that we dare to speak to affirm the goodness and righteousness in it, the virtue and the power of its core values, and to speak against the things that would do harm to it and to those core values. What is and has always been lovely about our country is our right and our duty to criticize those in power, to dissent from their policies if we think them to be wrong, and to hold our alternative vision to be as fully valid as theirs.

In 1952, a long time ago for many of you here in this congregation, but just yesterday for others, Adlai Stevenson was running for president against the patriotic and heroic Dwight D. Eisenhower, who was then, ironically, president of Columbia University. The university had said that it was trying to get Milton, but it got Ike instead, who had wanted to be president of something, and Columbia would do. Adlai Stevenson was running against Eisenhower in a run that was doomed to failure, and was asked to speak to the American League convention in New York City in the summer after his nomination. One can imagine, or even remember, the charges of egghead-ism, of intellectualism, of being soft on Communism and soft on patriot-ism—all those charges that had been leveled on the intelligent and eloquent Adlai Stevenson. Here is what he said on that very subject in a speech called "Patriotism in America," and, by implication, in response to the charges:

> What do we mean by patriotism in the context of our time? I venture to suggest that what we mean is a sense of national responsibility, a patriotism which is not short, frenzied outbursts of emotion, but the tranquil and steady dedication of a lifetime.

Note the careful choice of words: ". . . national responsibility, a patriot-ism which is not short, frenzied outbursts of emotion, but the tranquil and steady dedication of a lifetime." How carefully, poignantly, and aptly chosen are those words in comparison with some of the language we hear flashed about morning, noon, and night in recent days.

I wonder how many of you here this morning have ever seen or given much thought to the white marble statue of a British nurse standing just above Trafalgar Square and beneath Leicester Square in London, to the side of the National Gallery? Londoners and tourists, perhaps some of you, pass it in the to-and-fro of an incredibly busy thoroughfare, lingering at its island base if only to hail an elusive taxi. I have done so many times myself. It is the statue of Nurse Edith Cavell, one of whose claims to fame is that in the early morning hours of October 12, 1915, she was tied to a stake in German-occupied Belgium and shot as a traitor. Long before the war she had for many years headed a nursing home in Belgium, and even after war had broken out she had remained at her post, where, together with her nurses, she gave care to injured soldiers regardless of nationality—whether German, French, or English. Miss Cavell was arrested as a traitor by the Germans for the "crime" of assisting soldiers in their flight to neutral Holland. Determined to make an example of her, the Germans tried her under military law, under a military tribunal, and without adequate counsel she was presumed guilty, found so, and sentenced to death and executed within ten hours of the judgment: the whole episode was shrouded in vindictive haste and stealth. The debate about the exact nature of her so-called crime has gone on for years, but there has never been any debate about the heroic nature of her death, and it was this that turned her into one of the few true heroines of World War I. Some have even gone so far as to say that in her simple way, Edith Cavell was the Dietrich Bonhoeffer of that war. Her last moments, and her final words, are described as follows by an eyewitness:

> After receiving the sacrament, and within minutes of being led out to her death, she said, "Standing as I do in view of God and eternity, I realize that patriotism is not enough. I must have no hatred or bitterness toward anyone."

On the base of her London statue are carved the words "PATRIOTISM IS NOT ENOUGH." This is an impressive message from one who lost her life in the name of somebody else's patriotism.

Edith Cavell, an English vicar's daughter, lived and died a Christian, but her last words are almost too enigmatic and too simple, and they compel us to ask now, in a time of war and of rumors of war, what ought to be the proper relationship between love of God and love of country. If mere patriotism is not enough, what is it that will help us to be both conscientious citizens and faithful Christians? Are the two mutually exclusive, or is it possible, somehow, to live responsibly in the tension between those two claims? That is our business this morning, and that is always the business of any Christian who takes seriously his allegiance to Jesus Christ and his responsibility to his country and his society.

Perhaps a word from our text will help. Did you notice, in the text from Jeremiah, which is printed and available to you on the Order of Worship, that wisdom, might, and riches are set in clear opposition to love, justice, and righteousness? That is not my doing, and it is not even the translator's doing. That is what it says, and it creates for us a self-conscious biblical tension not easily resolved or explained away. Jeremiah knows that we are inclined to boast of our wisdom, particularly in the University, and that is what the Hebrew word that is translated as "glory" really means: boasting, and the thumping of our intellectual chests. We know how to do that about wisdom in the University, and we know how to boast about our might and our riches in this land of opportunity. Jeremiah knows that it is our natural penchant to seize upon and celebrate our achievements, for they define who we are, what we have, and what we do. This is the way of the world, and when we are "number one" in the world, it is "our way or the highway." How strange it is to think back on the relatively stimulating days of the Cold War, when the threat of another dangerous superpower actually helped to make us behave and believe. The prophet does not deny the reality of these claims, but over and against them he sets God's claims of love, justice, and righteousness. Not only is that intellectual symmetry; it is moral symmetry. He is unambiguously clear here—would that he were not so clear. If we as God's people are to glory in anything, we must glory in—that is, we must boast of, take pride in and responsibility for—the things that God values, that God loves, and that God blesses. Why should God bless America if America does not bless the things that God delights in? What are they? Here they are, right in front of us:

> ". . . but let him who glories glory in this, that he understands and knows me, that I am the Lord who practices steadfast love, justice, and righteous-ness in the earth; for in these things I delight, says the Lord."

If we do not delight in the things that the Lord delights in, why should the Lord delight in us? Try that one on for size. This will not fit on a bumper sticker or on a T-shirt, but you might carry it around to ponder in your hearts and minds.

The lesson we heard read from the Book of Joshua is a famous lesson about great choices. Joshua says, "Choose ye this day whom ye will serve." Will you serve the God of the Amorites, or those various other little domestic deities whom you love to serve but who don't deliver the goods? Will you serve them? Well, go right ahead, he in essence says: if that's what turns you on, lay your sacrifices before those little tin-pot gods; I understand it. Then, rising on his prophetic hind legs, Joshua says, "As for me and my house, we will serve the Lord." Well, of course they agree: "We'll serve the

Lord too." Joshua, however, counters by saying, essentially, "No, you won't. You can't. Not unless you are prepared to make the significant, ultimate choice, and sacrifice. If you are really willing to choose between your culture and the God who delivered you, and you choose the God who delivered you, then you can do it, but you can't have it both ways." Again the prophet is unambiguously clear. So, after a lot of to-ing and fro-ing for twenty-four more verses, the people come round to it and say, "Okay, okay, okay, we will serve the Lord who delivered us, and has done all these things." Joshua says, "All right, I trust you, but we're going to build a monument, and this monument, these stones, will remind you, and God, of these promises. Whenever you see this monument, remember that you have chosen the Lord and not the other, lesser deities." So they build the monument, and there it stands. Of course this doesn't really work, because if it did the Bible would end at the Book of Joshua instead of going on for another sixty books—but that's a subject for another story, and for a very good class that I'm teaching this term.

This church in which we stand, and hundreds and thousands like it across this country and around the world, reminds us of the choices we have made. "Choose ye this day whom ye will serve . . . as for me and my house, we will serve the Lord." This place has its great mission as a monument for peace, and we are reminded, on each day that we sit here or pass by these premises, that that is the choice we are required to make. It is a tension, however, and I have not easily resolved it, nor has the prophet.

That tension is even harder to avoid in the second lesson of this morning, where the apostle Paul begins by telling us—in J. B. Phillips's pungent translation—something we should listen to. You remember the Revised Standard Version translation, which we heard this morning: "I beseech you by the mercies of God. . . ." Now listen to how Phillips translates Romans 12; it is meant to grab us by our vitals:

> With eyes wide open to the mercies of God, I beg you, as an act of intelligent worship, to give him your bodies as a living sacrifice, consecrated to him and acceptable by him.

Note "With eyes wide open. . . ." Not in fake devotion or in pseudo-piety, but with eyes wide open as an act of intelligent, thoughtful worship. Your mind is engaged, and not on hold. That's what Paul says. He goes on:

Don't let the world around you squeeze you into its own mold, but let God remold your minds from within, so that you may prove in practice that the plan of God for you is good, meets all his demands, and moves toward the goal of true maturity. (Romans 12:1–3, J. B. Phillips)

Think about that call to nonconformity. Think about that call to transformation. Think of that in the context of a choice you have made and have to make. That tension simply will not go away; it will not easily be resolved, and we, like all faithful Christians and honest citizens throughout all time, will have to live with it and through it. If we are uncomfortable in this conflict of values, we are meant to be uncomfortable. The easy syllogism, that we go to war in order to keep the peace, ought not to comfort us or our Christian president. It is that same alleged "moral clarity" that led to the infamous Vietnam logic. Perhaps you will remember it—that we had to destroy the village in order to "save" it. If that is "moral clarity," then I am Peter Rabbit.

Yet, my beloved friends, we are not without guidance or hope. Many, and perhaps some of you, will argue: who are *we* to challenge the moral clarity and vision of our government, of people who presumably know more than we do, and who have the awful duty not only to protect and to serve, but to anticipate and to initiate? Who are we to kibitz from the sidelines without access to secret briefings, intelligence, knowledge, and all of the apparatus of government? Well, who, indeed, are we?

First, let us remember that we are citizens. They, experts and all, work for us, not we for them. We pay their salaries through the extortion known as taxes. Let us not forget that it is our government, and not theirs. They hold our government—and, indeed, our lives—in a trust. We have a right, we have a responsibility, we have a duty to speak, and we do not have to be experts to do so. We do not require degrees from the Kennedy School or the Wharton School or the Law School to have an opinion about the moral future of our country. In fact, it has usually been the so-called experts who have managed to get us into wars in the first place. We have a duty to speak, to dissent, and to demand a better case for compromising our most fundamental principles as Christians and citizens than has thus far been made. We deserve a better case than the one that is floating around out there at the moment. As a citizen I demand a better excuse than revenge, or oil, for the prosecution of a war that is likely to do more harm than good, that will destabilize not only the region but the world for years to come, and that, worst of all, will confirm for all the world to see our country's reputation as an irrational and undisciplined bully who acts not because it ought, but because it can: we make up the rules, so it seems, as we please. I love my country too much to see it complicit in its own worst stereotype. Right after September 11 a year ago, we asked, in some agonizing perplexity, "Why do they hate us?" Remember that question? Well, if we persist in making war the first rather than the last option, we will soon find out. The answer will be all too terribly manifest.

Now, I know that in the mighty roar of wisdom, might, and riches, the sounds of love, justice, and righteousness—those things in which God delights, and in which God's people are meant to delight—may seem thin, feeble, and anemic. Yet my Christian conscience tells me that these "soft" values should prevail every time over the "hard," even though they often do not. If I am compelled to compromise those Christian values in the service of the state, I had better be as certain as is humanly possible that such a compromise is worth sacrificing the things I hold most precious; and I certainly won't know that, nor will you, unless there is a great deal more thoughtful discussion, debate, and dissent than there has been so far. The most terrifying indictment of Christians in modern times was the general unwillingness of German Christians, with a few notable exceptions, to challenge in any meaningful way, from a Christian point of view, the political assumptions of their government in the years leading up to World War II. They stand indicted by their moral silence, and they know it. Since we are not Nazi Germany, and because we do claim love, justice, and righteousness not only as personal values but as national values, we have all the more responsibility to make the country we love a lovely country.

It pleases me that I am not alone in this enterprise. I am not brave enough to be alone, out front on the prophetic pinnacle; I am afraid that that is a weakness of my character. It pleases me to join with other religious leaders who are beginning to speak and be heard on behalf of a thoughtful case for peace and to engage in a rigorous debate: the *New York Times* only yesterday morning noted the broad antiwar sentiment of the religious leadership across America. Religious opinion is by no means unanimous: those evangelicals who have found little fault with anything that this administration has done or proposes to do, and who seldom met a war they didn't like, lined up to be counted on the president's side. Polls show that most Americans, frustrated, alas, by the ephemeral character of the "War on Terrorism," and still angry and confused about September 11, 2001, want to do something. As we know, however, in angry, vengeful moments, the desire to do "something" is easily translated into the will to do anything, and that "anything" may very well be the wrong thing. Bombing Iraq into oblivion as payback to those who have done us injury seems to me at this moment to be the wrong thing to do. Polls do not get at the truth. Thirty years ago, most polls showed significant majorities in favor of whatever it was we were doing in Vietnam, and eventually the majority in favor concluded that the minority opposed were, in fact, right. Polls simply tell us where we are, not where we ought to be.

The gospel, however, does tell us where we ought to be—tough, untenable, and difficult as that place may be. Wisdom, might, and riches must yield to love, justice, and righteousness. Love, justice, and righteousness are superior to wisdom, might, and riches. How often do we have to be told that? "And these are God's words," says Paul at the end of Romans 12, once again in the Phillips translation: "If thine enemy hunger, feed him; if he thirst, give him drink; for in so doing thou shalt heap coals of fire upon his head." Don't allow yourself to be overpowered with evil: take the offensive and overpower evil with good. That is what Paul is saying: take the offensive; overpower evil with good! Now, that is a radical foreign policy. That would scare the bejesus out of a lot of people, to know that with all of our power we decided that we were going to overpower evil with good—and what a topsy-turvy world this would be! That should give all the hawks in Washington something to think about—that if they want us to be noticed, the world would notice us if we took seriously the idea of overpowering evil with good.

Nurse Cavell was, and is, right: "Patriotism is not enough . . ." If we wish to be on God's side rather than making God into our own ally of American realpolitik, then we would do well to remember our text from Jeremiah. God's values are clear; so too ought ours to be.

> "Let not the wise man glory in his wisdom, let not the mighty man glory in his might, let not the rich man glory in his riches; but let him who glories glory in this, that he understands and knows me, that I am the Lord who practices steadfast love, justice, and righteousness in the earth; for in these things I delight, says the Lord."

If you love the Lord, you will love the things the Lord loves. There is no other way around it.

A Good Word for Harlots

Text: Jesus said to them, "Truly, I say to you, the tax collectors and the harlots go into the kingdom of God before you."

—MATTHEW 21:31

Some of you will remember my sermon *When They Think You're Crazy:* a number of people came up to me afterward and told me that that sermon had their name on it. Today I offer *A Good Word for Harlots,* and if your name is on this sermon, please do not be ashamed to let me know.

Harlots have had a bad rap. Not all of them have gone on to fame and fortune, not all of them have had famous customers, and no less a likable fellow than Hugh Grant reminded us this summer that the world's oldest profession is alive and well and flourishing in the Western world. I do not recall a comment by Senator Dole or Senator Gramm on Hugh's "misfortune," but I think we can safely say that they would disapprove, loving neither the sin nor the sinner.

Jesus, on the other hand, not a candidate for president, had a good word for harlots, a word that those of us who think ourselves morally superior to them, and to others, ought to hear, and this morning you heard it: right here in Scripture, with no compromising conditions, Jesus says, "Truly, I say to you, the tax collectors and the harlots go into the kingdom of God before you." The "you," here, refers to *you!*

Now, this could have been a sermon about tax collectors, but they do not appeal to our prurient interests, for, after all, they neither give nor get any pleasure. Harlots, though, appeal to the naughty and to the sensuous in us, and passion and pleasure combined illegitimately create a winning combination in a profession that of all professions has lasted longest though there is no instruction for it in our professional graduate schools. We are at our most morally anxious where sex is involved, and that is why Jesus gets our attention when he tells the uptight Puritans among us that harlots have a prior claim on heaven and will get there before we do. It is annoying, this illegitimate pleasure, and that it will get the harlots into heaven before us is not only annoying, but unfair.

Why is this so? I will save that for later in order to keep you awake and alert. For now, the question is not "Why?" but "Who?"

Professor Dudley Herschbach gave you a very clear clue in his wonderful reading of that long first lesson from Joshua. The harlot's name is Rahab, and Professor Herschbach gave it the correct Hebrew pronunciation, I am sure, but in my Sunday school her name was pronounced "*Ray*hab," and so to me for ever and ever her name is *Ray*hab. Her name is Rahab, and in Hebrew that name means "wide," "expansive"—and you don't need a degree in etymology to figure that out. Rabbinic tradition describes Rahab as "one of the four most beautiful women in the world"; her name alone is said to have inspired lust. In the various commentaries Rahab is described as a "giver of hospitality," which sounds like the term the Japanese used to describe the Chinese and other women forced to serve the needs of the invading army in World War II: "comfort women," a disgusting euphemism.

Rahab—and I have never heard of a girl called Rahab!—in Joshua 2, was famous, a well-known prostitute, a woman of pleasure, a harlot, who lived within the walls of the city of Jericho. The place where she dwelled was both well known and discreet, in an ideal location on the border between the city and its outskirts, conveniently situated for a house of ill repute. Rabbinic commentary says that in the forty years—a long time—in which she practiced her profession, no prince or ruler had been denied her favors. She was well connected to the great and to the very good; and in terms of who she was and of what she knew she was probably the best-informed person in the city, for prostitutes are always in the forefront in learning the news, through pillow talk, and no less so than in the city of Jericho.

She was also shrewd, and she was smart, and when the Jewish spies came to her house to scout out the city for Joshua's eventual attack, she bargained with them. She would protect them from the search party if they would protect her and her household when Joshua attacked and won the city.

The rest is history, and one of my favorite tales from Sunday school. The men were hidden under the flax of her roof, and escaped by being let down over the wall from her house by a scarlet—or crimson—cord, a sign of protection, redemption, and salvation. Rahab was instructed to display the scarlet cord from the same window, so that when the conquerors came to slaughter the inhabitants of the city they would identify the house and spare it. This, as a small matter of interest, is the source from which the color red came to be associated with prostitutes, and their district to be known as the red-light district.

Rahab was taken to Israel, her conversion to Judaism affirmed, and in Matthew's Gospel she is listed among the ancestors of David, which means that she was also an ancestor of Jesus. In Hebrews she is listed among the saints who are justified both by works and by faith.

For some of the early church fathers, uptight Christians that they were, it was difficult to think of Jesus as having a prostitute, an admitted harlot, among his ancestors—a skeleton in the divine closet, so to speak; and some of them tried to sanitize the text and story by suggesting that she was merely an innkeeper, or at the most the proprietess of the Jericho No-Tell Motel. That is a silly bit of tittle-tattle, hardly convincing, and it persuaded me, at least, that hypocrisy is a less honorable calling than harlotry.

This is the point that Jesus himself makes: that there is more truth in harlotry than in religious and moral hypocrisy, and here is where we must remember the substance of the text where Jesus gives the harlots pride of place. We are fascinated with the apparent facts of Rahab's life for forty years: we think of her as the prostitute who helped the spies, or as the English might say, "The tart with a heart." That is to us who she was.

But *why*, we may now ask, did she do what she did? How many men did she entertain? Did she or didn't she? What accounted for her charity to these Jewish men? The Book of Joshua is not an exercise in therapy, but we do know one thing: we know that Rahab earned her living on her back, and that she recognized where God was to be found, and that she understood on which side of the equation God was. She had sexual and political skills, and she now had moral insight into the kingdom of God, and she was determined to be on the right side. She confessed to the spies, "For the Lord your God is he who is God in heaven above and on earth beneath" (Joshua 2:11).

Rahab did not require a ton of bricks—or the walls of Jericho—to fall on her head. She had heard of the wonder working of God, and she acknowledged it: "Your God is going to win," she deduced, "and I want to be on the winning side." She had heard of the children of Israel being led dry shod through the Red Sea waters, and despite her devotion to pleasure and profit, she knew that in the end God would prevail. In order to save her life she changed her mind, and changed her ways: she "amended her lifestyle" might be the way to put it in the current language. She recognized the opportunity for salvation, she was not so immersed in her life that she couldn't change it, and, having seen her options, she *acted*. She didn't dither, she didn't speculate, she didn't procrastinate: she acted, and she was saved, and thus she was spared, and became an ancestress of the Lord.

To the early church fathers, all stuck-up, Rahab *lied:* she was not a saint, she was not a Girl Scout—thank goodness she wasn't—and she had not sunk so low that she could not look up, and out, and live; and good for her. Now, I know that some will say that the Plummer Professor of Christian Morals is preaching on prostitution and on lying in The Memorial Church, and that I will read about it tomorrow morning in the papers, but it doesn't matter. Rahab was not so much the victim of her circumstances, as we would like to say in this age of the sanctity of victimhood, that she could not recognize an opportunity for repentance and salvation, and grab hold of it with both hands. She was not so immersed in the seedy commerce of the world, stuck in her profession, locked into her options, that she could not see the way out and through to the other side. What is more, having seen, she acted: she struck a bargain, did what she had to do, and was saved. We have to admire her sense of the expedient, even though some of the fastidious among us might say that this was just the problem: it *was* all so expedient: She knew that she would die with everyone else if she didn't change, and so she opted for survival. *Tsk-tsk.*

Well, what do you want? Repentance is expedient. It is what you do if you don't want to go on as you are, and die. Salvation *is* expedient: it is designed to get you out of the way of an oncoming train. You don't stand in front of the train and hope that it will be derailed and not hit you; you don't try to gauge the speed of the train and the speed with which you could jump away; you don't wave your hand at the engineer, signaling him to stop because you are on the track. *No!* You do the only expedient thing: you get out of the way! When we speak of being "saved" we mean literally that: being rescued from life as it is in order to take on life as it can be and as it ought to be, because it is in the interest of eternal salvation.

Jesus is annoyed with the righteous, in Matthew 21, because he has presented to them the clear and present option for a new life, a life of peace and joy and righteousness, but the virtuous, so content with who, what, and where they are, find no need for repentance. They are like the Boston lady who found no reason to be born again, because she had been born once, on Commonwealth Avenue.

The virtuous, the respectable, the Christians of America have no need to hear the good news of Christ because we have already achieved a level of perfection consistent with our level of comfort: who of us thinks ourself so wicked and our life so bad that we have an urgent need to repent here and now?

No: we cannot, we will not see God's future, for we are so seduced by the conveniences and conventional wisdom of the present. Unlike Rahab, we are unwilling to give up what we have and what we know to risk going with God. Rahab had everthing to lose, and she gave up everything to go with God. The trouble with us is that we don't want to lose anything, and are unwilling to give up any of it. "Let me keep my intellectual superiority, my economic security, my social stability; let me keep my habits and my ways, and let me keep to my timetable and my priorities; and indeed, let me even keep my anxieties and my neuroses," we say to ourselves. "Then, if God can fit into that, I will pencil him in."

That is why the harlots, and even the despised IRS drones, will get into heaven before you.

So, what to do? Take up prostitution? Work for the government? Of course not. Look at your options; there has to be more than this. Take a long and hard look at the life you think you are trapped into, or to which you think you are committed. Look at what your priorities and anxieties are: you know that life has more to offer than what you now have of it, no matter how much you own or how smart you are or how important you are. There has to be more than this, and there is, and you can have it if you turn around and claim a place for God in your life.

What Rahab found is free and available to you in Christ, for the good word for harlots is good news for you as well: "Come unto me, all ye that labor and are heavy laden, and I will give you rest." That is what Jesus says to the harlots and to the tax collectors, and to you and to me. Try it and see!

How to Ruin Your Reputation

Text: The Son of man has come eating and drinking. . . .

—LUKE 7:34

The text this morning is the thirty-fourth verse of the seventh chapter of the gospel according to St. Luke, which, in the more vivid and archaic King James version, goes on to say of Jesus, "Behold a gluttonous man, and a winebibber. . . ."

As a rule I rarely advertise books from this pulpit, especially books written by somebody else, but I make an exception this morning because a half-page advertisement in yesterday's *New York Times Book Review* caught my attention. It was for a new book, written by Donald Spoto, entitled, *The Hidden Jesus: A New Life,* and the teaser to the ad, of enormous cost, asks, "What do we really know about Jesus?" The author is credited with the following conclusions:

- Nowhere in Scripture is there anything against women becoming priests.

- Sexual morality was not an issue of great concern to Jesus.

- No true Christian can endorse capital punishment.

- There are ancient anti-Semitic passages in the New Testament that Jesus himself would certainly have rejected.

The book is endorsed by no less a spiritual writer than Thomas Moore, and I intend to get it to see if it follows through; and I hasten to add that I do not know, nor have I ever heard of, Donald Spoto, so we are not in league together.

Now, those of us in the business of talking and writing about Jesus might ask, "Does the world need yet another biography of Jesus?" Bookstore shelves are groaning with books about Jesus, and the world never seems to grow better for it; in fact, it seems to get worse. Apparently we cannot get enough of Jesus, when all we need to know is contained in the four Gospels, read out in church every Sunday, which tell his story but pale in weight and in number to the books *about* him. Is this another story about Jesus written because we don't like the one we have? Perhaps the reason there has been such an industry in the life of Jesus is that we don't necessarily know or like what we find about him in the Gospels, and are hoping for something better. If we keep working at it we just might come up with an agreeable, attractive, acceptable Jesus who is worthy of our literary efforts, and worthy of a half page in the *New York Times Book Review*. If this new book pays any attention to the gospel portrait of Jesus and gives him back his life, then it *will* have justified its publication, it *will* be worthy of our efforts, and of a column in the *New York Times*. I intend to get it and read it, but I do wonder if this cynical and hypocritical age can endure the truth about Jesus, whom we have managed to neuter and re-create in our own image. If Donald Spoto's book tells the truth about Jesus, can you and I bear it?

Take today's lesson, for example, from the Book of Proverbs, a book of wisdom with which our Lord as a good Jew would have been familiar, which justly sings out the praises of a good reputation: "A good name is to be chosen rather than great riches. . . . ," which is the same sentiment found in Ecclesiastes 7:1: "A good name is better than precious ointment. . . ." This is the text inscribed on a memorial tablet in one of the St. Grottlesex school chapels that will go unmentioned, where in very large bronze letters is declared, "Endicott Peabody Saltonstall: A Good Name Is Better Than Great Riches"; and if you can have both, why, all the better.

Well, this is a sermon about reputation and these are texts about reputation, and you are curious people who came here today to address the question of who we are, who people think we are, who we aspire to be, and to hear how to *ruin* your reputation. Reputation, we are told, is what both precedes and follows us, and, for better or for worse, a reputation is formed early and lasts long, and its image is hard to break. Here it may be useful as

a helpful aside to offer a mild but pertinent distinction between "reputation" and "character."

"Reputation," I was told as a young man, is what people think of you;
while "character" is what God knows of you. I rather like that, for character, despite all of the talk by such virtue mongers as Bill Bennett and his
Republican friends, is ultimately rather elusive; God looketh upon the
heart, man and woman looketh upon the outward appearance, and so it
would appear that character is that which is ultimately known to God,
while reputation is that which passes in the meantime. Reputation is the
stuff with which human beings work most of the time, the visible tip of the
iceberg, the character of which is way below the surface. Whenever I see
Charles Colson on the television I know that I am meant to see a born-
again Christian who now preaches virtue with the authority of a convicted
and converted felon, but I still see, God help me, the arch–Watergate bur-
glar. I try, but a reputation is a terrible thing not to be able to shake.
Richard Nixon had more lives than a cat, but his reputation is still that of a
crook: only God now knows the difference. Character is elusive, and I
would be very suspicious of those who run on theirs, and you should be
too: a "good" character may simply mean either a lack of information or
imagination, or of opportunity.

Reputations, however, are to be taken quite seriously, as we discover in
today's second lesson, in which it is clear that Jesus is being compared with
his cousin John the Baptist, at this moment a rival prophet of exceptional
moral and ascetic qualities: John the Baptist, who would make Independent
Counsel Ken Starr look like Johnny Rotten. We understand what the New
Testament paints as a picture of John the Baptist: John the Baptist, prophet
of righteousness, locusts, honey, wearing a hair shirt and wandering around
without shoes all over the desert, who would certainly be no fun at a cock-
tail party—but, if you were looking for someone to save your soul, he is
numero uno. "John the Baptist," says Jesus, "has come eating no bread and
drinking no wine." He had a good reputation as a prophet.

At this point, though, Jesus, a rising new young prophet, was gaining a
reputation as a healer of the sick—always a good way to gain such a reputation, for to take someone who is sick and make him well and allow him to
testify about it is a very good and useful testimonial and endorsement.
Earlier in today's gospel he goes beyond merely curing someone from the
common cold: he raises from the dead the son of the widow of Nain—a

remarkably sure way to establish a fine reputation. Passing through a village, he comes upon a funeral procession of a widow who has lost her son and therefore the source of her support. Here is this dead boy on his bier, borne aloft by mourners and pallbearers, and Jesus confronts the scene and, as Luke tells it, says to the young man, dead as a doornail on the bier, "Young man, I say to you, arise"; and then, according to Luke, "the dead man sat up and began to speak." Now, that is a remarkable occurrence; even you would be impressed if that happened here in The Memorial Church at some memorial service, and we said to one of our colleagues, presumed to be safely and finally dead, "Get up!" and he did, and, more than that, began to talk. What does the gospel say? "Fear seized them all," reports Luke, "and they glorified God, saying, 'A great prophet has risen among us!' and 'God has visited his people!'" Now, I know that some of you don't know the Bible and think that I am making all this up, but I am not. It is all there. Read it; it's in Luke 7:16, and it's an incredible story. "And this report concerning him," Luke continues, "spread through the whole of Judea and all the surrounding country." He was gaining a reputation, he was building up credits; people heard about him and wanted to see and to hear him.

So Jesus' reputation began to grow so fast and so remarkably that even John the Baptist wondered, "Are you he who is to come, or shall we look for another?" Jesus refuses a direct answer, an annoying characteristic of his throughout the Gospels, but he praises John, saying, "I tell you, among those born of women none is greater than John; yet he who is least in the kingdom of God is greater than he"—the sting in the tail.

This is the context of that famous scene of hospitality where in Simon the Pharisee's house—not Simon Peter; don't confuse them—Jesus creates a scandal by accepting the intimate ministrations of a woman of the streets, of low repute. What did she do? She crashed the party, she wasn't invited—like someone popping in to a party saying they know Fred when they've never heard of Fred. So, the woman crashed the party, she stood behind Jesus trying not to be noticed, and she washed his feet with her tears, wiped them with her hair, and anointed them with precious ointment.

Now, even the dullest of you knows that this is pretty intimate stuff—playing with feet, weeping, washing, anointing; it's very tactile. This is not a metaphor: this woman was all over him, or at least all over his feet—and who was she to be doing this in the first place? For her to be there at all was little short of scandalous, for who was she, to be in the presence of the prophet? That is scandal of the first order, for a woman to be in the same room as the great prophet when she was supposed to be outside or in the kitchen, or anywhere but near the scene of the great visitation. That raises other questions. Where did she get the precious ointment? What did she do to get the money to pay for the ointment? Maybe it's best not to ask, not to inquire too closely. By what right did she presume the intimacies of a friend, a host, even of a lover? Only the most intimate of relations allows somebody to do this to somebody else; it is only a host who washes the feet of a guest in his house, only a lover who washes the feet of his or her spouse or companion. Who is she to do this, and what was she trying to advertise? What was her game? What was she up to?

She was well known in the town—she had a reputation, we might say—and so the criticism falls on Jesus, for, when the Pharisee Simon, who had invited Jesus home, saw this, he said to himself, "If this man were a prophet [i.e., a true prophet], he would have known who and what sort of woman this is who is touching him, for she is a sinner" (Luke 7:39). The assumptions are that if Jesus had been a real prophet he would have known who she was, and that if he had known that she was a sinner he would have had nothing to do with her. Those two assumptions hold this story together.

Here was a situation in which the woman had nothing to lose, and Jesus, it would appear, had everything to lose: his rising credentials as a prophet with a deep knowledge of people; his moral purity, which should be preserved against the contamination of sinners; and, most of all, his simple good judgment and gravitas. If he didn't value his own reputation, at least he should have valued the reputation of his host, in whose house these intimacies were publicly and unashamedly displayed. Had he no sense of place? No judgment? No sense of pride? He embarrassed his host, yet he rebukes the host and not the woman, saying to Simon, "Do you see this woman? I entered your house, you gave me no water for my feet, but she has wet my feet with her tears and wiped them with her hair. You gave me no kiss, but from the time I came in she has not ceased to kiss my feet. You did not anoint my head with oil, but she has anointed my feet with ointment. Therefore I tell you, her sins, which are many, are forgiven, for she loved much; but he who is forgiven little, loves little" (Luke 7:44–47).

One cannot imagine such behavior from John the Baptist, or even, for that matter, from anyone whose job it is to varnish one's reputation for probity and morality. Virtue, as we all know, is keeping a conspicuous distance from vice; but, as our text puts it so clearly and unambiguously, "The Son of man has come eating and drinking"; and, as is also very clear, the son of man consorts with people of low degree. Eating and drinking, consorting with people whom you and I would either raise an eyebrow about or spend very little time with.

The King James version of the Bible is wonderfully vivid here, translating Luke 7:34, "Behold a gluttonous man, and a winebibber"; and the only other time that that word, *winebibber,* is found in Scripture is in Proverbs 23:20, where in good advice to the would-be moral Jew it is written, "Be not among winebibbers; among riotous eaters of flesh"—a direct prohibition against the very thing that Luke describes our Lord as being. Both St. Luke in his description, and Jesus in his action, knew what they were doing: this is no accident, no editorial slip of the tongue, no casual mistake, for Jesus does not conform to the moral dictatorship of the many; he accepts neither the conventional wisdom nor the conventional virtue. In this he makes some formidable enemies—and isn't it often said that we should be known by the enemies we make? Who are your enemies? Who really doesn't like you? Who would seek to do you in? Then you have to ask if it is worth it. To be known by one's enemies is to have a catalogue of those things against which many might well object.

Pharisees, for example, do not like to be rebuked, especially publicly, and particularly in their own houses. Jesus' grandstanding in the house of Simon, taking the part of the fallen and brazen woman—and later more notoriously drinking with publicans, tax collectors, and those outside of the chosen few—would earn him the enmity of those who had better reputations than his to maintain. They would succeed; we know that they succeeded: they would see him on the cross, and it doesn't get any better than that if you wish to put your enemy out of business.

Jesus' greatest crime was that he disturbed the balance of power and destroyed the serenity of those who believed in the immutability of the social order and in the superiority of their own moral vision; and he makes them, and us, all nervous and upset. Our lesson from Luke is just one of dozens of examples in which he does this, all with an eye not to what is apparent to the human sensibility—reputation—but to what is known to and loved by God—dare we call it character? In this way he ruined his reputation for classic prophethood, which usually means the absence of vice, and replaced it with an affirmation of virtue, which consists in the nature of one's own heart and its relationship to God. If that is described in Donald Spoto's book, it's a good book; and if it is not described in Donald Spoto's book, it is a wicked book and not worth the paper it is printed on. It is this consistent, vivid, and confrontational system of morality that characterizes the life and the teachings of Jesus and makes him so fundamentally unacceptable to us, to all of us, his followers.

Most of the time we do not worship the Jesus of the Gospels but rather a pale construction, a pale imitation who reflects the rather weak virtues of our culture. We like his healing of the sick—who would be against the healing of the sick?—but we do not like his condemnation of the righteous. We think his parables interesting and perhaps worthy of study in the Divinity School or the English Department, but we do not like his judgments about money. We are sorry that he ends up on the cross, a tragic ending to a noble life, but we cannot accept that his resurrection is for the sinful and not for the virtuous.

I hope that Mr. Spoto, in his book, spends a great deal of time on Jesus' social teachings on wealth and money—those who have it and those who want it, which just about covers everybody in this congregation—for if he does he will learn that Jesus is much more interested in the burden of money than he is, for example, in the vices of sex; and this is only one instance in which we edit out what we know of Jesus. We, on the other hand, are much more interested in sex ourselves, and we define our virtue in terms of it but leave our money, and talk about it, alone.

Jesus spends his time with and risks his reputation for those noticeably different and cast out from conventional polite society. We segregate those different from ourselves, and in the terrible logic of a climate that permits this, we kill them, as was done to that poor gay boy in Wyoming, news of whom cannot have escaped any of us.

If we tame the social conscience of Jesus, we allow the savage in every one of us to escape, to run rampant, and there is nothing in this world more dangerous or destructive than savagery done in the name of religion. Did you notice that the funeral of Matthew Shepard was picketed by members of a fundamentalist Christian church that bears the name of Baptist—God spare us identity with such wicked people—and that they had signs saying, "God Hates Fags," presuming to quote from the Epistle to the Romans? This was done in the name of the gospel. There can be no moral cover either for such a belief or for such a behavior; you cannot hide under the cushion of "I feel sincerely and strongly on this point of view." You may try to hide, but you are wrong.

The week's news was not all bad, however, thank God. On Wednesday, the *Boston Globe* reported that the Dutch Reformed Church in South Africa publicly repudiated its old racist theology and its reading of the Bible in order to support apartheid. It adopted a "resolution rejecting apartheid as wrong and sinful not simply in its effects and operations but in its fundamental nature." The resolution called apartheid "a travesty of the gospel" and apologized for what it called "sinful." It took the Southern Baptist Convention one hundred and thirty-five years after the end of the War Between the States, as they delight to call it, to apologize for the same sins.

Thank God it is never too late to repent—that is, until Jesus comes. Where will we be, however, when the Church at last repents of its destructive treatment of homosexuals and its reading of Scripture that allows society permission to act upon its innate savagery? Where will we be when the apology is written? The moral equivalent of the scene in Simon's house in today's gospel would be cast in gay terms, and if that distresses you, it should, and so should the gospel.

A good reputation is a terrible thing to lose, a better reputation a glorious thing to gain. Jesus was a winebibber: "Behold, a glutton and a drunkard, a friend of tax collectors and sinners!" That means that in Jesus' fallen circle of friends there may yet be room for you and for me. His ruined reputation may just help us to rehabilitate ours, and for that we should say, "Praise God!" and "Amen."

Outer Turmoil, Inner Strength

**Text: Set a straight course and keep to it, and do not be dismayed
in the face of adversity.**

—ECCLESIASTICUS 2:2 (THE APOCRYPHA)

My text is the second verse of the second chapter of the book of
Ecclesiasticus, and the lesson from which it was taken was read in the
Revised English Version. I am taking the King James translation of that
same opening verse, which says: "Set thy heart aright, and constantly
endure, and make not haste in time of calamity."

Let me begin with an observation, one might say, of comparative religion.
I understand that in the traditions and liturgies of the Greek Orthodox
Church, our brethren in the East, when a child is baptized—and by "child"
I mean an infant, not a squalling seven-year-old but a real infant, literally
still damp—after the baptism has been performed, the minister or priest or
bishop takes his very large pectoral cross—twice the size of mine—and
forcefully strikes the little child on its breast, so hard that it leaves a mark,
and so hard that it hurts the child and the child screams. In the West, we
give the child roses. What is the difference here?

The symbolism of the Eastern baptism is clear, indicating that the child
who has been baptized into Christ must bear the cross, and that the cross is
a sign not of ease or of victory or of prosperity or of success, but of sorrow,
suffering, pain, and death; and by it those things are overcome. It is important to remember that. The symbol of our Christian faith is this very cross
that you see on that holy table, carved in that choir screen, worn around

the necks of many of us and held in honor and esteemed by all of us; and it stands to remind us of the troubles of the world that placed our Savior upon it for sins that he did not commit. We Christians, therefore, like those Greek Orthodox babies, ought to expect trouble, turmoil, and tribulation as the normal course of life. We don't, however; and we have been seduced by a false and phony version of the Christian faith that suggests that by our faith we are immune to trouble.

Because we have been nice to God, our thinking goes, God should be nice to us. Because you have interrupted your normal routine and come here today, God should somehow take note of it, mark it down in the book, and spare you any trouble, tribulation, turmoil, or difficulty. Tribulation, we know, happens only to bad people: should it therefore be happening in spades to all those people in Canaday Hall as I speak, who are not here this morning but just getting up out of bed, recovering from a night of pleasure and satiety? Tribulation happens only to the nonobservant and the bad people; and when, as Rabbi Kushner so famously and quite profitably noted, bad things happen to good people, we feel that something has gone terribly wrong. God is not supposed to behave that way, we think, for that is not part of the deal; and we ask, "Where is God?" I'll get back to that question, but that is what we ask.

Now, let me hasten to say that the answer to that conundrum is not a false conception of God. The issue has nothing whatsoever to do with the so-called death of God, and everything to do with the life and the faith of the believer. It is not the death of God that should concern us; it is the questionable state of the life of the believer. God does not spare us from turmoil, which even the most casual observance of the Scriptures tells us: God strengthens us for turmoil, and we can find that in the Good Book as well. It is a shabby faith that suggests that God is to do all the heavy lifting and that you and I are to do none. The whole record of Scripture, from Genesis to Revelation, and the whole experience of the people of God from Good Friday down to and beyond Tuesday, September 11, suggest that faith is forged on the anvil of human adversity. No adversity; no faith.

Consider the lessons we heard this morning. In the first lesson, from one of the ancient books of the Jews, the book of Ecclesiasticus in the Apocrypha, could it be put any plainer? "My son, if thou comest to serve the Lord, prepare thy soul for temptation. Set thy heart aright, and constantly endure, and do not make haste in time of calamity." You don't need a degree in Hebrew Bible or exegesis to figure out what that is saying. What is the context for these words? Trouble, turmoil, tribulation, and temptation: that's the given, that's the context. What is the response for calamity? Endurance. Don't rush, don't panic. What are we to do in calamitous times? We are to slow down. We are to inquire. We are to endure. Tribulation does not invite haste; it invites contemplation, reflection, perseverance, endurance.

Where may we turn for examples of what I am trying to say that the Scriptures say to us? We are in the middle, with our Jewish brethren, of the great "Days of Awe," with the beginning of the new year and the Day of Atonement; and when the Jewish people celebrate these Days of Awe and begin their new year and atone for their sins, they always remember two things. First, they remember the troubles and the tribulations through which they have been, and they recite the history not of their victories but of their sorrows and their troubles. They remind themselves and one another, and everybody else, of how they have been formed and forged through the experience of trial and tribulation. They remember those things.

The second thing they remember is how the Lord delivered them out of those troubles and helped them to endure and bear and eventually overcome them. They are reminded of that, and they remind themselves of it over and over and over again; and when it is said that "It is not the Jew who keeps the law, but the law which keeps the Jew," it is to this process of remembrance, endurance, and deliverance that the aphorism speaks. Again, it says in the book of Ecclesiasticus, "Look at the generations of old, and see. Whoever did put his trust in the Lord, and was ashamed? Or who did abide in his fear, and was forsaken? Or who did call upon him, and he despised him?" The history of the Jews in the world is not a history of escape from trouble; would that it were, but it is not. It is the record of endurance through tribulation, an endurance that would have been impossible without God. If any people had the right to claim that God was dead, or at least on sabbatical, it was the Jews, but they never have said it, and they never will, for they know better. They do not worship a metaphor or a simile, or a theological construct. They worship the one who stands beside them and who has been with them from Egypt to Auschwitz and beyond, and who enables them to stand up to all that a world of tribulation can throw at them. If we want to know about outer turmoil and inner strength, we need look no further than to our neighbors the Jews. Remember, they wrote the book on the subject.

We may also look a little closer to home. We may look to the authentic witness of the Christian faith to which we bear, in this church, unambiguous allegiance. We do not just believe in God in general, or in a spiritual hope: we believe in Jesus Christ, who is all that we can fully know about God. So, we look at this tradition for inner strength in the midst of outer turmoil.

Consider St. Paul, a Jew and a Christian, and consider his view of things in a less than agreeable world. I hope you heard that second lesson read this morning in J. B. Phillips's pungent prose; I chose it so it would get your attention. Listen to what St. Paul says: "We are handicapped on all sides"—a very fashionable translation of the word, but apt—"but we are never frustrated. We are puzzled," he says, "but never in despair. We are persecuted, but we never have to stand it alone, and . . . "—this fourth part is the part I like the most—"we may be knocked down, but we are never knocked out."

Now, Paul is not an abstract theologian, like so many of my colleagues: Paul speaks from the experience of a frustrated but not defeated believer. This is not the "How to be leaders and win" sort of stuff that he writes; this is not the kind of CEO book that they trot out in the Business School and in motivational seminars. No. Paul writes out of failure, frustration, and conflict, but never out of despair. If you are looking for something to read in these troublesome times, do not turn to books of cheap inspiration and handy-dandy aphorisms; do not look for feel-good and no-stress and lots-of-gain-and-no-pain kinds of books. They're all out there, and you will be sorely tempted, but if you want to read something useful during these times, my brothers and sisters in Christ, read the letters of Paul. Read them and weep! Read them and rejoice! Read them and understand that neither you nor I are the first people in the world ever to face sorrow, death, frustration, or terror: we are not the first, and there is a record of coping here that is not merely of coping but of overcoming. If you do not wish to succumb to the tidal wave of despair and temptation and angst that surrounds us on every hand, you will go back to the roots of our faith, which are stronger than any form of patriotism. I don't despise patriotism, don't misunderstand me; but there is no salvation in love of country. There is salvation only in love of Jesus Christ; and if you confuse the two, the greatest defeat will have been achieved. Remember that. Read the letters of Paul.

When you look at that fourth chapter in 2 Corinthians, the chapter with which we have been working today, you will discover that this is not a faith of evasion, a faith of success, or a faith of unambiguous pleasure and delight. It is reality, a reality that believers have always been forced to face. "In the world," says the apostle John, "we shall have tribulation." Jesus says,

"Be of good cheer; I have overcome the world." Well, that's all very right and good for Jesus, who in fact has overcome the world; and good for him, I say again, but for us who have not yet overcome the world, John's Gospel is as true as ever it was. In the world we shall have tribulation, and anyone who promises you otherwise is either uninformed or lying, and perhaps both; and owes no allegiance to the gospel. When we face the world as believers, we face it with tribulation on every hand.

From this very pulpit my venerable predecessor Willard Sperry used often to quote Georges Tyrell, who was one of the famous Catholic modernists of the first third of the twentieth century. In a time when World War I was still fresh and World War II was clearly on the horizon, Sperry preached week after week to congregations like this—to your grandparents, three generations removed. One of his favorite quotations of Father Tyrell's was Tyrell's definition of Christianity; and this is what Tyrell said, what Sperry quoted, and what I now quote again: "Christianity is an ultimate optimism founded upon a provisional pessimism." In this world we shall have tribulation.

So, a reasonable person—and we're all reasonable persons here, are we not? That's why we're here and not in some other church—might ask, "From where has this notion come, that Christians are entitled to a free 'Get out of Jail' card, an exemption from the world of turmoil and tribulation?" This misreading of the Christian faith—for that is exactly what it is—comes from the fashionable, cultural faith with which we have so often confused the Christian faith. Most of us aspire to be believers in the Christian faith, but all of us to one degree or another, alas, subscribe to the cultural faith; and that cultural religion in times of prosperity is often easy and always dangerous. Be suspicious of religion in times of prosperity and ease. Why is it dangerous? It is dangerous because prosperity itself can become a terribly tempting false god and a substitute for religion; and in the name of the religion of prosperity, success, and control, most of us will do anything, and almost everything—and we have.

In times of prosperity either we make prosperity our religion, or we imagine that we can do without religion altogether. Who needs it? When turmoil happens to others we can be mildly empathetic, perhaps even sympathetic, and maybe we can even utter that famous aphorism, "There but for the grace of God go I"; but when turmoil hits us, when we are knocked flat, when all of our securities and our cherished illusions are challenged to the breaking point and break, then comes the great question we must both ask and answer: what is left when everything we have is taken from us?

What is left when everything you have is taken from you? For the last decade I have asked on commencement morning, in my sermons to the seniors about to leave this College, questions like this: "How will you live after the Fall?" I don't mean autumn; I mean the Fall. "How will you manage when trouble comes? How will you manage when you are tested and fail the test? How will you cope with frustration and fear and failure and anxiety?" Many of them have thought those to be quaint and even rude questions, perhaps the kind of rhetorical excess that preachers engage in around commencement time, a kind of raining on their parade.

Since September 11, however, these are no longer abstract, philosophical, or theoretical questions, and people have gravitated in astonishing numbers to the places where such questions are taken seriously. Every rabbi, minister, priest, imam, and spiritual leader whom I know or have heard of reports, as can I, the incredible turn toward faith in this time of our current crisis. Probably not since the Second World War has there been such a conspicuous turn to the faith in our country, and both our ordinary and our extraordinary services here in the last ten days bear profound witness to this. On Tuesday afternoon, September 11, the day of the terrorist attacks on the World Trade Center and the Pentagon, and the downing of the plane in Pennsylvania, we saw thousands in the Yard in an ecumenical witness; and on Friday of that same week we saw almost as many here at a Service of Prayer and Remembrance, on a day especially designated a national Day of Prayer and Remembrance. Last Sunday's service was like Easter day, and this one is very close to it. The daily service of Morning Prayers in Appleton Chapel is nearly standing room only, and this past week the president of this University asked if he could come and speak at Morning Prayers on Friday, thus proving beyond all shadow of a doubt that there is a God. With his opening words from our lectern he said that this was the last place he expected to find himself so early in his administration. This is from a secular man who, by the standards of this secular place, is as close to God as many aspire to reach.

These are extraordinary times, this is an extraordinary moment, we are witnessing extraordinary things, and I ask you this: is it not an incredible irony that, in the face of the most terrible and tangible facts available to us, the destruction of those monuments to material success—the brutally

OUTER TURMOIL, INNER STRENGTH 145

physical worldly reality, with the violence before our very eyes—men and women instinctively turn to the very things that cannot be seen? They turn not to the reality of the visible but to the reality of the invisible, which, when compared with what can be seen, ultimately endures. Seeking faith amid the ruins is the subtext of these days. There's a terrible parable there: that as the very temple to which we offered our secular worship is destroyed before us, we seek the God who precedes and who follows these temples made and destroyed by human hands. People are seeking inner strength beyond the outer turmoil; that is what I see and that is what I hear on every hand, in every paper, in every magazine, on every talk show, and on everybody's lips.

In light of this, the question, "Where is God?" seems almost irrelevant. This was the question of the day for the religion editor of the *Boston Globe* last weekend, and a host of my clerical colleagues attempted an answer or two. I was not asked—another proof of the existence of God—but had I been, I would have said what I now say to you, which is that it was the wrong question. The question is not where God is when disaster strikes; the real and interesting question is where you were before disaster struck. Where were you two weeks ago? Three weeks ago? Where will you be three weeks from now, or four weeks from now? God has not forgotten you, but is it not reasonable to suggest that before September 11 many of us had forgotten God? God is where God always is and has always been; it is we who have to account for our absence.

Be certain of one thing, however: we should not be embarrassed that now in adversity we seek the God whom we had forgotten in prosperity; for what is God for if he is not to be there when we seek him? We should not be embarrassed that in trouble we have remembered one profound theological truth: that God is to be found where God is most needed—in trouble, sorrow, sickness, adversity, and even in death itself. Over and over and over again the psalms make this point, as we sang in the sermon hymn, in paraphrase of Psalm 46: "God is our refuge and strength; a very present help in trouble."

Isn't this Luther's point in his great hymn, "A Mighty Fortress Is Our God"?

> Let goods and kindred go,
> This mortal life also;
> The body they may kill;

God's truth abideth still,
His kingdom is forever.

You don't have to be a Lutheran to know the truth of that. Then remember that one of the few bright spots in the National Cathedral Service of Prayer and Remembrance, one week ago, came in Billy Graham's sermon when he quoted the old hymn "How Firm a Foundation":

Fear not, I am with thee, O be not dismayed!
For I am thy God and will still give thee aid;
I'll strengthen thee, help thee, and cause thee to stand,
Upheld by my righteous, omnipotent hand.

Those hymns weren't written yesterday. They were not written by people who did not know turmoil. They were written by people who in the midst of outer turmoil had inner strength.

This last week, as I've thought about this morning and my obligations toward you, two images have flashed in my mind. One was the indelible image of those burning towers and those terrible encounters with the airplanes, a kind of conflict of our own magnificent technologies coming together in a horrible parody of our skills and our strengths. That was one image. The other goes back to one of my favorite movies, which will identify all of my phobias and predilections and will also give away my age. Between Dunkirk and Pearl Harbor there was produced one great film: *Mrs. Miniver.* How many of you here have ever seen *Mrs. Miniver*? Show me, please; I need some help here. Thank you! You young people, look at these old people and go out and rent *Mrs. Miniver.* She's a film, by the way. Go rent it; go see it. Those of you who know it know that I'm referring to that last scene in the bombed-out church on a Sunday morning, where, with the window destroyed and the cross standing in the broken window, the people of the congregation, though ripped apart by Hitler's bombing of their little village, still are able to sing, "Children of the heavenly king / As we journey sweetly sing." I know it was a great propaganda film, I know it was designed to rouse the souls and the spirits of the British people, I know it was Hollywood's version of Britain, with Walter Pidgeon and Greer Garson. I know all of that, and I believe it! So did the British people, and so do you need to believe that in that construction somewhere rests that image of the God who was with us at the most terrible moment of our time. The answer to the question "Where is God?" is that God is where God is always—by the side of those who need him. He is not in front to lead, not behind to push, not above to protect, but beside us to get us through: "Beside us to guide us / Our God with us joining."

I cannot imagine those heroic firefighters and police officers and workers and volunteers, amid the rubble of Ground Zero in New York, indulging in the luxurious theological speculation about where God might or might not be. They *know* where God is: he is right there with them, enabling them, empowering them, strengthening them, even when hope itself has died. If you want to know where God is, do not ask the prosperous. Ask the suffering. Ask the sorrowing. Ask those who are acquainted with grief.

In the Book of Common Prayer there is a collect that begins, "God of all comfort . . ." To some who don't know any better, that sounds like mere consolation, something soothing, adequate words in troubled times of turmoil and tribulation, a kind of Band-Aid on cancer, if you will, like the "comfortable words" in the old Book of Common Prayer, which were not very comforting to a church and a culture that had grown too comfortable. Do you know the proper meaning of the word *comfort,* by the way? You're about to. It means "to fortify; to strengthen; to give courage, even power," and not merely consolation. The God of all comfort is the one who supplies what we most lack when we most need it. As Paul puts it, God gives us sufficient capacity that when we are knocked down we are not knocked out. The God of all comfort is not the god who fights like Superman, or Rambo, or Clint Eastwood, or any of our conventional cultural heroes. The God of all comfort is the one who gives inner power and strength to those who would be easily outnumbered, outmaneuvered, outpowered by the conventional forces and the conventional wisdom. Inner strength is what is required when in the midst of turmoil we do not know what to do with our outward power and our outward might.

Let us also not forget one powerful fact that we are tempted to forget, which is that the world has always been a dangerous and precarious place. The fact that we have just discovered this terrible fact for ourselves does not make it any less true, or any less dangerous. Outer turmoil is no longer the fate that falls to others: the shrinking world that has allowed us to export technology abroad has now, alas, permitted terror to be imported to us. The great question now is how we stand and how we manage in a world now less brave, now less new than ever it was.

Inner strength, I believe, comes from the sure conviction that God has placed us in the world to do the work of life, and not of death. This is what St. Paul says in Corinthians. "We are always facing death," he writes; "but this means that we know more and more of life" (2 Corinthians 4:11). Faith is not the opposite either of doubt or of death but the means whereby we face and endure doubt and death, and overcome our fear of them. Our inner faith as believers comes from the sure conviction that neither death nor doubt nor fear is the last word. This is not a policy statement for the nation; this is a sure conviction for Christian believers. Therefore, because we believe that, and because that belief is testified to by the experience of our ancestors in the faith, and our contemporaries who labor beside us, and for God in the rubble, we are able to endure. We are able to go through the worst for the best, come what may. Endurance is what it takes when you have nothing left. Phillips Brooks once said that we do not pray for lighter loads, but for greater strength to bear the loads we are given. Heavy loads have been placed upon us in these days, and even greater burdens and sacrifices are to come: of that there can be no doubt; and, like Jesus in the Garden, we would be less than human if we did not pray that this cup might pass us by—but it won't. The real issue for us, then, as it was for Jesus, is, How do we manage?

Inner strength in the midst of turmoil, I suggest, is not simply stoic endurance and perseverance, important as they are, especially in tough, demanding times. Nor is inner strength simply a form of mind over matter, a kind of moral escapism that says that you "may have captured my body, but my mind is free." It's not only either of those. When I tried to think of what it was, I remembered a story told by old Dr. Ernest Gordon, for many years dean of the chapel at Princeton, and more famous because of his book about his captivity on the River Kwai during World War II. In that Japanese prison camp, Ernest Gordon said, he and his fellow British who were captives were initially very religious, reading their Bibles, praying, singing hymns, witnessing and testifying to their faith, and hoping and expecting that God would reward them and fortify them for their faith by freeing them or at least mitigating their captivity. God didn't deliver, however, and the men became both disillusioned and angry, and some even faithless. They gave up on the outward display of their faith; but after a while, Gordon says, the men, responding to the needs of their fellows—caring for them, protecting the weaker ones, and in some cases dying for one another—began to discern something of a spirit of God in their midst. It was not a revival of religion in the conventional sense, but rather the discovery that religion was not what you believed but what you did for others when it seemed that you could do nothing at all. It was compassion that gave them their inner strength, and it was from their inner strength that their compassion came. I owe this insight to Dr. A. Leonard Griffiths, from *Illusions of Our Culture.*

Could it be that amid the cries of vengeance and violence and warfare, and the turmoil that is attempting to sweep us all up in the calamity of these days, the inner strength we so desperately seek is the strength that comes from compassion, from hearing and heeding the cry of the other?

In one of the books in Theodore Parker Ferris's library—*The Beatitudes,* by Hugh Martin—I found underlined these words about strength:

Some people's strength is all drawn from themselves. They are like isolated pools with limited reserves. Others are more like rivers. They do not produce or contain the power, but it flows through them, like blood through the body. The more they give, the more they are able to draw in. That strength is theirs, but it is not their own.

Then the author says, in words that I wish were mine:

The strength that God gives is available to those who care for others, for they are showing the spirit of Jesus. The power of God's spirit fortifies them.

Can it be that inner strength is the capacity not simply to endure, but to give? Can it be that compassion is superior to power? Can it be that amid the turmoil of that violent crowd on Good Friday, from his inner strength Jesus showed compassion? He forgave his enemies, he reunited his friends, and he redeemed the criminal.

When in the midst of turmoil and calamity you seek the inner strength that helps you not only to endure but to overcome, do not look for what you can get: look rather for what you have been given, and for what you can give. We begin with calamity, but we end with compassion. Remember the quotation that Theodore Ferris had underlined: "The strength that God gives is available to those who care for others. . . ."

Some Things Worth Fighting For

Text: Fight the good fight of faith. . . .

—1 TIMOTHY 6:12

We have two marvelous lessons this morning, and most of you must be relieved that you recognized the first, the story of David and Goliath, and were encouraged by the second, in the letter to Timothy. Two lessons, one text; and that is from 1 Timothy 6:12: "Fight the good fight of faith. . . ." It is in paraphrase of that verse that John Monsell wrote the hymn that we have just sung; and I wish to talk this morning about some things worth fighting for.

Let me start at the beginning—at the very beginning, that is, of my ministry here, now thirty-two years ago, and before many of you were born. Let me start with my very first sermon in this pulpit in the fall of 1970, which I recall giving as if it were yesterday. Perhaps there are a few of you here who can remember it as well, although I suspect that not many of you will confess to that fact. Remember, if you will, what 1970 was like—a time of social upheaval, of struggle on every imaginable hand. The 1970s cannot really be described; they can only be painted by crazy, demented artists, for there was the antiwar movement, and there were battles at home and battles abroad, fightings within and fears without. There was the civil rights movement, the struggle for the soul of America; there was the feminist movement just aborning, with all of its edges; and there were the cultural and the generational wars and gaps growing into a chasm. It was a terrible time, and here was I, a very green, very young, very anxious new assistant minister eager to prove myself and to discern the temper of the times. What should be my first words?

Well, I took my first text from Jacob's wrestling with the angel, in Genesis, and gave as my title "The Art of Militant Living." *Pretty cool,* I thought, *the "art of militant living."* *Militant* was the operative buzzword way back then, when people were described as "militant" or "nonmilitant," and everyone, it seemed, was militant about something. I stood up here in this pulpit on an October morning, with an Afro that would put Cornel West's to shame—he was a freshman in that year—and I went on about militant living. Everybody in those days called their particular agenda a "struggle." Remember the "struggles"? Are you in the "struggle"? If you're not in the "struggle" with us, you're in the "struggle" against us—and thus the idea of "struggling" was born, of struggling with God and religion, struggling with faith, and struggling with the whole establishment. This was the language of the day, and I spoke it as well as any twenty-eight-year-old might speak it, for at twenty-eight everything seems so clear, so absolute, so unambiguous: find the right cause, do the right thing; either you are a part of the solution or you are a part of the problem. Oh, to be twenty-eight again!

I dip into this little autobiographical bog in order to make a larger point, because I think that it is in that spirit of militant struggle that most of us read or hear the story of David and Goliath. That's why it's popular; and why not? It is a scene right out of the World Wide Wrestling Federation. There was a giant of a bully and a virtuous stripling youth: you can cast the characters— manifest evil and manifest virtue—and we know how the story begins. The bully mocks the youth, paws the ground, and brandishes his weapon. The youth takes on the bully; the bully underestimates the youth. I remember Bill Coffin preaching on this very text in this pulpit, placing this memorable line in the mouth of Goliath: "Hey, kid, whatcha got in the bag?" We know the answer, and we are particularly pleased when the little David stands on the fallen bully's chest and hacks off Goliath's head with Goliath's own sword. There is some manipulation that has to be done here, however, because the Scripture tells us that Goliath was hit in the forehead with the stone and fell on his face, so David either has to get some help to turn Goliath over in order to stand on his chest; or there is a more unseemly picture but more accurate, according to Samuel, that David stands on Goliath's back and then hacks away at his head. Now that's militant living with attitude! All makes sense in this wonderful narrative—all, that is, except for a few slightly ambiguous lines and moments at verse forty-six, where, before David does the deed, he says these words to the giant. Listen carefully:

This day the Lord will deliver you into my hand, and I will strike you down, and cut off your head; and I will give the dead bodies of the host of the Philistines this day to the birds of the air and to the wild beasts of the earth; that all the earth may know that there is a God in Israel, and that all this assembly may know that the Lord saves not with sword and spear; for the battle is the Lord's and he will give you into our hand. (1 Samuel 17:46–47)

What about those lines: ". . . that all this assembly may know that the Lord saves not with sword and spear. . . ."? It appears very well that the Lord saves with sword and spear, or their equivalent in terms of one round stone. I know that it is Goliath who is destined to lose, despite his power and his sword and his spear; and, remember, when Saul offered David his sword, his spear, and his armor, David said, "This is too heavy. I can't wear it; this is not my sort of stuff." There is something disturbing, mildly disquieting about the notion that the Lord does not deliver the goods with sword and spear—not with anybody's sword and spear.

A strange moment of placidity appears in the middle of this wonderful and predictable scene of fighting, violence, and war. What we know later of David, after he has won this victory and thousands more, and after he has achieved all his worldly and political ambitions, is that his greatest battle is not the one with Goliath. Scripture tells us that he won that battle; the greatest battle that he was to fight, however, was with himself, which Scripture, with equal candor, tells us that he lost. The struggle with Goliath was easy, even predictable; but the struggle David had within himself when he had his best friend killed so that he could take his widow as his wife was not only wrong and difficult; it was tragic, a tragic failure—for he lost the ultimate battle within. Fighting without is easy; fighting within is very difficult, and even dangerous.

Hold that thought as we turn to St. Paul, who speaks of a different kind of struggle from that of David and Goliath, in a different kind of fight that is equally compelling, equally dangerous, but different. Remember, it is Paul, the older, wiser, more seasoned person, who says to his young timorous friend Timothy—Paul is a senior and Timothy is a freshman—"My boy, fight the good fight of faith." How does he put it, in 1 Timothy? Listen:

"But as for you, man of God, shun all of this. . . ."—which is what preceded the sixth chapter: the love of vanity, the love of riches, the love of power, the love of all the things that the world values. Paul says to Timothy:

. . . shun all of this: aim at righteousness, godliness, faith, love, steadfastness, gentleness. Fight the good fight of faith; take hold of the eternal life to which you were called when you made the good confession in the presence of many witnesses. . . . I charge you, Timothy, to keep the commandment unstained and free from reproach until the appearing of our Lord Jesus Christ. (1 Timothy 6:14)

That's the advice Paul gives to Timothy. Those are the things he tells him are worth fighting for, that is, in the good fight of faith. What could this possibly mean? How may we interpret it? How may we understand it? Well, remember the famous line of Mark Twain, who said that the problem he had with the Bible was not with what he could not understand, but with what was perfectly clear and that he could understand? Paul says that the things worth fighting for are righteousness, godliness, faith, love, steadfastness, gentleness. These are the things for which Christians—not everybody, but Christians, those who profess the Lord Jesus Christ—are meant to fight, these the things for which we are meant to be known to one another and to the world. Righteousness, godliness, faith, love, steadfastness, gentleness: this is not just another New Testament list of virtues, and when you scratch us, these are the things you are supposed to see and to recognize. If you're not sure whether or not a stranger is a Christian, you should be able to tell if he exercises righteousness, godliness, faith, love, steadfastness, gentleness. Which of these words do we not understand? What do we not get? Where is the conundrum? It seems pretty clear to me.

Now, I know that such a list as this is bound to disappoint those of us for whom fighting against others is a fundamental part of our human nature and our human identity. Dean Colin Slee declared from this pulpit last Sunday, as a foreigner—he's English, but a foreigner—that the world perceives us—that is, Christian America—as a fundamentally violent culture that celebrates the execution of more people than almost any other country in the world, worships the gun, beats people up, and loves television violence. When he said from this pulpit that the world sees us as a culture of violence, I watched, and I saw many of you squirming, although I couldn't tell if you didn't like the preacher for saying what he said, or didn't like the fact that what he said was actually true and that we stand guilty as charged. He touched a nerve in a culture that always seemingly defines itself as at war with something or somebody. We are now in a war on terrorism, and our president—George, that is; not Larry—has declared that we shall be on a war footing indefinitely, a position that has been ratified by astronomical poll ratings in his favor. Good for George; too bad for the rest of us.

We have been in a war on drugs for as long as anybody can remember; and do you remember that Lyndon Johnson once waged a war on poverty? Most of us grew up in the Cold War, and when it ended with our "victory," we as a culture, without a visible and external enemy to fight, did not know what to do, because we are better trained to war than we are to peace. That is presumably why we took to fighting each other in the culture wars of the 1990s: we needed someone to fight. Thank God the Republicans had Bill Clinton, and Bill Clinton had the Republicans. There was a fight in which we could all engage at some level or another, because we are trained to war and not to peace. Some people now are actually relieved to have a real war to fight once again.

When Tony Campolo was preaching among us with great power two weeks ago, he shocked many a conventional admirer in these pews when he asked, "Have you prayed for Osama bin Laden lately?" I thought that some of you probably thought, "What a rhetorical question. Oh, that clever Tony Campolo, he knows how to press our buttons." He meant it, however, and he reminded us that if we have enemies, we are supposed to pray for them. I realized that I stood convicted, for I hadn't prayed for Osama bin Laden lately, and I haven't heard many intercessions offered here in his name; but if he is our enemy, he is by definition someone for whom we should be praying. Most of us believe that the Christian fight gives us permission to fight righteously, and that we are called to what in my first sermon here I called "the art of militant living." We can conjure up chapter and verse in the Bible to support that position, for nobody wants to be a wimp for Jesus, and, in fact, Jesus embarrasses those of us who look to his example for a definition of "battle" and "fighting," because he wimps out on us. We want him to fight back—as, for example, when he is arrested in the garden on Maundy Thursday, and the soldiers come after him with swords and sticks and staves, and Peter, our kind of can-do guy, hacks off the ear of the high priest's servant. When I was child that was the highlight of the Passion narrative as far as I was concerned, and the rest was downhill all the way.

What does Jesus do in this situation? He doesn't say, "Well done, Peter," or "Let's get the bastard." He doesn't say that. He scolds Peter and says, "You shouldn't have done that. Come, take me to Pilate. I want to chat with

Pilate. Here I am, all yours." That's a wimpy sort of scene; and rather than rising from the dead, he should have stayed dead, for this is no example to set before people like ourselves who want heroics in every spot. On the cross, when Jesus ought to have brought down the wrath of God upon his executioners instead of rending the veil of the temple in twain after it was all too late, and instead of sending the earthquake long after it could do any good—when he should have churned up all creation—what does he do? He pardons, he forgives, he promises paradise, and he finally gives up the ghost. If that is an example of righteous resistance to evil, then forget it; no wonder evil triumphs in the world if the example that the gospel offers us is that of one who simply surrenders all.

St. Paul has more moxie than Jesus, and yet St. Paul tells us that the only things worth fighting for are "righteousness, godliness, faith, love, steadfastness, gentleness. Fight the good fight of faith," he says; "take hold of the eternal life to which you were called when you made the good confession." This list is to make the "good confession" issue-specific: righteousness, godliness, faith, love, steadfastness, gentleness—that's Paul's list.

In some very real sense, humanly speaking, the easiest thing that we can do in this world is to fight. That is probably why we do it so often—not because we're good at it, but because it's easy to do. It is the simplest, most apparent way to settle grievances and differences. You hit me and I hit you, and because you would hit me first if you had the chance, I will hit you first in a defensive, preemptive strike. You show me attitude, I'll show you attitude, and we'll set our attitudes at one another. We start this behavior on the playground, we carry it out in the school, we exercise it in the workplace, we take it into the family, we take it into the nation, and then we take it into the family of nations; and because fighting is the only way we can define ourselves, we can do nothing but fight: if we stop fighting, not simply will we lose, but we will no longer be certain of who we are. We lose not the battle but our identity, our being, and our purpose.

One of the most chilling television docudramas I ever saw was on the BBC a few years ago, about the so-called hard men of the IRA, who were terrified of the Irish peace process because not only would it put them out of work, but, since they were defined by their work, which was blowing things up and killing people, they would lose their identity and purpose. They would be made "redundant," as the British put it; they would be put out of work, and the effect would be the same as when steelworkers are put out of work; and when they can no longer work with steel, who are they? When policemen are retired and can no longer police, who are they? When bankers are downsized and can no longer bank, who are they? The hard men of the IRA would be retired by peace, they would literally cease to be, and real war, the story went, was preferable to real peace, for real peace is riskier, it being the great unknown. I sometimes think that this is the case in the Middle East, personified by those two calcified professional warriors Sharon and Arafat, neither of whom can contemplate existence in the absence of war, since they have been defined by war and use war to define themselves. Our ever-wise colleague David Gergen pointed out to our Visiting Committee last week, in answer to a question about the Middle East, "What the Middle East needs is a Nelson Mandela." Instead we have Sharon and Arafat. What a bad exchange.

Some of you will remember our late colleague here in the University, Larry Hill, that robust Presbyterian musician chaplain, agent provocateur, founder of the Pro Arte Orchestra, and a peace and justice warrior of the first order. Larry knew all about the art of militant living, and one of his most successful and confrontational ministries here twenty years ago was a program that he called "Waging Peace." He argued that we had to fight for peace with even more energy than that which we expend when we fight in war. As a good Presbyterian he also understood that it was harder and thus even more necessary to wage war against our inner demons than it was to demonize our enemies, for it is easy to demonize our enemies and incredibly difficult to fight our demons; it is easy to fight the enemy on the outside and to ignore the enemy on the inside. Every day I am in a pitched battle between my inner self that knows what I ought to do and even what I want to do, and my other inner self that tempts me to "act out," as the psychologists say, my paranoia, my anger, my depression, and my fear; and the trouble with that inner battle is that it doesn't always stay within but is contagious, just like measles and television. Sit or work with a depressed person fighting his or her demons and they do not fight alone, they drag you into it and you spread it, and pretty soon there's a gray cloud over everything.

Thus we all kick the dog, even if we haven't a dog, when we can't win the inner fight for our own souls; and that is to what the Epistle of James refers when it asks, in James, chapter 4, "What causes war, and what causes fighting among you? Is it not your passions that are at war in your members? You desire and do not have, so you kill, and you covet and cannot obtain, so you fight and wage war." What's the problem here? This is James speaking: "You do not have because you do not ask; you ask and do not receive because you ask wrongly." We ask for "victory" when we should be asking for reconciliation. We ask to win "them" over to our side instead of first asking to win ourselves over to the right side. We think we are called to war when we are called to struggle, and to fight for the things that are worth fighting for, which we think are country, property, prosperity, power, and our personal liberties. The Bible gives no such list. The Bible tells us that the things worth fighting for are righteousness, godliness, faith, love, steadfastness, gentleness—the things that we confess and profess in Jesus Christ. That is why the Bible is a more demanding and superior document than the Declaration of Independence, the Magna Carta, the U.S. Constitution, and even the Mayflower Compact.

Perhaps this Pauline stuff is a little too abstract? Too religious, all this talk of righteousness, godliness, faith, love, gentleness, and so on? After all, Paul didn't have to live in the kind of world that we live in. Perhaps we would hearken more to another voice, a secular voice, about the things worth fighting for? I will give such a secular voice, with which few of us would choose to argue. Here is what Gandhi had to say when he described the seven social sins that not only can destroy nations but also are capable of destroying persons. To fight against these social sins is to fight for their opposites. Here are what Gandhi said are the seven social sins:

1. Politics without principle

2. Wealth without work

3. Commerce without morality

4. Pleasure without conscience

5. Education without character

6. Science without humanity

7. Worship without sacrifice

These may all be civil, corporate, public values, but they all begin with the struggle within, the conquests of the apparent by the ultimate. These are some of the things worth fighting for.

The British Baptist preacher Charles Haddon Spurgeon, who routinely preached to thousands a century ago all across Britain, and whose books were read in Christian households around the world, said:

There may be persons who can always glide along like a tramcar on rails without a solitary jerk, but I find that I have a vile nature to contend with, and spiritual life is a struggle with me. I have to fight from day to day with inbred corruption, coldness, deadness, barrenness, and if it were not for my Lord Jesus Christ my heart would be as dry as the heart of the damned.

Does that sound familiar? Do you know who that person is? If you do not, then look in the mirror, for there will be at least one person you will recognize.

I have no cheap, quick, easy formula, no fast analyses, no quick fixes, no "lean thighs in thirty days," and neither has the gospel; and we should be very suspicious of anyone who offers such things. The things that are worth fighting for are hard to define, and hard to defend. Who dares to be righteous in an unrighteous world? Who dares to be godly in a godless place? Who dares to be faithful and loving in a faithless and loveless world? Who can afford steadfastness? Who, in this ego-centered, id-obsessed, power-hungry world dares to be gentle? Yet, we are told that these are things for which we should be fighting daily and forever, and struggling and contending; and if this gospel were really and truly preached, I guarantee that there would be many fewer people in church to hear it.

In this most churchgoing country in the world, one of the reasons the churches are so filled with people is that those people do not hear a compelling, demanding, defiant gospel that challenges the conventional wisdom and says that the things worth fighting for are not what they think they are, but are what are listed here in the good news. Those who did remain in church, after hearing such a gospel, would turn the world upside down. Think of the noble few who did: Jesus, Paul, Gandhi, King, Mandela, and Tutu, just up the street here in Cambridge. Heroes, yes, but their fight, and what enabled them for the fight, can be ours as well. It is not esoteric, it is not limited to the moral elite; the struggle is ours and it is now, and if we lose this fight no other fight will be worth winning. Paul, who describes the Christian life as one constant struggle, with no cheap or easy victories, also shows us how the impossible can be possible for us.

How is this all to be done? How can this happen? How can people like us take up righteousness, kindness, gentleness, steadfastness, faith? How can we do it? Paul gives us the answer in another of his letters, when he says, "I can do all things through Christ, who strengthens me." It is not we who do

Christ the favor of worshiping him; it is Christ who empowers us by strengthening us, and enabling us to fight for the things that are worth fighting for, the things that endure; and that is a promise worth fighting for, worth dying for, and worth living for. So let us, for Christ's sake and our own, begin the struggle afresh, anew, today, here, and now. Fight the good fight of faith.

What Have You Done for Me Lately?

Text: Is the Lord among us or not?

—EXODUS 17:7

Yesterday, while many of you were enduring yet another of our humiliating defeats on Soldiers Field—34–24, I believe, was the fateful score—I was enjoying myself mightily as the grand marshal of Plymouth's Thanksgiving parade. Now, we have lots of old traditions in Plymouth, but this parade is a relatively new one, only five years old, with Thanksgiving on an international scale as its theme. Instead of a small pageant of the usual Pilgrims and Indians, or as Macy's celebration of Thanksgiving as one big commercial for Christmas shopping, yesterday's parade was meant to celebrate the community of nations, their peoples, and their hopes. It was in the spirit of the United Nations proclamation, which many of you may not know, that has declared this year the International Year of Thanksgiving.

As grand marshal, I had the extraordinary opportunity to sit in the reviewing stand and watch a two-and-a-half-hour parade of nations and their cultures pass by, represented by dancers in the streets, children, marching bands, drum and bugle corps, and mariachi bands; and to see an Irish pipe band following a group of dancers from Senegal; and Hondurans, Pakistanis, and Germans all sharing their splendid colors, music, and marching styles as they passed the Pilgrim landmarks of Plymouth Rock and the *Mayflower.* It was a sense of Thanksgiving that would have blown away the minds of those poor frightened little Pilgrims and their Native American hosts and guests, and an extraordinary thing to behold. One woman nearby observed, in a good midwestern American stage whisper to no one in particular but within perfect earshot of us all, that being in Plymouth for Thanksgiving was like being in Bethlehem for Christmas, only that it was a lot safer in Plymouth.

I mention all of this to remind us how easy it is to feel good at this time of year. Basking in that international splendor, and looking at the many representatives of those nations marching in our streets who are in the headlines not for the joys and peace of their lands but for the trials and tribulations they have endured and are enduring, it is easy to rejoice in our own good fortune and to celebrate the fact that we invented this holiday, it is uniquely ours, and we have a right to feel good. It is also easy, however, to feel bad at this time of year, especially if we feel we haven't sufficient reason to feel good. We have had, for example, bad financial news; the medical diagnosis is not encouraging; there are serious strains in the marriage; the relationship is breaking apart; and either Al Gore or George Bush will be president. I know people who have profited enormously in the stock-market boom of the last few years who, instead of rejoicing and being grateful to God for their unmerited windfall of wealth, are in a semipermanent state of depression and anxiety because they know it all must end sooner or later.

Some old Pilgrim friends—Pilgrim-descendant friends—go into hiding at this time of year, and curse their ancestors. "I hate the Pilgrims," says one of them, "for just because they were always cheerful in tough times, and thankful, and worked hard, and all of that, everybody thinks we should do the same. It was an ill wind that blew the *Mayflower* into Plymouth Harbor."

When these moods hit, and they do or they will; when we are not grateful or thankful or happy on cue; when the calendar and culture tell us we are to be pleased, happy, thankful, and joyful whether we are or not; when we remember the advice of Flanders and Swann, that "We should always be sincere whether we mean it or not"—at such moments we are likely to respond as did those difficult Jews in this morning's lesson, tempting and taunting God, and asking, "Is the Lord with us or not?" Are you on our side or not? Are you going to deliver the goods or not? Not way out there, not way back then, but now? Moses "called the name of the place Massah and Meribah"—which means, in translation from the Hebrew, places of "testing and strife"—"because of the faultfinding of the children of Israel, and because they put the Lord to the proof. . . ." The lesson takes place in a place of testing and strife.

They were annoyed, as you will recall, by their privations in the wilderness, and some had even wanted to return to Egypt, where at least they had had three meals a day, drink, a certain familiar routine, and guaranteed employment. By the time we encounter them they have forgotten the facts of their oppression, and, worse, they have forgotten the facts of their liberation. They have forgotten how they were wonderfully led out of Egypt and through the Red Sea. They have forgotten their charismatic leader, Moses, and his great services to them; and they have forgotten God. We cannot say that they had forgotten the psalm that we read this morning, which lists all of those things, because the psalm had not yet been written. So, we cannot blame them for forgetting the psalm, but we *can* blame them for forgetting that the steadfast love of the Lord endures forever.

Didn't you revel in the cadence of that psalm as it increased and we kept repeating that phrase, "The steadfast love of the Lord endures forever"? Would that those complaining, kvetching people at Massah and Meribah had had the benefit of the responsive reading of that psalm, to be able to implant all this upon their memories—but memory was of no use to them. They were thirsty, impatient, doubting, fearful, paranoid, and so angry that they were about to stone Moses to death. Moses said, "What am I going to do with these people, God? They are about to destroy me." They taunted not only Moses, but God: "Are you among us or not?" Are you with us or not? If you are with us, do something now. Don't just remind us of our glorious past or our bright future. We are thirsty here and now. What good are memory and hope if we die of thirst? What have you done for us lately? What have you done for *me* lately? Are you with us or not?

My colleagues in the Hebrew Bible and the Old Testament define this set of verses from which the text comes as the "murmuring tradition," where there is not yet outright rebellion but a low-grade grumbling fever, not outright war but an undercurrent of moaning and groaning, of complaining and kvetching, the sort of little irritants that make up the day, the week, the year, our lives. The murmuring tradition is one we all know; nothing worth causing a fuss about yet never quite settled. Your partner asks, "Is there anything wrong, dear?" and you answer, curtly, "No, nothing's the matter; everything is perfectly all right." Then, "May I help you in any way?" "No, of course not; everything's fine. There's nothing wrong at all . . ." So it goes. We all know about this murmuring tradition, and you're all a part of it, charter members of the murmuring tradition, vaguely remembering great things, longing for great things to come, yet right now pretty annoyed, pretty irritated, pretty unsatisfied. We maintain stiff upper Yankee lips and a good stern eye toward the future, although we are very unhappy right now.

It is an impertinent, nasty little scene that is described here in Exodus, and God is not pleased. "Did I go to all this trouble, getting damp and wet to bring such a disagreeable people out, to be treated in this way? To be provoked, challenged, questioned as to my loyalty to you?"—to put a few words into God's mouth. Yet, for Moses' sake, not the people's—the lesson is very clear—God saves the day by telling him to strike the rock with the very rod with which he had caused the Red Sea waters to part. Moses does so, and, wonder of wonders, out comes potable, drinkable, Poland Spring water. The people are satisfied for the minute, until the next time, when they ask, "Is the Lord among us or not?" What have you done for me lately? The passage ends on an ominous note: "And he called the name of the place Massah and Meribah, because of the chiding of the children of Israel, and because they tempted the Lord, saying, 'Is the Lord among us or not?'" Places of testing and strife.

Now, you have perfectly good reason to ask what we, on the eve of Thanksgiving, are to make of this, and what points the preacher wants us to take away. Well, I am going to make it simple, because I want you to remember that there are three things to be learned from this lesson, and I hope they will see you through lunch, through Thanksgiving Day, and through the rest of your life, however short or long that may be.

First, remember to remember. The thirsty Jews, so obsessed with their present privations, forgot to remember the God who had brought them out of Egypt in the first place, through all that water, and forgot to remember that that God would not bring them this far to let them die of thirst in the desert. That would be a wasted investment—all that trouble and annoyance for nothing. This Thursday, as you gather around your tables with your dysfunctional families and friends, I invite you to remember not the usual good things, not the list of the blessings you have received, like an audit at a stockholders' meeting, but the bad things, by name, that have happened to you, the terrible things, the worst things.

Think of your worst moments, your sorrows, your losses, your sadness, and then remember that here you are, able to remember them. You got through the worst day of your life; there may be yet a worse one in store for you, but that's for next Thanksgiving. This Thanksgiving you got through the trauma, you got though the trial, you endured the temptation, you survived the bad relationship, you're making your way out of the dark and out of the miry clay. Remember who got you through. You got into the mess on your own, but remember that it was the Lord who got you out of it, got you through it, and was with you in the middle of it. There are more troubles to come, infinitely more troubles to come, and you may be in trouble right now, but if you remember to remember you will remember, as the old spiritual says, "How I got over." How I was spared, how the Lord did a wonderful thing in bringing me through to this present moment; and how he did it I will never know, how I got here I will never know, but I will remember to remember to thank God. Remember to remember, and not just the good things—you'll take those for granted— but remember the bad things, and then look to see where you are. That's the first thing: remember to remember.

Second, and this is a little more sophisticated than the first point: Thanksgiving is not an event or a day or a moment; it is a process. The children of Israel were on a journey in the wilderness, moving from one place to the other, not where they had been and not yet where they were going, but in the "middest"—as the Middle English word has it—or middle of it, as are you and I. Although life was an unsteady motion, the direction was generally forward. Tender mercies do not happen always at once: sometimes there are long parched periods where we are dry, without guidance, and without inner or outer strength, and we have to function like the camel, living on what we have stored up. Like the camel we have to keep moving nevertheless, and then mercies come in bunches like bananas, and we pause in amazement.

Great is Thy faithfulness, O God, my father;
Morning by morning, new mercies I see.

All I have need of, Thy hand hath provided:
Great is Thy faithfulness, Lord, unto me.

THOMAS CHISHOLM (1866–1960)

An old pastor of mine cherished a very old Sunday bulletin where the printer had made a mistake and had listed the service for the fourth

Thursday in November 1936 as "Thanks*living* Day." What a wonderful mistake! What a wonderful blessing that little mistake can make in an attitude, a life, a world! Don't make the mistake of the children of Israel, and mistake a moment's privation for the end of the world. Thanksgiving is a process; it is Thanks*living*.

Finally, against all perils remember this: do not tempt God. Do not put God to the test. Do not put God to your puny little proofs. You are not to tempt God; you are to trust God. Do not make God give you constant proofs of loyalty, power, and affection. You can tell in a relationship that the lights are going out when one of the parties is constantly saying to the other, "Do you love me? Prove it." Love is based not on proof but on trust. Infidelity is based on proof—have you ever thought about that? Love, however, is based upon trust. God is not to be tempted. He never forgot how the people at Massah and Meribah tried to tempt him and his providence in the wilderness; he forgave them, but he never forgot, and this incident is referred to at least a dozen times throughout both the Old and the New Testaments. God is to be trusted in good season and in bad, when we win or when we lose, whether we live or whether we die. God is to be trusted, for God is trustworthy and true; and the evidence of our own being is sufficient evidence of that. So:

1. Remember to remember—the bad things, not just the good.

2. Thanksgiving is Thanks*living,* a life of gratitude, a work in progress.

3. God is not to be tempted but to be trusted.

It is the case, as every Pilgrim knows, that our best days are ahead of us and not behind us, and for that we thank God; and it is indeed the case, as every Pilgrim knows, that we have not yet arrived at where we are meant to be. This is not our destination, and for that we thank God; and it is indeed the case that the Lord has not brought us this far to abandon us in the wilderness of our own despair and disappointment, and for that we thank God.

Thus we know the answer to the impertinent question of the text: "Is the Lord among us or not?" You bet your lives he is, for how else would we be here to ask that question and be assured of the glorious answer? Thanks be to God. Amen.

Sin and Sympathy

Text: For we have not a high priest who is unable to sympathize with our weakness.

—HEBREWS 4:15

As always, I have a text, and my text today is from the fourth chapter of the Book of Hebrews, the fifteenth verse, which is the fulcrum, or middle, or balancing point of three verses that you should keep in mind from this remarkable chapter. First is the thirteenth verse: "And before him no creature is hidden, but all are naked and laid bare to the eyes of the one to whom we must render an account." Second is the text above. And third is the sixteenth verse: "Let us therefore approach the throne of grace with boldness, so that we may receive mercy and find grace to help in time of need."

God knows all and sees all. God loves us despite all that he sees and knows, and because of that we have confidence to draw near to God. That is the gospel, the good news, the summary and essence of our faith.

This morning I am talking about sin and sympathy. That is the title I invented for this morning's sermon, and that is what I put on the notice boards and in the *Boston Globe,* and that is what it says on the top of my manuscript. "Sin," said one of my secular, worldly friends, "what a dreary title word. What a tiny, nasty little word. That's all you Christians can talk about. Why don't you talk about people?"

When I invented this title I recalled that conversation, and then I thought of the perfect reply to my friend, but, as usual, I came upon this reply long after the conversation had passed. I should have said to him, "I do talk about people, all of the time: it is called 'sin.'" Most of my best lines in riposte or repartee occur after the fact, giving rise to the title for my next book: *Things I Wish I Had Said.*

Sin: what a turnoff! You don't find business leaders talking about "loss"—or lawyers talking about "guilt," unless you are Alan Dershowitz—so why do preachers spend so much time talking about sin? Is it simply the economic motive—that if there weren't any we'd all be out of business?

Sin: we can speculate, we can imagine, we can remember Calvin Coolidge's famous remark about the Sunday sermon. His wife, Grace Goodhue, asked, upon her husband's return from church, "What did the preacher talk about?" "Sin," answered the president. "Well, what did he say?" she persisted. "He was agin' it," said the president. End of story and, presumably, end of sermon, but you all know better than that.

Sin: contrary to the popular opinion of my theological colleagues, I do not believe that we have lost our sense of sin. Not at all. We may live in a permissive society, a glitzy, cheap, and sensational society, and it may appear to some that civilization and Christian values are all going to hell in a handbasket. Remember the Flanders and Swann routine of forty years ago, about "rude words," and the part where they say that we now say in public things that we would never dare to say in private? Values and standards all seem to be falling down around our ears.

There is a cottage industry—no, a real industry—in the so-called crisis of morals and values. We have lost our way, we are told. We are like lost sheep. We no longer know or care about what is right and what is wrong. Our standards are low, and even they are easily transgressed. A perjurer like Oliver North is a credible candidate for the U.S. Senate on a reform ticket, no less; what an extraordinary thing! and biblical literacy in our Bible republic has never been lower. Did you read in yesterday's *Boston Globe,* where a poll conducted by the Barna Research Group on biblical literacy in America revealed that many Bible readers identified Joan of Arc as Noah's wife? It's in the *Globe;* read it for yourselves.

We have lost our way, and our sense of wrong, and sense of guilt, and sense of sin. So goes the conventional and familiar litany, but it is not as simple as all of that; even here at Harvard it's not as simple as all of that. In my years of ministry here, now nearly twenty-five years in this place of achievement and ambition, tender egos and tough minds, I have never encountered anyone with an inadequate doctrine of sin, with the possible exceptions of my colleagues in the Law and Divinity Schools, and that is only temporary. Most people could outdo the most fire-breathing evangelists in a catalogue of their own sinfulness—or inadequacy, as they might prefer to say. We, more than most, know our own flaws and weaknesses: we are on intimate terms with all of our demons, as well as with the demons of all the rest of us, and with the world.

It is not the sense of sin that is missing in any of us or in our culture, for we know wrong when we see it, we know wrong when we hear about it, we know wrong when we do it. It is not the sense of sin that is missing; it is the sense of grace, sympathy, and forgiveness that is absent. We know what is wrong; we do not know what is right. The British writer Cyril Connolly, in *The Unquiet Grace,* written in 1944, put it for the modern condition: "Those of us who were brought up as Christians and have lost our faith have retained the sense of sin without the saving belief in redemption. This poisons our thought and so paralyses us in action."

I would put it another way, in the title of a paperback book I could imagine becoming a bestseller: *Guilt Without Sex: The Worst Side of the Equation Without Any of the Benefits.*

The dilemma for most of us is that we have a perfectly vivid doctrine of sin, while we have a less vivid certainty of sympathy with it or redemption from it, and that is, in my view, the worst of all possible conditions. Our problem is not ignorance of our sins; our problem is that we know we cannot overcome them, and we are not certain that anyone cares. We are not driven by our virtues; we are driven by the fear of our vices, and thus, like T. S. Eliot's figure in one of his *Four Quartets,* we work so hard at devising systems "so perfect that no one need ever be good."

Sin: it is not an abstraction, a doctrine to be proven. I don't have to argue you, any of you, into a sensibility of sin. All you have to do is look in the mirror and look into your hearts to know the reality of sin, or if not at yourselves, look at your neighbors: the burden of conscience, what the old evangelicals called the "sin-sick soul," is not an abstraction. We can name our sins faster than our blessings. Ask the dying at the gates of death. They do not ask for explanations; they ask for forgiveness. They know the reality of the sense of sin, and if that were all there was to know, what a miserable state we would all be in.

Christianity did not invent sin, nor did the Jews. That is not the claim of the gospel. The heart of Christian faith, the good news, is that we know someone who not only knows our sin and sympathizes, but can do and does do something about it. Sympathy is entering into someone else's situation, and understanding and still loving them both in it and beyond it. Take, for instance, sympathy notes. We write them because we have known the experience of sorrow, and heart calls out to heart: we enter into the experience and share the love. That is what sympathy is, and ours is a sympathetic religion. We know someone who sympathizes and knows our sin: God. The gospel is about sympathy and salvation; and, contrary to the rantings of radio and television preachers and those who traffic in guilt and angst, the gospel is not about sin but about sinners who discover that there is life and hope and redemption beyond and after and in the midst of their sins. The gospel is first about sympathy, and then about salvation, and who does not need both?

On Wednesday afternoon there was a service of thanksgiving in this church for the life of Erik Erikson, and one anecdote told of the students and teaching fellows who sat at the feet of this great man, who was almost godlike to his students: in one session, a long time after everyone was well acquainted, a teaching fellow asked of Professor Erikson, "Are you a Jew?" To which Erikson replied, "If you are an anti-Semite, then I am a Jew." That is sympathy. That is entering into the experience of someone else, and that is what the servant passage is about, in the fifty-third chapter of Isaiah. That is also the point of our text from the Book of Hebrews, not the easiest book from which to preach, but this text is as accessible and true to us now as it was to those Jewish Christians who worried that they were required to be perfect in order to be saved: "For we have not a high priest who is unable to sympathize with our weakness."

Without compromising the sinless nature of Jesus, the ideal high priest for whom the writer longs, he assures us that Jesus knows who we are and knows our condition. Jesus knows temptation, and the temptation to do the right thing for the wrong reason, which is the substance of the temptation stories in the wilderness at the beginning of Jesus' ministry. He knows the temptations to anger, to virtue, and to power. He knows the temptations to doubt oneself and one's ability, and to doubt one's God. In short, he knows who we are: in the words of the psalmist, "He knoweth our frame;"

and because of who we are, he is who he is. We can trust him because we know he knows who we are, not who we would like to be or who we pretend to be, or who we need to be, or who we hope people think we are. The divine sympathy is with us beyond all our illusions. Jesus sees beyond them, and still cares.

I knew an old woman once who, when ill, would never go to the doctor. She always said, "I'll go when I feel better." That same old woman hired a weekly housekeeper, and on the day before she was due to come, would clean the house from top to bottom. When asked why, her reply was, "I can't let her see my house like this."

The good news of the gospel is that Jesus sees us as we are and does not turn away. The conundrum of the gospel is that he forgives us. That's it, pure and simple. It is all right for God to see us as we are, for that is what God is supposed to do; but to see us as we are and to not turn away or destroy us is something else, and that is called the gospel.

In my old church in Plymouth, the old First Baptist, there was cast in stained glass—in yellow, blue, green, and red in all the appropriate places—in the ceiling over the pulpit a single eye, almost pulsating, and terrifying to a child, almost like that Masonic eye on our currency. It was a terrifying sight, and the text with it equally so: "Thou, God, seest me." It would be many years later and a degree or two down the way before I would recognize that eye, and with it Milton's powerful line about "living in my great taskmaster's eye." What terrified me was the fact that my God and that incredible eye could see all that I had hidden from the world and even from myself, and I knew I was seen to be the fraud that I knew I was. The image of that eye was like the equally terrifying secular image of Santa Claus— "He sees when you're sleeping, / He knows when you're awake, / He knows if you've been bad or good, / So be good, for goodness' sake." That is the easy and terrifying part, but when I discovered that the God who sees me, all of me, the real me, loves me in spite of what he sees, that became the incredible good news that is as implausible as it is true.

A judgmental God, a just God, even a good God I could understand, but a sympathetic God? A high priest who can identify with me and who knows my sin, and who cares for me beyond it? Well, that is news enough to turn one's life around. That is nothing less than love divine, all loves excelling.

We used to sing, beneath that all-seeing eye of God in the First Baptist Church in Plymouth, this old hymn:

There's not a friend like the lowly Jesus, no not one, no not one;
None else could heal all our souls' diseases, no not one, no not one.
Jesus knows all about our struggle. He will guide 'til the day is done;
There's not a friend like the lowly Jesus, no not one, no not one.

That is a sympathetic God who sees sin and turns not from it.

There is a danger, I know, in the domestication of salvation—in the making of Jesus so personal and private, the private property of our own piety—that we lose the majesty and grandeur, the awesomeness, the solemnity of God; and that we lose as well our own sense of unworthiness and our need of correction. We might become flippant: as the French cynic said, "It is my job to sin, God's to forgive me." I know all of that, but if I had but one sermon to preach, one case to make, one argument to put forward about the Christian faith, it would be about none of those larger, cosmic issues; it would be this one: we have a high priest, a savior, a friend who knows us as we are, loves us as we are, and wills us to be as he is without limit or condition. To know that we are loved of God is to know everything worth knowing.

Therefore—and that is the biggest word in the gospel—let us with confidence draw near to the throne of grace, that we may receive mercy and find grace to help in time of need. Amen.

PART TWO

Sermons for the Liturgical Seasons

Facing the Future

Text: Say to those who are of a fearful heart, "Be strong, fear not!"

—Isaiah 35:4

These words from the book of the prophet Isaiah that say to those of us with a fearful heart, "Be strong, fear not!" are good words with which to begin the new year, which is, of course, today. This is the beginning of the church's year, not of the calendar year or of the fiscal year or of the academic year or even of the social calendar, but of the Christian new year; and here we begin once again the cycle of praise and prayer centered first around the birth of our Lord, and ordered by his resurrection. Advent Sunday is a great day for Christians, for we begin at the beginning all over again, but important as it is, you would hardly notice it, tucked away behind Thanksgiving and before Christmas and the end of the "real" year. Here in Cambridge and at Harvard it is even more obscure, a Sunday in which people are still away for the Thanksgiving recess; and there are no Advent cards in the stores, no Advent holiday parties, and no Advent television specials. We Christians have the day all to ourselves, and here we are yet again as we have been for nearly two thousand years, daring to face the future.

In a sermon that was preached here now over a decade ago by the then provost of Southwark Cathedral in London, David Edwards reminded us that the Christian faith is a religion of the dawn, of the morning, of the new day, and he did this by reading the opening accounts of the resurrection in the Gospels. They all begin in the morning, at dawn, at the start of the new day, at the rising of the sun; they all put away the past and face the future, for the direction of the Christian faith is forward, ahead of time, always ahead of where we are at the moment, and always into new and uncharted territory.

That new day begins today.

Is this a surprising fact for Christians who are used to finding, in the past, justification for everything we do? We pride ourselves on the fact that we are a "historical" religion, and that we have a past of great glory and great achievement. We are by nature a remembering people, as I try to remind you on Remembrance Day in November, the month of remembering; and in a memorial place such as this Memorial Church it is easy to think that our duty is simply to remember. Advent, however, is meant to remind the people of God that we look ahead, that our only destiny is ahead of us, that which has not yet happened, and that all that we really possess, all that we really love, is in the future. Religions that try to recapture the past, that live in the past, that glory in the past, are dead; and this Memorial Church cannot be a church built to the glory of Harvard and in memory of God. It, and we, must understand, on this Sunday if on no other, that our best days are ahead of us, despite the fact that the alumni return at commencement and recall their days of derring-do when they were students: these cannot, however, be the best days of our lives. What a dreadful thought! We live in anticipation and not in memory—which is a hard concept, a hard bill of goods, because we suffer under the tyranny of the past. Oh, it may not seem like a tyranny to many of us; it may rather seem like a comfort: "the good old days," "things as they once were," the politics and piety of nostalgia, of past times.

There is another form that that tyranny takes: our obsession with the past; our nursing of past wounds, of past anxieties, of past fears and doubts. There are people who are seemingly kept alive in the difficult present by the memories of an even more difficult past, and you know them; perhaps you are even among them—people who actually cherish old feelings, and who find reconciliation hard. What is that old motto of clashing clans who cannot remember why they have hated but wallow in the fact that they always have? "When I hate, I know that I am alive."

Advent bids us confront the tyranny of the past, chuck it, get over it, put it away, and get on with the future; and that is the invitation of this morning.

That, however, is easier said than done, for if we are subject to the tyranny of the past, we are also subject to the tyranny or the fear of the future. Things may be difficult now, but at least we know these difficulties. What, though, does the future hold?

Ask a senior in this College or in any other college what she or he is doing next year and you will find just how fearful the future can be, and how hostile the question seems. Ask those of us who invest so heavily in the present about the future, and like all of the stock markets on earth we tremble and we shake. If we have something, we fear losing it all; if we have nothing at all, we fear more of the same in the future, and so we live in a world so fearful in the present that we are tyrannized by the past, so fearful of the future that we idolize the present.

Advent, then, comes to us as a shock, for its only direction is forward, its only word is for the future, and it will tolerate neither fear nor idolatry. Think of it: no one in the New Testament looked backward; they looked only forward. There is no sweet and pious nostalgia in the New Testament: the people anticipated that their best days were yet to come. What happened to Lot's wife in the Old Testament when she did look back? There she stood, and there she stayed, and there she is today. History will not save us; the present is incapable. Our only chance is in facing the future. Why? Because it is in the future that God is to be found, it is to the future that we are called: "Say to those who are of a fearful heart, 'Be strong, fear not!'" This is the essence and substance of the gospel, and that is why we look ahead and not back: our best days lie before us, the best is yet to come; and this is not a pious utterance—like Monsieur Coué, who every morning said, "Every day in every way I am getting better and better." We are not getting better and better: just look at the person next to you, just look into the mirror. We are in the care of God. The lesson of the prophet Isaiah is filled with hope, for he utters words that give us a vision of things to come that is almost too good to believe: "The blind shall see, the deaf hear, the lame leap, and the dumb speak." The future is the time that is to be, the land of verbs of action and renewal where things now unimagined become real.

Christians possess the future because that is where God intends to meet us once again. That is why we must always look ahead and not back, and why we must always trust and not fear: for the Christian the imperishable slogan must always be "Our best days are before us!"

When we celebrate the Holy Communion, as we soon shall, we engage in the most radical act of facing the future that is possible for humans: we take the ordinary creatures of the present, the bread and the wine; we remember the past out of which this action comes, the history of our redemption; *but,* and this is a very great *but,* we eat and drink as an act of faith and courage for the future. By this we say that we will not be held hostage to the bondage of the past or to the fears of the moment but that we live for tomorrow, we begin anew, and we celebrate and anticipate our redemption.

Who, then, can be afraid? What is there to worry about? We wait for the Lord with the last gesture we make as we pass from this world to the next. We are people of the dawn, people of the new day, people of the day that is to come, and we are never too old, never too young, to embrace the dawn and the rising sun; and if this is true, what is there to worry about? The only place to go, the only game in town, is the future, and we join on Advent Sunday with those who await the coming of the Lord and of his day. This is the God who will "strengthen the weak hands and make firm the feeble knees"; this is the God who says to those of a fearful, anxious, and unsettled heart, "Be strong, fear not!"

Our best days are ahead of us, the best is yet to come. Hallelujah! Happy new year! Amen.

The Courage to Hope

Text: For whatever was written in former days was written for our instruction, that by steadfastness and by the encouragement of the scriptures we might have hope.

—ROMANS 15:4

Advent is the season of hope, and we worship the God of things that are not yet, the God of things that are to be. That is both true and easy to say, and I have just done so; but hope, real hope, Christian hope, is not quite so easy to come by. Sometimes our hope fails us for lack of imagination, lack of courage, or for not thinking or hoping "big" enough—cheap and inadequate hope. Let me illustrate.

Our good friend Lord Runcie of Cuddesdon, the 102d Archbishop of Canterbury, told a marvelous story a few weeks ago in London of his friend the British ambassador to the United States, Sir Nicholas Henderson, who at the height of the Cold War was interviewed at just about this time of year by a features reporter from the *Washington Post*. The question, a features sort of question, was, "Mr. Ambassador, what do you want for Christmas?" Sir Nicholas, a master of British reserve and understatement, and not wanting to appear greedy but wanting also to be truthful, replied to the reporter that all he really wanted for Christmas was a jar of fruit preserved in ginger, such as you could get at Harrod's or in Fortnum and Mason. Apparently he liked that and that was what he would like for Christmas, and he hoped that Lady Henderson or somebody would give him such a jar. A few days later the *Washington Post*'s Christmas feature article described in detail what the diplomatic corps hoped for for Christmas: the Russian ambassador hoped for peace and goodwill; the Swiss ambassador hoped for genuine disarmament around the world; the Spanish ambassador hoped for Gibraltar to be given back; the Israeli ambassador hoped for peace in the Middle East; and so on and so on and so forth. Sir Nicholas, the British ambassador, was recorded as hoping for a jar of preserved fruit. Now, obviously of all those things hoped for, Sir Nicholas's hope was the most obtainable, and he was doubtless the only one who got what he wanted for Christmas; but by comparison, as Lord Runcie pointed out, his hope seemed to lack a little in imagination or in courage. Sometimes we do not hope enough.

Sometimes, however, our hope seems doomed and we dare not ask for more than we can see amid the bitter reality in which we live. Let me illustrate again. Yesterday I got my Christmas letter from an old friend and colleague, formerly Episcopal chaplain here in the University, now twenty years ago. You here, I know, are all also experiencing these fat, reproduced letters on colored paper, badly printed up with all sorts of news you are not really interested in receiving. I dutifully read through mine, and I came to his penultimate paragraph, which reads as follows:

> As the holiday season once again approaches, I want to wish you all the joy and happiness possible in a world so filled with poverty, hunger, and violence, and in a country so rife with anger and hatred that a black man is dragged to his death behind a truck, a gay man is hung on a fence like a scarecrow, and a doctor is shot for performing a legal procedure. While the Congress and the press and many ordinary citizens are preoccupied with petty matters, major issues of foreign policy and domestic consequence go unattended, or at best are given short shrift. My hope is that somehow this tide can be turned. . . . I must confess, however, that I have little, if any, confidence in this occurring.

Sometimes, particularly at this time of year, hope seems shabby and miserable, inadequate, when we are surrounded by the mendacity and the mediocrity of this world. I think, in part, this is why more of us applaud rather than deplore Thomas Johnson, who is fast becoming one of my heroes, the man who for ten years lived underground in a hole on Nantucket undiscovered and undisturbed, living in the bowels of the most expensive real estate in the world until his hideaway was discovered this past week; we've all been reading about this in the papers. "How nice it would be," thought I, "to scamper into the ground like Thomas Johnson, and to pull the earth over me like a character in *The Wind in the Willows.*" Now poor old Johnson is forced to join the rest of us, however, while some of us say, "Why should he enjoy those dark and private comforts while the rest of us have to contend with Christmas and our noisy, difficult neighbors?" We haven't heard the end of his saga, but, alas, I think we all know how it is likely to end.

Hope, you see, is not an act of will so much as it is an act of imagination and of courage. Hope, it strikes me, is not that word that we utter at the bedside of the dying when we say unthinkingly, "I hope that this will all end well," and what we mean is that we hope that this life will not continue to go in the direction in which it is going. That is not hope but a kind of mindless optimism, of which we shall say more a little later. The substance of hope is that somehow we will get through and go through this inevitable direction, because on the other side is that hope into which we believe we have been called and for which and by which we have been prepared all our lives. It is that kind of hope that the doctors simply do not understand at the bedsides of the dying; it is that kind of hope that is the ultimate resource available to the faithful, an act of imagination and courage, and imagination and courage are required, for hope deals with what has not yet happened. Hope allows us to see beyond what is and to imagine, to see with our inner eye, what might and what ought to be. When we say, as we often do, that hope triumphs over experience, that is precisely what we mean. Left alone to a life of experience, where we deal with nothing but the facts, where we are content to address only the tangible, the material, the really real, the mundane, we are doomed to the accumulation, the sum total, of that experience. Experience tells us only where we have been, like driving a car by the light of the rearview mirror; and there can be no ultimate satisfaction in the accumulation of that experience. Christian hope is meant to guide you into the place where you have not yet been, and into becoming the person you have not yet become.

That is the radical dimension of the Christian faith, and it is not content with the notion of Christianity celebrating the things that are or, worse still, of Christianity celebrating things as we imagine them once to have been. There is no good place in history to which Christians can turn; I defy any of you to show me a Christian time better than this one. This is as good as it gets, and that is always the case, and it is never good enough. Those who live by the faith of nostalgia or some sentimental history, some imagination of the good old days or the good old times, or some time, any time other than this time, clearly are not seeing clearly. They are seeing only a partial picture, and refuse to see that the gospel is not interested in either the confirmations of the past or the confirmations of the present.

The Christian faith is, and has always been, prophetic, speaking of the time to come, of things that are not yet, of places we have not yet been to, of people we have not yet become. That is the image: none of us, and no place, and no time, is good enough, not yet. No past and no present is superior to the future that is yet to be. That is not just any old future, not just what happens at the end of divine service, or at the end of your undergraduate career, or even at the end of your life. It's not just any future; it is God's particular future, where certain things are meant to happen, and we know what those are. We know what they are because the Bible tells us what they are, and in Advent we are reminded of the content of God's future. You heard it twice this morning, first in Isaiah's old prophesy, "The wolf shall dwell with the lamb, and the leopard shall lie down with the kid, and the calf and the lion and the fatling together, and a little child shall lead them" (Isaiah 11:6). You heard it all, and some of you have seen it in that marvelous work by the Quaker painter Edward Hicks, called *The Peaceable Kingdom*. Many of us have sung it, even, in the marvelous setting of "The Peaceable Kingdom" by Randall Thompson, who wrote our second anthem this morning. We have all seen and heard, routinely, that vision of what the content of God's future is meant to be.

We are too smart, though, for that: been there, done that; it doesn't work; we're too shrewd, too realistic, to take this image of the peaceable kingdom too seriously, for we know better. Our bitter experience of the past has taught us to expect little of the present, and even less of the future, and so we have substituted a shallow optimism for a deep hope. Basically, way down deep, we are very shallow indeed. Maybe it's a national characteristic, but we Americans describe ourselves and are often described by others as optimists, natural-born optimists. We are a people carved out of the failures and disappointments of the rest of the world, and our cultural and political isolationism is meant to protect us from the negativity of the rest of the world. That is why we have always been suspicious of immigration in this country—of course, after our own ancestors made it here—and why we are suspicious of people who don't look like ourselves or talk like ourselves, or who come from different places: because they will spoil our optimism. We like to walk on the sunny side of the street; we like to wear a sunny face and to wish everyone a happy and nice day. We want our movies to have happy endings, as in *It's a Wonderful Life;* we want our Broadway musicals to be upbeat, and that is why every Broadway musical sounds the same and certainly ends the same; and we know that the air around this time of year will be filled with "Tidings of comfort and joy, comfort and joy; O, tidings of comfort and joy."

Our optimism, however, characterized by these attitudes and habits, doesn't square with our perception of reality. We know that there is no genuine peace on earth, we know that there is no fundamental lasting goodwill to those with whom he is well pleased. We know that the holiday season tends to bring out the worst, not the best, in people, particularly in our own families. I know, and I know you know, how much we dread Christmas Day, because we are living with the paradox of great expectation on the one hand and grim reality on the other. We know that for ourselves constant good cheer is hard to manufacture and even harder to maintain. It is this contrast between our hyped expectations, aided and abetted by the salespeople and the ads of the *Boston Globe* and the *Boston Herald* and all of the media outlets, by all of the window designers in all of the shops, by places like the Harvard Coöperative Society and every department store that you can imagine, jingling and jangling for weeks: it is these hyped expectations of this season on the one hand, and their inevitable capacity to disappoint us on the other, that creates the well-known seasonal depression to which for many people alcohol, or some other stimulant, alas, is the only solution.

Advent hope, my friends, is meant to be the sobering antidote to false Christmas cheer. That is why the church drags you kicking and screaming through Advent; that is why it forces you to confront the promises and their lack of apparent deliverance now; that is why the church requires that you look ahead and not back to the manger of Bethlehem; that is why we light these Advent candles: to lighten the darkness and not simply to allow you a better rearview window view. That is why it is my job and that of every preacher and priest in Christendom, on these four Sundays in Advent, to place these facts and these promises and these hopes before you, and it is your duty as the faithful in Christ to consider them. You have no choice. This you must do. Advent is not celebration; it is not the moment for dancing around the light pole. Advent hope is not an exercise in nostalgia or seasonal optimism. Advent is not celebration but fortification against the very forces that would drive us to despair and drag us downward. Advent is an exercise in endurance, in preparation for the long journey to a time and a place where we have not yet been, and for which all of the past and all of the present are mere preparation. This is what Paul, the apostle to the Gentiles—that is, to us—means to suggest when he writes in Romans, "For whatever was written in former days was written for our instruction, that by steadfastness and by the encouragement of the scriptures we might have hope." In other words, the Bible is not a record of human achievement, or even of divine achievement, but a record of divine promises and a constant tale of human folly. We are meant to learn from these instructions and these experiences, not to reenter "Bibleland," as Krister Stendahl once described it, but to be encouraged and prepared for that time that has not yet been. These things were written for our instruction, that by steadfastness, holding on, by the encouragement of the examples within the Scriptures, both positive and negative, we might have hope.

Paul was writing to a people who knew the promises, and he cites them in this chapter when in verse twelve he recalls Isaiah's vision of the lamb and the wolf. He was writing to a people who knew the promises but who also knew the bitter experience of disappointment, of "hope deferred," in that marvelous phrase of the playwright Lorraine Hansberry: "Hope deferred, which is like a raisin in the sun; it dries up and turns hard." These people knew the experiences of a world not yet ready for God's prime time, and that is still our world—not yet ready for God's prime time. He was writing to a world in which black men and gay men and others are still murdered by Christians, he was writing to a world in which violence flourishes in the name of the pro-life movement, and he was writing to a world in which the Christian faith is used so often to consecrate the *status quo* of the favored and the privileged, a people like you, and like me. He understood that the optimist among us says that this is the best of all possible worlds, and the pessimist agrees.

Optimism—I'm prepared to be quoted on this—simply doesn't cut it: it cannot stand the sharp ray of experience or disappointment. Optimism alone drives people into fantasy, and sometimes into terrible rage and disappointment.

Sometimes it is difficult even for me to remember anything other than happiness and the bright promise that lay ahead for me in the Plymouth, Massachusetts, of the 1940s and early 1950s. There were very few black families living in town, maybe four or five of us, and most of us were related in one way or another, and we were "colored" then, not black, and we'd all lived there for a very long time. We were totally socialized, totally adapted, black Yankees—Afro-Saxons, if you will, every one of us—and they all talked as I do and I talk as they did, if that helps to explain anything for any of you. Once a month, on Sunday morning after church, when my mother and father and I left to get into our car to drive home for Sunday dinner, there would have been placed on the front seat, through the open window, a brown paper bag, carefully sealed and tied up, and when we got home we would find in that parcel a modest treasure trove of magazines, the only copies in the entire town of Plymouth of the newly founded *Ebony* magazine; its down-market offspring, *Jet;* and well-thumbed copies of the *Pittsburgh Courier,* the nation's then-leading black daily newspaper. These periodicals, kind of black *Life* magazines, were subscribed to—under cover of darkness, it seemed—by only one of our families, and circulated quietly among the colored families. We read them quietly and faithfully and passed them on until we all had read them, and in addition to their stories of uplift and achievement in the black America of fifty years ago, they also contained gruesomely vivid accounts of murders, rapes, lynchings, and race wars in far-off places like Detroit and Atlanta. They contained a vivid chronicle, a vivid account of a segregated America, and of most of America's desire to keep it that way.

It was almost an embarrassment to read such things in the "land of the free and the home of the brave," the "land of the Pilgrim's pride," and it was hard to take when my parents, in an understandable desire to protect me from the consequences of a false optimism, reminded me that this was the real world, and that the world in which I was living was a world of illusions. Contrary to how it may appear, and to what some of you may think, I have never forgotten that; not for one minute, as your pastor these many years, have I forgotten that. Black people in America have never been optimistic, for we know better; but we have always been hopeful, full of hope. That is why we continue to sing James Weldon Johnson's "Lift Ev'ry Voice," and respond particularly to the words:

> *Stony the road we trod,*
> *Bitter the chast'ning rod*
> *Felt in the days when hope unborn had died;*
> *Yet with a steady beat,*
> *Have not our weary feet*
> *Come to the place for which our fathers sighed?*

That, my friends, is not a statement but a question, and for the faithful in Christ the answer must continue to be a resolute "No, we have not!" We have not yet come to the place for which our fathers and mothers sighed, and neither have you, not even the most well off of you, not even the brightest of you, not even the best of you; and to think that we have is to be sadly deluded. The Advent hope reminds us that this is true, and the Advent hope reminds us that it takes courage to hope in spite of circumstances, courage to persevere beyond the apparent and the convenient, courage not to be satisfied or dissuaded with our circumstances, not to take for granted who we are, or where we are, or what we do. There must be among us all a divine discontent, a constant irritant that can never be satisfied until we are where we are meant to be—and this is not that place.

To imagine Isaiah's peaceable kingdom as still possible, still expectant, still desirable, is to have the courage not of our convictions but of our imagination and our hopes; and perhaps the most courageous thing to do in desperate, disappointing times such as these is to affirm a steadfast hope out of all proportion to what passes for reality. Let me illustrate for the final time.

Over the west door of an English country church, in the county of Leicestershire, is an inscription written in the seventeenth century at the time of the English civil war between the Royalists and Puritans, a nasty, unpleasant confrontation:

> When all things sacred were throughout the nation either destroyed or profaned, Sir Robert Shirley, Baronet, founded this church whose singular praise is to have done the best things in the worst of times, and hoped them in the most calamitous.

"To have done the best of things in the worst of times, and hoped them in the most calamitous." Sir Robert built a house of prayer in the middle of the carnage of a brutal civil war, and, except in the minds of the historians, that war is long over, long forgotten. Yet the church at Staunton Harold in Leicestershire still stands; you can see it today, a monument to the courage to hope, to have done the best of things in the worst of times.

Our war with our world, our spiritual war and the war for our souls, is no less serious than that one, with the stakes even higher; and to wage it, especially in these Advent days, "May the God of hope fill you with joy and peace in believing, so that by the power of the Holy Spirit you may abound in hope."

Impatience Is a Virtue

Text: . . . Where is the promise of His coming?

—2 PETER 3:4

Peter asks the hard questions, "Where is he?"; "What are we waiting for?" My sermon cuts across the grain of the conventional wisdom and asserts as the true but painful proposition that Christianity is a disappointment, and so too are most Christians, and I include myself among them. Christianity is not what it is cracked up to be and neither are we, and this is a dreadful secret of colossal proportions that for very good reason is not usually acknowledged in public. In Advent, the Church has given us a season for truth telling and for facing sad facts, and one of those facts—if we listen carefully and with candor—is that Christian faith and Christian living have not delivered the goods as promised or as expected. The world doesn't give two figs for Advent: the world is "into" something called "Christmas," and real Christians are "into" Advent.

Now, we are not supposed to say that or even think that: it is disloyal, and what would our secular or Jewish or Muslim or Hindu friends think of us and of our religion if they knew that we knew that it did not perform according to expectations? It would be an embarrassment. Look at our record, however, and then look at our experience, and see what we have.

The record we think we know, and we have heard two lessons this morning from the Bible, for that is where the history of the lessons is to be found. In Micah 4:1–4 there is that almost luxurious lesson of the vision of the establishment of the House of the Lord in the highest mountains to which peoples and nations will come, where they will learn the lessons that the Lord means for them to learn. Here is perhaps the most hopeful verse in all of scripture: "They shall beat their swords into ploughshares, and their spears into pruning hooks; nations shall not lift up sword against nation, neither shall they learn war any more. But they shall sit, every man under his vine and fig tree, and none shall make them afraid; for the mouth of the Lord of hosts has spoken."

As Bertrand Russell, that raging atheist of the twentieth century, might have said, "Show me where this is even remotely true, or has ever been true, and I will convert to Christianity tomorrow!" You do not have to be an atheistic English earl with a doctorate in physics to know that no such place and no such time have ever existed or are even likely to exist.

At Morning Prayers on Friday last my colleague and friend Dean Eleanor Shore of the Medical School, in an elegant talk, asked of the Beatitudes what is meant by "The meek shall inherit the earth." She made the point that meekness is not a quality sought out or desired or exhibited in any of the persons whom Harvard rewards as students for admission, or professors for promotion. Meekness is not in the Harvard job description, and most of us cannot imagine a world owned by the meek, nor would we want to live in such a place if it existed, for we associate meekness with weakness and incompetence. It is all well and good to say—as I have said to you before, let the record show—that meekness is not the opposite of strength but of pride. That is very true, and the meek are not likely to come into possession anytime soon: we know that a world in which meekness is a quality to be admired is a world that is impossible to imagine, and we can be reassured that no such world has ever yet existed.

The text itself, from one of the so-called pastoral or "minor" Epistles in the New Testament, is one of expectation, but it is mostly an exercise in disappointment, consisting as it does of the question, "Where is the promise of his coming?" Remember that television commercial of a decade ago, with its fifteen minutes of fame, and the question asked by the little old lady: "Where's the beef?" Well, this is the same sort of question: "Where is the promise of his coming?"

Scoffers say to the Christians of 2 Peter, "For ever since the fathers fell asleep, all things have continued as they were from the beginning of creation." In other words, they say that nothing has changed: People still cheat, lie, and die. Life is still nasty, brutish, and short. The wicked still prosper, nice guys come in last, things are not much better than they ever were. So, "Where is the promise of his coming?"

Now, I know that we all know what we are expected to think and how we are expected to feel on this matter: in fact, the Epistle tells us in essence to relax, to calm down and wait, that we have got the timetable wrong, that for with the Lord one day is as a thousand years. The bottom line for impatient Christians is verse 13: "But according to His promise we wait for new heavens and a new earth in which righteousness dwells." That is what we are supposed to do: wait. That is the watchword of Advent: wait, and we are supposed to wait *patiently!*

Everywhere I look, patience is held up to be a virtue. "O rest in the Lord, wait patiently for Him, for He will give thee thy heart's desire. . . ." The Puritans named their daughters Patience; St. Augustine says, "Patience is the companion of wisdom"; St. Gregory says, "Patience is the root and guardian of all the virtues"; the Chinese proverb has it that "patience is power: with time and patience the mulberry leaf becomes silk"; and when we see heroic sufferings, pious Christians are inclined to say that those sufferings were endured with "the patience of Job."

All of that is well and good, and it keeps the fortune-cookie industry in business, but it does not answer the impatient question of Christians at Advent: "Where is the promise of his coming?" Where is the Lord? Where is Jesus? Where is the age of gold and of peace, and where are that vine and fig tree? Things do seem pretty much to be where they have been since the beginning of creation, and we do live by the golden rule—that is, by the rule that those who have the gold, rule.

Advent forces us, much against our wills and hearts, to face the bleak and sad truth that we have not yet seen "the promise of his coming," and we don't know when he is coming. We try to drown out the grim truth by the noisy, tawdry diversions of Christmas, hoping that in a binge of Bing Crosby and George Bailey we can overcome the darkness within and without, and we imagine that Hollywood can fulfill what Christ obviously has not yet fulfilled. Our secular friends are not possessed of any anxieties about this season: they know that it is a time to make money and to make as much of it as possible, and they are craven in their desire to do so. So we keep the stores open twenty-four hours a day for seven days a week, with the music blaring, the lights shining and blinking, and the hype going so that we will have no time for silence or for the opportunity to notice that nothing and no one has changed. Why our Jewish friends think that Christmas trees and boughs of holly, candles in windows and even civic manger scenes have anything to do with the religion of Christ is beyond me. They should enjoy these pagan symbols along with the rest of the pagans: their religious integrity will not be challenged, because these symbols have little if anything to do with our religious integrity.

No! Impatience is the only virtue that counts today, and we *ought* to be impatient. The tinsel Christmas is not what Christmas is, and it seems to me that the virtue of this season for the faithful, or even for the curious, and certainly for hopeful Christians, can *only* be impatience, and not patience—an impatience with things, with people, and even with ourselves as we are. The trouble with patience is that it is so close to self-satisfaction, to self-contentment, and to acquiescence to things as they are and to ourselves as we are that the edge of expectation and transformation has been dulled or lost altogether.

I know that we should honor John Milton, who tells us in one of the greatest poems of the English language, "They also serve who only stand and wait." I, however, heretic that I am, prefer Margaret Thatcher, who said, "I am extremely patient provided I get my own way in the end."

Well, where is "the promise of His coming"? Where is the time to which Christians aspire? Where is that new heaven, that new earth, in which righteousness dwells? Is the argument in 2 Peter a little lame? Has it come and we missed it? I will lay a bet with six percent interest that we will still be asking this on Advent III in the year 2001. Did we miss the Messiah's coming?

There are some who think so, perhaps some of you. If you are a liberal, you think that perhaps it was in the days of the Great Society, or the New Deal, or the New Frontier, or in some moment other than today, when things appeared to be better than they are or were. If you are a conservative, you imagine that new world order as the last time that you felt that you were in charge and felt happy about yourself, and God only knows when that was. When people like Bob Dole and Bill Bennett and others talk about getting back to basics and putting this country back on the right track, again I cannot imagine what it is that they are talking about: was there some golden age when all was well here, and I missed it?

If Advent does nothing else, it should remind and warn Christians that there is no comfort or scintilla of consolation in the past, that there is no

Eden, that there is no moment when we had it and lost it; and I defy any-one, Christian or otherwise, to demonstrate counterwise: it cannot be done unless the definition of the golden age, or the idealized past, is when *you* were in charge; and if so, if you were ever in charge, then you have a lot to answer for.

The risks and dangers of an Advent patience are that it implies a false virtue to the *status quo:* it tends to sanctify the culture, and it can easily be confused with moral laziness and spiritual indifference. Advent demands an impatience on the part of those who take the gospel seriously: we are impatient not for the return to some falsely idealized past; there is not a moment that I would want to repeat, for example—not a day, and certainly not my sixteenth birthday, which was a terrible day, by the way. We are impatient, as we ought to be, with the present and its dim passions, its feeble ambitions, and with the terrible reign of the second-rate shoddy secularism that is paganism without the fun: who wants to celebrate that?

We are meant to be impatient for that future in which the promises are fulfilled. Impatience is not the opposite of waiting; it is the opposite of self-satisfaction, and there is no one here who in Christ's name can be satisfied with where we are, with what we have done, or with who we are. Advent does not celebrate things as they were or as they are. It speaks only of things that are to be, and of our impatience with anything until those things—that "new heaven and new earth wherein righteousness dwells"—are achieved, and things are not as they were but as they are to be.

So, then, what's it all about? Here we are, a week before Christmas, and here is where you are to get psychically pumped up for that season, and where you are supposed to get hope. You all like lists: we are all David Letterman types, and I will give you a list of three things to help you to remember the virtue of impatience:

1. We are not what we ought to be; so pray.

2. We are not where we ought to be: Cambridge is not our destination; so hope.

3. What we have, no matter how much or how little, is not what we need; so work.

Pray, hope, and work. These are the engines driven by impatience and a discontent with things as they are; nothing has changed, and we are still with those early, anxious, and impatient Christians. "Where is the promise of His coming?" Where it has always been: out there, in front of us, waiting for us even as we pray, hope, and work for it. Read 2 Peter 3 for yourselves, especially verses 17–18, and see.

> You therefore, beloved, knowing this beforehand, beware lest you be carried away with the error of lawless men and lose your own stability. But grow in the grace and knowledge of our Lord and Savior Jesus Christ. To him be the glory both now and to the day of eternity. Amen.

Gifts

Text: For the grace of God has appeared for the salvation of all men. . . .

—TITUS 2:11A

O come, let us adore him
O come, let us adore him
O come, let us adore him
Christ the Lord.

I know that you know the gospel for Christmas. Those of you who made your Holy Communion last night heard it here or elsewhere, and those of you here this morning have heard it once again; you know the glorious words of St. Luke. I suspect, however, that you might not be as familiar with the equally glorious words of the letter of Paul to Titus, which is why I will read again for you the passage that was read for us by Professor George Hunston Williams:

For the grace of God has appeared, bringing salvation to all, training us to renounce impiety and worldly possessions, and in the present age to live lives that are self-controlled, upright, and godly, while we wait for the blessed hope and the manifestation of the glory of our great God and Savior, Jesus Christ. He it is who gave himself for us that he might redeem us from all iniquity and purify for himself a people of his own who are zealous for good deeds. Declare these things; exhort and reprove with all authority. Let no one disregard you.

The gift of God for the people of God.

I plan my preaching agenda in the summertime, when I am not over-whelmed by the business of business and can think for two or three hours without interruption. It is a wonderful thing to think, on a balmy day in July, of a sermon for December, and I decided last July on topics for my Advent sermons, and to preach, God willing, on Christmas Day, today—on that rare occasion when Christmas Day and Sunday are simultaneous—on "gifts." This I did not out of sophisticated thoughts of the season, but because the word most associated with Christmas is *gifts*—gifts purchased, gifts given, gifts received, gifts anticipated, even gifts returned. Gifts is what it's all about, and gifts is what I decided on for this sermon.

When we think of gifts, most of us first recall the ruins of Christmas mornings when we were children: piles of paper and ribbons scattered about, beautiful bows cast aside—bows that someone had taken time to prepare and to crimp and to pat beautifully into shape—all ruined in a great rush to get inside that mysterious box or parcel. For many of you with children, and for many of you who are children, that scene is not history, that was this morn-ing, it is a current event, an existential moment. In our frugal family it was our custom, at my mother's insistence—who had been impressed and depressed by the Great Depression and thus saved every bit of string and elas-tic band—that we open our gifts carefully so that we could save the wrapping paper and use it again another year. This we did: the paper was carefully pressed and put into a big drawer in the pantry, and while we didn't know *what* was in the parcel with the green stripes and red stars, we knew *who* had received something in that same paper last year, and we could put our minds to work and figure out who was giving us something this year; and so there was continuity amid the excitement and newness of Christmas morning.

Perhaps the second sense of gifts comes when we recall what we have given, what we have put together for our family and our friends. In the best of circumstances the search and careful thought given to gifts to present is rather a spiritual pilgrimage that allows us to at least initially attempt a match between the gift, the giver, and the gifted one: a sort of trinity of the right present for the right person from the right person. We rehearse their lives and our relationship to their lives, imagining what gift, what tangible token, will capture the spirit and the soul of the person and bring alive our relationship. That is the ideal. I cannot remember all my presents over the years, but I do remember the relationships.

Then there is the reality, for the rest of us, who race about at the last minute, shopping on the day before Christmas and hoping that the combination of shortage of time and good intentions will produce inspiration. For us the giving of gifts is very much like the thrill of the chase: it is not the finding of it, but the seeking of it and *then* perhaps the finding of it, that counts. When I think of gifts, invariably I think not only of the present itself but of the relationships that generated the gift. When I think of my childhood Christmases, now long ago, I recall not simply the annual supply of sensible sweaters from Cochrane's in Cambridge, but I think of my Cousin Annie who gave them, and with whom I will dine this afternoon. When I think of the presents I really wanted—not the socks, or the handkerchiefs, or the pen and pencil sets, but the one toy I really wanted: the sled, the record player, or the game of the moment—I remember my Cousin Marjorie, who always knew what would delight a hard-to-please child. How did she know? Because I always told her, knowing that my sensible mother and father would never in the world give me what I wanted: I shall dine with Marjorie this afternoon as well. For the next generation, I recall not so much the books and toys and trinkets that I give to the children in my life, to my godchildren, my young cousins, the children of neighbors, and of friends and relations, the children tied to me by ribbons of kin and affection with ties that cannot be broken; rather, I recall why I am giving them anything at all, and all that is symbolized by these presents.

This reminds me, and I hope you, that the gift is but the means to define and develop and express the relationship that we have. We are all reticent, and we do not squander affection on the people to whom we are devoted: the gift is the way we say what often we dare not say without it, the gift gives us permission to say I love you, I really think you're special, I care about you, I am devoted to you, and I want you to know it. The gift says volumes.

"Thank you," we say on receiving a gift, face radiant, eyes glowing. "You shouldn't have done it."

"Oh, it's nothing at all," we say in reply . . . and it is everything, it is *everything*.

So, the gift gives us permission to understand and to say I love you and I love being loved by you.

For those of us who believe that the greatest gift is the gift of love, Christmas is the ultimate and most intimate expression there is. The child in the manger, heretical as this may sound, is not the end or even the object of this holy day: the child in the manger is the means whereby God's love is presented to the people whom he loves. The birth of Jesus is many, many things: it is miracle, it is mystery, it is mercy, it is ensign of hope, it is word of justice, it is truth, it is the sign of hope. It is all of that, but much more than that it is as we often say at the Holy Communion: *the gift of God for the people of God.* That is what Christmas is about. If the flesh had anything to do with it, Mary and Joseph would have had other plans and would have made other arrangements. If reason had anything to do with it, this wouldn't all work, because it doesn't make sense. Here we have an unwed mother and a father, vagrant migrants out of their own district disrupting shepherds and confusing the heavenly host, and this is not reconciled— because it is not our show, but God's. Christmas is God's initiative, it is God's work, when God begins to establish a relationship of love with us; and of this love Jesus is the sign, the substance, and the symbol. *The gift of God for the people of God.* The gift is the renewal of that love, and the main- tenance of that love even against all the forces of this dark and cold and unremitting world.

Let me tell you a little about that dark and cold and unremitting world. Yesterday the *New York Times* ran an article by Christopher Durang entitled "Hope for the Seasonally Challenged." Are you seasonally challenged? People are stressed out: expectations are high; Bing Crosby croons of a per- fect white Christmas; people are expected to trust that trust will be returned and renewed, that they will get what they want for Christmas, that the turkey will taste good and not be dry—and it isn't going to be like that, and so people get depressed. Even the newspapers tell us of holiday depres- sion, and this is not news, this is not new news: the world is never going to be perfect, never filled with peace on earth, good will toward men; this world cannot deliver Christmas to you as you want it. I suspect that you already know that that is the case, and I suspect that you are not surprised by it: and it *is* the case. It is into that dark world, not into some Dickensian fantasy, or Radio City Music Hall wonderland, that Christmas comes, the gift of God for the salvation of us all.

We are tempted to imagine Christmas as an "out-of-body experience," an antidote to the reality and brutality and crass commercialism of a world that has lost its way, but remember that the gospel begins with Caesar Augustus, in a real and fallen world. Understandably we want Christmas to be apart from such a world—an island of purity in a sea of corruption. I see these "hopes and fears of all the years" each year when I assist, as I did last night, at the Christmas Eve midnight communion at Trinity Church in Copley Square, and it is wonderful to see people desperate to get into a church instead of into a rock concert or a sale, hordes of people pounding at the doors to get, as the poet described it, "a whiff of incense"—not available at Trinity—"and a hint of hope;" and I understand and appreciate their need. The very durability of the gift of Christ, *the gift of God for the people of God,* is that it happens in the midst of what the *Crimson* calls the "real world," the world of homelessness, the world of war in Bosnia, the world of broken homes, of broken dreams, the world of aging and dying—and that is its great gift. *The gift of God for the people of God* comes into the needy, dangerous, bitter, and cynical world where babies are born with inherited diseases and little chance of hope; where politicians continue in the crooked ways of their spiritual ancestor, King Herod; and where it is easier to believe a plausible lie than an impossible truth. The *Boston Globe* prints implausible lies and we believe them; the gospel preaches an impossible truth, and we believe today that it is written in truth.

It is into a world of such darkness and despair that the gift of light and hope comes, and it is the sense of what I will call "this invincible reality" that draws the helpless, the hopeful, the faithful, and the confused to the manger. It has done so for thousands of years, and it will do so until the kingdom of this world becomes the kingdom of our God and of his Christ. Indeed, if God waited for a world worthy of the gift of himself, he would never come at all.

Come he has, however, and come he does, and come he will; and our response to this? Surely we cannot explain it—God help all of the clergy in Christendom today who are trying to explain Christmas—and we can much less understand or comprehend it; all we can do is fall to our knees and adore. All we can do is to receive the gift and say, "Oh, you shouldn't have . . . ," and we will discover that it is not nothing at all, but all and *everything.*

Some will say that it takes an act of will or of imagination to see all of this; I say that it takes courage: it takes courage to acknowledge our need, and even more, it takes courage to acknowledge our joy at the discovery that we are not merely tolerated, not merely observed, but loved—loved so much that God cared enough to send the very best. It takes courage and it takes joy to accept what this day above all others has to offer; it takes courage to be a generous receiver of a generous gift, and that is what it is all about: *the gift of God for the people of God.*

In her poem "Love Came Down at Christmas," Christina Rossetti tells us:

Love came down at Christmas,
Love all lovely, Love divine;
Love was born at Christmas;
Star and angels gave the sign.

Worship we the Godhead,
Love incarnate, Love divine;
Worship we our Jesus,
But where-with for sacred sign?

She answers the question:

Love shall be our token;
Love be yours and love be mine,
Love to God and all men,
Love for plea and gift and sign.

The gift of God for the people of God. Thanks be to God who gives us the victory, through our Lord Jesus Christ.

So Far, So Good; So What?

**Text: Forgetting what lies behind and straining forward to what
lies ahead, I press on toward the goal for the prize of the
upward call of God in Christ Jesus.**

—PHILIPPIANS 3:13–14

As I cast about in my mind for a text to take for the first Sunday of the
new year, I must say that I had not one second's struggle, not one moment
of doubt, and that I spent not one minute in shuffling through the Prayer
Book, the Concordance, or the Lectionary. There is only one text for New
Year's Sunday, and I have chosen it; these verses that Paul has written in
Philippians 3: "Forgetting what lies behind and straining forward to what
lies ahead, I press on toward the goal for the prize of the upward call of
God in Christ Jesus."

"Forgetting what lies behind and straining forward. . . ." It doesn't get
any clearer, any better, than that; and if you don't get it now, you may as
well leave. This is crystalline, and even after a three-day orgy of new year,
new century, new millennium—faux—celebrations, you still ought to be
clear enough in head and heart and mind to hear what St. Paul has to say to
those of us who are still in our mid-course.

I want you to take your minds back, if you can—and if you can't, you
can imagine—sixty years, to Christmas Day 1939, when on the radio King
George VI spoke to his very nervous, troubled, and fearful people in the
British Empire. There was reason to be nervous, troubled, and fearful in
1939, for the world stood on the precipice of war yet again. It was a dark

and dangerous time, especially for the English-speaking world; and Hitler was not just a comic German running about the stage looking like Charlie Chaplin, but a threat to anything that was civil, holy, or moral. In the face of galloping danger, and in seeking reassurance, the king addressed his people in perhaps the most famous Christmas message of the twentieth century, and in doing so he quoted from an obscure Canadian woman named Minnie Louise Haskins. He made her famous by using her lines, quoting at the end of his speech from a little piece that she had written called *The Gate of the Year:*

> And I said to the man who stood at the gate of the year:
> "Give me a light that I may tread safely into the unknown."
> And he replied, "Go out into the darkness, and put your hand into the hand
> of God. That shall be to you better than light and safer than a known way."

I looked in vain over the last two or three days for any citation of Minnie Louise Haskins in all of the year's-end summaries, and all of the newspapers, and naturally I saw none. Partially I was disappointed; another part of me was delighted, for what they don't know, I do, and that is always satisfying. The tone of the end of the year, however, has been remarkable in its dissonance and confusion. When I was young, we Baptists spent New Year's Eve in church in what was called, in those simple days, "Watch Night" services, which perhaps some of you will remember. There we recalled our blessings over the year past, and committed ourselves to Christ's service in the year to come. We hoped not necessarily to be better, but to carry on. These were rather plain and simple services, nothing to be compared with the midnight services at Christmas and the secular revelry that took place in Times Square, but there was among us a quiet confidence, perhaps even a naïveté, that believers should face the new year and the future with prayer, thanksgiving, and serenity, with eyes wide open. We should be sober, and filled with great expectations.

Well, that was then, and this is now. The secular world, I believe, has always looked upon New Year's Eve with more fear than love. Think about the devices with which the secular world chooses to greet the new year. The ritual of the secular new year celebrations is to get as many people as possible together in one place to make as much noise as possible, and to drink as much drink as possible, all to make certain that we are giving a very good facsimile of having a very good time: one of the best reasons to spend New Year's Eve with strangers is that they don't know whether or not you are really having a good time. A cultural anthropologist might say that our Western New Year's Eve customs are signs of wholesale paranoia, that we are a culture afraid that if it closes its eyes it will not wake up. That is why we stay up so late; that is why we make so much noise. We are a culture convinced that noise is a sign of life, that "If I can scream I am still alive; if I can hear other people screaming, they are still alive." We are a culture afraid of the dark, believing in sophisticated twentieth-century logic while actually believing that the sun has died; and we're uncertain of whether it will appear again, so we're uncertain of the unknown and untrusting of the future. It sounds like an undergraduate party, with noise, lots of light, lots of sound, lots of strangers, and lots of activity all giving the illusion of fun and pleasure, but really rather tiresome.

George Orwell describes such a scene in his essay "Pleasure Spots," in which he writes about the opening of a spa somewhere in the Western world after the close of World War II, where all of the pleasures that have been denied long-suffering people during rationing would now be supplied for the asking, and in abundance. He described the place in this way:

> *The lights must never go out,*
> *The music must always play*
> *Lest we should see where we are;*
> *Lost in a haunted wood,*
> *Children afraid of the dark*
> *Who have never been happy*
> *Or good.*

The twentieth century seemed so much like that haunted wood in which we have been lost, afraid of the dark, never happy, never good.

. That's the secular world's view of all of this, and it is not made any less real or any less paranoid by the conveniences through which we can observe it simultaneously in every major capital of the world. If this were the only view with which to be concerned that would be bad enough, but toward the end of this last decade we have noticed that large numbers of religious people have seemed equally obsessed with the end of the age, with a sense of paranoia and gloom and fear. Lots of religious people were looking forward to yesterday in the firm conviction that it was the beginning of the end. Perhaps you noticed, in yesterday's *New York Times,* of January 1, 2000, on page A20, the headline, "More Christians Believe Second Coming Is Near"; and the article went on to say, "One in three in the *Times* poll expects to see events. Despite explicit biblical warnings against trying to predict the end of the age, and despite the embarrassingly bad track record of all those who have tried to do so, many believers believe in the year 2000 as the time to reckon with. The virus Y2K"—what ever happened to it?—"was the technologically correct sign of the end time, and a vengeful judgment would be unleashed for which many have fervently prayed." It has always seemed remarkable to me that those who predict the coming judgment of the Lord always manage to have themselves on the winning side and not subject to that very judgment. Toward the close of last week the papers reported a large number of the outspoken prophets of the last three or four years quietly recalibrating their predictions and their dates; and I even saw an article in which The Reverend Jerry Falwell said that he would not be afraid to fly in an airplane on New Year's Day, and I wonder if he did.

What is it about the future that makes both believers and unbelievers so frightened, so anxious, so fearful, and so driven to all kinds of bombast and anxiety that in retrospect prove only to be embarrassing? Why is it that our Christian way of life, when it comes to the future, seems much more driven by fear than it is by faith? Few of the great religions of this world base their faith upon a dreadful apprehension of the future, but I would argue that the dark stain, the underside of the Christian faith, is its petulant anxiety about the time to come, and its unwillingness to leave that time to God.

St. Paul, for all his faults—and there are complications and difficulties that any of us could enumerate with St. Paul—is a much more reliable guide to the Christian attitude toward the future, and that is why it is a pleasure to turn to him at the beginning of a new year. To read Paul after reading the *Boston Globe* or the *New York Times,* or listening to the natterers on the television or radio, is like a glass of fresh, cold spring water. It is not only a pleasure, therefore, to read Paul; it is also instructive for us to do so, for here is the most authoritative voice of early Christianity, a voice that in nearness to the great Christian expectation is a voice that is not afraid of the future, not intimidated by the past, and not seduced by the moment.

Paul is that person who, with clear and steady eye, is able to right the balance between the fear of the past and the terror of the future, and he does so boldly, and particularly so in his letter to the Philippians, from which we have heard today.

Before the part that we had as our lesson, he writes of his own credentials as being a real-world, secular-credentials-bearing realist. He writes that while he has attained a great deal in this life on this world's terms and has accomplished much that anybody could recognize and accept, all of those accomplishments, all of those distinctions, and all of those achievements are as nothing if he cannot lay a claim on the future. Everything that you have done in the past, interesting as it may have been, is of no use if you cannot face the future unafraid. The longest entry in *Who's Who,* the longest entry in the *Quinquennial,* the finest list upon which you may find yourself, the greatest achievements you may feel you have developed or have been ascribed to you, are as nothing if you cannot face the future unafraid. That is the point he is making.

He says, *Look. If you want credentials, I have credentials:* "If any man thinks he has reason for confidence in the flesh, I have more." Now, the thing I have always liked about St. Paul is that he has an ample-sized ego. He is not one of the cringing, shriveling little people who say, "After you, my dear Alphonse." Absolutely not. This is a man who was a super-Jew, a super-Greek, a super-Roman, a super-Christian, and proud of it. He gives consolation to those of us who suffer with outsize egos, and that is why I like St. Paul. He says to the likes of you and me, "You people think you have achievements, you people think you have credentials, but I have more than all of you: let me tell you what I have." He goes on, in the first part of chapter 3, to summarize his credentials, and they are impressive. He says, "I was circumcised on the eighth day of the tribe of the people of Israel, of the tribe of Benjamin": I am a Jew, A-number-one, beyond which there is no one better than me. He says, "I am a Hebrew of the Hebrews": don't try to outfox me with your genealogies and your laws, I come at the top of the line. He says, "As to the law, I am a Pharisee": I am a super ecclesiastical lawyer, I am a Harvard Law School graduate, don't mess with me on the point of the law. As to zeal, enthusiasm, I was the best persecutor of the church that the church ever had; if I had kept going, there would be no church, so, "As to zeal I was a persecutor of the church; and as to righteousness under the law, I am blameless": you can find no fault in me. All of this he has, he says, and all of this he counts as loss. He calls it all, in various translations of the Greek word in this text, "refuse," "rubbish," "trash," or "junk" in comparison to what he has found in Jesus Christ. This is the distinction that he makes. I take my credentials, I take my experience, I take my past, I take my authority, I take all of these things that not only the world but I count as important, and I regard them as expendable junk. I toss them away as worthless, as they are in comparison to what I have found in Jesus Christ. To know Christ, Paul says, is to know all, and Paul wishes to know him and the power of his resurrection, and that is what he says. It is important to realize that he is talking about throwing away what he has and knows in order to attain and strive after that which he seeks and desires.

It is also important to remember that this is the man who encounters the living God on the Damascus road. This is the man who was thrown from his horse and ended up on his hind side, the light coming down from heaven, the voice of the encounter of the ultimate Christian experience. This is the man who has had more narrow escapes than Houdini, all with the assistance of God. This is the man who preaches before high and low and preaches Christ and him crucified; and for us, this is the man without whom the world would know next to nothing about Jesus Christ. If our Christian faith depended upon the four evangelists we would have some lovely pastel stories, and some interesting narratives lost among the great narratives of the Western world. It is Paul who translates the life and story of Christ into the living witness of a new and revolutionary community. That is why Paul is called "the Apostle to the Gentiles," the apostle to us, the apostle to the rest of the world; and if anybody could afford to rest upon his spiritual laurels, as it were, it would be Paul. Here in Philippians, however, he tells us that he doesn't care to do so.

I've often thought about that phrase, "resting on one's laurels." Think about the physical difficulty. Your laurels are usually on your head, and to rest upon them is a form of contortion that really doesn't bear looking into. Paul says that he wants to forget all about his laurels; he wants to forget about all of that—to put it in the trash, as it were: "Forgetting what lies behind, I strain forward to what lies ahead; I press on; my best days are before me." "Forgetting what lies behind" is a very brave thing to say, and a very difficult thing to do. How easy it is to live in the past and to use the past as a determining factor for all that happens thereafter in the present and in the future. We think—because we have been taught to think this way—that the one who forgets history is bound to repeat it. How many times have you heard that old canard? There is enough truth there, enough but not enough, for there is an even greater truth, which is that to forget nothing is to learn nothing. Think about that. If you forget nothing, if you retain everything you've ever known, every experience you've ever had, and keep it up there in your mind, imagine how difficult it is for anything else to get in, and how difficult to adjust the balance of what you remember against that what you must now anticipate. To forget nothing is to learn nothing.

A few months ago I went to a conference on reconciliation and forgiveness sponsored by the Templeton Foundation at the Museum of Science down the street. There were lots of us there from greater Boston, and I think that none of us really knew what this conference was about, but the invitation was beautifully printed and it came from the Templeton Foundation, and so we all had our price and went to see just how much we were willing to pay; and I found the experience worth the not-so-good dinner. I heard speaker after speaker observe that the remembrance of past grievances was the single most significant obstacle to reconciliation and forgiveness. An archmentor of this occasion was none other than our old friend Desmond Tutu, who, as chairman of the Truth and Reconciliation Commission in South Africa, experienced in a public stage this conflict between remembrance and reconciliation, the likes of which the world has never before seen. He was quoted as saying that the delicate balance between acknowledging the truth and the terrible things that it revealed, and the effort at reconciliation that meant going beyond that truth, was one of the great cultic burdens of our age. It is very hard to let go of grudges. You know and I know that eventually a well-nursed, well-nourished grudge defines the person who holds it. The person becomes the expression of the grudge that was just a small and negative part of the person, for sometimes the memory of a grievance is greater even than the grievance itself.

It is not only the remembrance of grievances against ourselves, but also the remembrance of things we have done wrong to ourselves and to others, that is the intolerable burden. The reason that we confess our sins is that, in the words of the Book of Common Prayer, "The remembrance of them is grievous; the burden of them is intolerable." Whenever I say that confession in the Prayer Book Communion Office, that is the acute moment of crucifixion for me. I remember the burdens of things that I remember, and the burden is intolerable, and there is no place to be relieved of that burden except at the altar of Christ. The only way to be free of such an intolerable burden is to put it where it belongs: into the past, where we can forget it in order to move forward. "Forgive and forget" is another canard with which we have been brought up, and we like it because we can have it both ways: "I forgive you"—the magnanimity of forgiveness—"but I don't forget the wicked thing you did to me; I maintain this little power. I forgive you, I love you, but I maintain the power because I won't forget." You cannot carry the weight of the past into God's future. "Let it go," said St. Paul: drop it, give it up, hand it over, and follow my example and me into the future. That is what he is saying here not only to himself but to us, and that is why—at this most burdened moment in our culture, where we stand at the edge of one age and are about to enter into another—his word is so important for us to appropriate for ourselves this morning.

"Forgetting what lies behind and straining forward to what lies ahead. . . ." There is almost an athletic metaphor here, in that second part— the straining, when you can almost see the runner in the race who cannot afford to look back or consider the past in any way, but who uses his head and upper body as a projectile in the race. It is not just the feet that carry the runner forward; it is the head and neck and upper body outstretched, moving aerodynamically into the future, that helps to carry the feet forward. Now, many of you are quite surprised that I should know anything at all about so athletic a venture: I can see the wonderment in your faces. "In what book did he read that? What film did he see? Was it *Chariots of Fire*?" I confess that in my youth I was not a great athlete, but the one thing I did enjoy was cross-country, for they left you alone in cross-country; and if you weren't keen on winning you could arrive at any point that you wanted to, at the other end of the line—but there was a moment where a good sprint was in order, and I was good at that. I remember the one thing that my coach said: "It's not your feet that carry you forward, my boy; it's straining forward." It didn't always work, but it's a figure that I have never forgotten. "Forgetting what lies behind and straining forward . . . ," you put yourself ahead and into the wind, and it will take you where you need to go.

Now, I may not be much of an athlete, but I met an athlete not many years ago one day at lunch in Lowell House, a boy I knew who usually flaunted a luxuriant head of hair. This was in the age of great heads of hair, and this boy had an enormous, leonine head of hair, but at lunch on that day he was as bald as an egg, and I thought, *Well, perhaps he's ill.* I wondered and worried, in that instantaneous analysis that we do when we see strange sights, that perhaps he was undergoing chemotherapy or some other dreaded treatment for that dreaded cancer. I wasn't quite sure how to begin, so I began gingerly by saying, "How are you?" "Fine!" he said, his old self. Then I think he noticed the mild apprehension, and he said, "Oh, you mean my head?" I said, "Yes, I was a little curious about that . . ." He thoughtfully explained to me, saying, "I'm on the varsity swim team and we have a meet tomorrow, and I have shaved my head to cut down drag in the water. It's all about physics and aerodynamics." Then, with a big boast and a naughty smile he said, "I'm as hairless as the day I was born; trust me." I said, "That's fine, that's fine, I believe you," but in my ignorance and curiosity I asked, "Does it really make a difference to shave your head and your mustache and your underarms, and so on and so forth?" He replied, "I don't want to take the risk that it doesn't." *Well done,* I thought; *impressive,* and we did win the meet over Dartmouth— which wasn't very hard to do, apparently, in those days.

"Straining forward . . ." as St. Paul put it, getting rid of any kind of impediment, going with the flow and making the flow take you. Straining forward is not only confidence in the future; it is confidence, for St. Paul, in the worthiness of the goal that is worth striving for, the prize of "the upward call of God in Christ Jesus." That is worth shaving your head for, in Pauline terms. Now, Paul, neither here nor elsewhere—and this is an important point—speaks of Jesus as his "personal Lord and Savior." That's a phrase that always to me sounds possessive, exclusive, and proprietary; and I ought to know, because I grew up with it! I didn't read about it in books; I grew up with that kind of piety. Not for Paul, however, is Jesus a private little totem, a kind of Phi Beta Kappa key of spirituality emblazoned upon the chest or the breast. No. He sees the upward call of Jesus as something that moves him forward toward it, that literally fuels him as he pursues that goal, and this is the point to be savored at the beginning of a new year: that which he seeks is in front of him, not behind him, and not beside him. Jesus remains in front of him to be followed, not to be dragged by him by a chain from the past. The only place for faith such as Paul has, and to which you and I are invited, is in the future. That is where it is, and that is where he is going, and no other place will do. You will not find God in your mother's faith or your father's faith, or your childhood faith, or in yesterday's faith: you will find God only in the future that awaits you; and if you're not prepared to go there, then you're not prepared to find God. You'll find lots of gods, interesting gods, gods that you can tie up and put on your mantel, gods that you can bow down to and worship, gods that you can possess and manipulate; but the living God is the God who goes before you, and if you want that God, then that is where you have to be and to go.

How does St. Paul propose to get there? How does he propose to meet that goal? It's all there in Philippians 3; he lays it out so clearly for us, saying, "I press on." Now, it is here that we must drop the speed and velocity metaphor of the athletic race and take on the purpose and endurance metaphor of the pilgrimage, the adventure, the climbing of the mountain— Everest, as it were—or the crossing of the desert as the wise men of old, or the sailing of the seas like the discoverers of the poles and Antarctica. "The only way forward is forward," as Dick Allen of Princeton likes to say. The only way toward the goal is to press on. That is what Paul says. Marathon runners, long-distance walkers are often asked, "How do you do it? How do you get from Hopkinton to Copley Square? What secret method, what sneakers, what formula or method do you use to guarantee success? Is it Evian water, or is it water from the tap? What is it that will help you to get there?" Usually they reply something like this: "You put one foot in front of the other and you press on, and you don't stop until you get there." I think there's nothing more to it than that, and I think that that is essentially what St. Paul means when he says, "I press on." He doesn't say, "I expect Jesus to come in in the last few seconds and move the goal upward toward me, or move me physically and take me to the goal. I don't expect Jesus to come in and call the game on account of the Apocalypse; I don't expect Jesus to turn things upside down. I must press on. There's not going to be any quick, short way to do this; no interference is going to prevent the burden of pressing on."

One can press on only, however, with confidence that the goal is worthy of the effort. You don't press on for an insincere or an unnecessary or an unconvincing goal. You press on not necessarily working for speed or an easy triumph, but persisting, remembering that the one who endures to the end shall be saved. If there is one single ingredient necessary to the human experience in this or in any other century, it is for believers the quality of persistence and endurance. Many of you have been trying this "Christian thing" for many, many years, and you and I know that you haven't got it right yet, and some of you are just starting out and want a quick shot; and you're still going on. What we all require is endurance and persistence.

My old friend Mason Hammond, of the Class of 1925, still gloriously living, told me that he had been coming to Daily Prayers for seventy-five years; and somebody listening said, "Oh, Professor Hammond, you must be a very holy man." He said, "I am a very wicked man, and that is why I come every day." Hardly a wicked man, but the point is crystal clear.

Paul calls this "maturity." We all have different meanings for the term "maturity." For the young, maturity means old; for the mature, maturity means death; for the Development Office, maturity means death with interest. Maturity has a very mixed set of meanings, but for Paul it means that, having cast away all other, less sensible and appealing options and objectives, this is the way right-thinking people think and behave. He says this in Philippians 4:15; "Let those of us who are mature be thus minded." A mature faith is not just an old faith or a faith for old people; it is an old faith for all people who are prepared to grow up and put away childish fears and fantasies. What does it mean for you and for me in the year 2000 to seek maturity in our faith? It means, "Don't be hasty, don't be intimidated, don't be discouraged, don't be seduced, don't be taken in, don't be diverted." This is the way for true believers who, "Forgetting what lies behind and straining toward what lies ahead, . . . press on toward the goal for the prize of the upward call of God in Christ Jesus."

What are you carrying into this new year that hinders you, that impedes your walk, that is a burden? Is it some old grudge? Some bad news? Some unfinished business? Something you want to settle? Some anxiety that constitutes the leftovers from the past? I don't know, I can't read your minds, but if I know you as well as I know myself, I know you have something there, for the turn of the calendar page does not expunge the past. You can, however, do something about it. You can put it down, you can drop it, you can let it go, you can forget it, you can do what the Boston Irish Catholics always say at a moment like this: "Offer it up." Forget what's at your back. Forget what lies behind. Forget your old pride. Forget your old wounds. Put it down, let it go; be ambitious to try again, straining forward to what lies ahead. Shave your head like my young friend. No matter how dismal or distinguished your past, in Christ your best days are ahead of you. Press on to the God who awaits you and is always ahead of you, and always worthy of your best efforts. Will you win? Will it all turn out right in the end like a good American ninety-minute movie? Will you hold up under the pressure? Is Miss Haskins right? Will the prize be worth the risk? It's all right for St. Paul to take on great things; that is what he is there for, but what about *me?*

Over the Christmas season I have, as have many of you, been watching image after image of the pope, the most ubiquitous presence in the last ten days; and I was struck by how aged, how frail, and how old he looks. My heart went out to him as he had to endure the endless Vatican liturgies and all that caterwauling of the Vatican choir, and yet I was struck by the comparison between his frail and obviously failing body and his brave words to a world literally afraid of its own shadow, a world in which even the religious people move more by fear than by faith, more paranoid even than the Pilgrims. I recalled that in 1994 the pope wrote a best-selling book called *Crossing the Threshold of Hope.* On the back cover of that book, the place where you usually put the promotional blurbs written by your friends, there appeared only three words, in the pope's own handwriting, and they are the three most powerful words in all of the Bible. In his own hand he had written, "Be not afraid!"

At the beginning of a new year, at the approach of a new century and the third Christian millennium, and in a world not much better than it ever was, these are the words that allow us to "press on toward the goal for the prize of the upward call of God in Christ Jesus." Be not afraid!

Let us consider the words of W. H. Auden from his poem "For the Time Being: A Christmas Oratorio":

> *He is the Way.*
> *Follow him through the land of unlikeness;*
> *You will see rare beasts,*
> *And have unique adventures.*
>
> *He is the Truth.*
> *Seek him in the kingdom of anxiety;*
> *You will come to a great city*
> *That has expected your return for years.*
>
> *He is the Life.*
> *Love him in the world of the flesh;*
> *And at your marriage all its seasons*
> *Shall dance for joy.*

The Real Presence

Text: This, the first of his signs, Jesus did at Cana in Galilee, and manifested his glory; and his disciples believed in him.

—JOHN 2:11

I take as my text the eleventh verse of the second chapter of St. John's Gospel, those words that conclude that remarkable occurrence at Cana, of Galilee. The story of the magi and of their offering of gifts to the infant king, and that of the remarkable wedding at Cana in Galilee, are both what we call in the trade "epiphany" stories; and you should become increasingly intimate with the meaning of *epiphany*. It is an appearance, a manifestation, a demonstration, and from these two wonderfully vivid and familiar stories this morning we are meant to learn of Jesus' real presence in the world. These stories are meant to get our attention, to hook us, to draw us in even as Jesus is meant to get our attention, to hook us, and to draw us in. In these two stories the same function is served: by the star in the first lesson, and the wine in the second; and in the Gospels of Matthew and John, which are as different as two Gospels can possibly be, there is a common enterprise exercised by the star in the one and the wine in the other. They are signs that are designed to lead us to discover where Jesus is, who Jesus is, and what Jesus does. The star and the wine answer the question "Who is Jesus?"

Now, all of us have survived many a Christmas pageant, and many of us survived the knock-out Christmas pageant here in this church two Sundays ago, when, with eyes keen to observe, you noticed the exotic collection of royal personages that came down our center aisle. Kings and queens, they were of various ages, stations, and degrees, and not simply men, not simply three, and not simply children in bathrobes. Tradition has the magi as three, custom has made them men, and romance has made them kings or astrologers, professors or wizards; but it is truly irrelevant who they were, how many they were, or what they looked like. The one thing that is consistent over the centuries in the variety of their depiction, and in every version of their journey, is that they always ask the same question: "Where is he that is born King of the Jews?" It really doesn't matter who they were, how many they were, what they looked like, or where they had come from; and what ought to matter to us, therefore, on this Sunday of the Kings, is clearly what mattered to them. They were looking for a king, a child of royal birth, a child of high degree, and so, in their search they ask a king— Herod—about *the* King—Jesus—whom they suppose to be at least as royal as the nominal sovereign of the land.

Think for a moment about that nominal sovereign of the land—powerful but anxious, a king yet insecure, who, upon rumor of a rival, goes into collapse, and all of Jerusalem with him. The arch sign of a politician in trouble is insincerity: "Tell me where he is that I too may come and worship him," says Herod; and we can see through him and all of his ilk, as could the wise men. They weren't wise for nothing. One thing, however, that we should give to Herod is that, unlike Mary—dear, blessèd, beloved Mary—it didn't take several drops of the penny for him to understand what was going on. He figured out immediately that there was a rival sovereign out there, and he knew that any king other than himself was a threat to the *status quo,* to the stability of the times, to the image of peace and prosperity, and to all of the comfortable certainties people need in order put up with less than the best. He understood it: "He was troubled, and all Jerusalem with him."

So, we have to credit Herod with getting the picture and knowing that this was serious, and we have to credit the magi with knowing what was *in* the picture, and for knowing what they were looking for, or whom they were looking for. It was a king, a sovereign, someone invested with transforming and transcending power whom they sought; and they recognized that the one whom they had not yet seen was a king with whom the world would have to reckon. Homage by kings to kings is the most ultimate of homages, for royalty is confirmed when royals acknowledge each other. When the magi found the king, they paid homage—they are always depicted on their knees—and they offered gifts, opened their treasures, and understood in their worldly wisdom that here was one who, in the apparent weakness and simplicity of infancy, would make a difference in the world. They understood that. This is no great mystery, no great secret conspiracy; and by their travel, their presence, and their worship the kings acknowledged that here was somebody who would make a difference.

We fast-forward now a few generations, into the earliest period of the Christian church. The earliest Christians living within memory of the lifetime of Jesus had the simplest of creeds—not the Apostles' Creed, so-called; or the Nicene Creed, so-called—for they did not have the variety of credal developments and formulations that litter the first three centuries of the Church. No, these earliest Christians had a very simple creed, which consisted of three words: "Jesus is Lord." That was all it was, and that was all that it needed to be. Jesus is Lord. He was the one to whom all other powers and principalities were subordinate, no matter what the circumstances or the preponderance of evidence might suggest. When we say that "Jesus is Lord," as did the earliest Christians, we mean that neither anyone else nor anything else can claim more of our loyalty or our love than can he. When Jesus is Lord, he is superior to the claims of one's family; and we read over and over again in the New Testament that family is important, clan is good, but that Jesus is Lord, and therefore one leaves one's mother and one's father and acknowledges one priority, which is that Jesus is Lord. When Jesus is Lord, he is superior to the claims of the nation, to the claims of the state, to any social organization. When Jesus is Lord, he trumps the claims of race, of class, of economic status, and of gender. When Jesus is Lord, he is superior even to the tyranny of time.

In one of our great hymns, Jesus is described as the "Potentate of Time." He is superior to time itself, and when Jesus is Lord, time itself falls in subordination. When Jesus is Lord, even death and hell are subordinate to him. Those three words, *Jesus is Lord,* make it possible for the frightened faithful in all ages, usually overwhelmed by the powers that be and their superior forces, to stand up in courage because they know that the one whom they serve is superior to the ones who could, and would, destroy them.

On the scaffold in a Nazi prison, within months of the end of the Second World War, Dietrich Bonhoeffer was superior to the might of Adolf Hitler because he knew that Jesus is Lord. This is the testimony of countless witnesses and martyrs throughout the ages, some known to us and many unknown to us. This is the witness when, on our deathbeds, in our dying moments, the faithful in Christ triumph over the failures of medicine and of the body, because we say and we know that Jesus is Lord. Those three words, affirmed by the magi, become the first, the best, and the last words for all believers. Who is Jesus? Jesus is Lord; and as long as there are people in the world who, in the worst of times and under the most dangerous of circumstances, yet declare that Jesus is Lord, this world and all of its powers will never ever have the last word. You may not remember the Apostles' Creed, and indeed, you may never have learned it; and you may be confused by the Nicene Creed—it wouldn't do you any harm to know both, by the way—but surely you can remember that all you need to know is that Jesus is Lord! That's who he is, and that's who the kings saw, and recognized.

So, if he is Lord, where is he? Where is he exercising his lordship? Remember, that was their question and the principle part of their question: "*Where* is he who is born king of the Jews?" Where is he to be found? Well, the first and most obvious answer is that he is to be found in the manger, the lord of the manger. One of the great paradoxes of the gospel is that in this manger, in this tiny little box of hay, is the Potentate of Time; and the manger is a very safe place in which to have the Potentate of Time, a very safe place in which to place Jesus, because in a manger he is not much of a threat. Who is? In every Christmas pageant, even in our own with a real, live baby, the child in the manger is the most passive participant in the show. He has no lines: imagine how shocked we would be if the child in the manger said, "Hail, Mary, full of grace! How nice of the rest of you to come to see me. I am the Lord and the Potentate of Time!" That would be shocking, almost as impressive as turning water into wine, but in the conventional reading the baby says nothing, he has no lines, he wears next to nothing at all, and he is easily upstaged by everybody else—angels fluttering, shepherds adoring, parents cooing, and kings worshiping. Even the animals have more to say and to do, and bigger parts, than the child in the manger. The next time *I* write a pageant, I'm going to write some lines for the baby, but you will have to wait a while to see that. So, if we want to really answer the question of where Jesus is, we have to look beyond the manger.

It is to this morning's second lesson that we must turn if we are to get a decent answer as to where he is; and it is no accident that St. John places Jesus—for his debut, if you will—in the context of a Jewish wedding. If any of you have ever been to a Jewish wedding, you know how important that occasion is, how full of expectation and excitement. You might even think that, because weddings are suffused with the myths of happiness and of joy making, that was the reason St. John placed Jesus in the middle of one. Ask those of us, however, who have to deal with weddings on a full-time and professional basis, such as the clergy and musicians, and our sexton, and you will learn from us that a wedding is a public occasion in which the worst is usually brought out in the largest number of people, and that whatever can go wrong usually does and will. It falls to us, by and large, inadequately paid for these combat hours, to try to sort it all out. St. John was no fool, and this wedding at Cana was no exception.

For example, despite what it says in the text, there is a long-standing countertradition that Jesus and his merry band of disciples were neither invited nor expected at the wedding at Cana. I know John says that "Jesus was invited also," but there is a large tradition to the contrary. That, how-ever, was the least of the trouble. The wine ran out, and it ran out possibly because there had not been an accurate count due to the failure then, as now, of so many people to "RSVP" properly. To run out of wine at any wedding is a disaster, because wine is the lubricant that makes that impossi-ble scene bearable, but no wine at a Jewish wedding is a catastrophe—a "catastrostroke," as Jimmy Durante used to say—for reputations are ruined, the host embarrassed, the bride's family shamed, the caterer made to look incompetent, and general chaos soon sets in and people get, as Al Gore said quite recently, "snippy." St. John knew precisely what he was doing when he placed Jesus in that context, and, as we all know, Jesus saves the day.

You notice too, for example, St. John's account of where Jesus and his mother have a great little tiff. She comes up to him, and she says, essentially, "My boy, they've run out of wine!" and he says, essentially, "I *know* that, Mother, but my time has not yet come." She, in exasperation, turns and says in an aside to the servants, "Do whatever he tells you. My son, he is the Lord; he can do everything." That's the setting in which we ask the ques-tion, "Where is Jesus?"

Now, I wish to make sure that you leave the service this morning know-ing clearly what is and what is not the miracle in John 2. The miracle is not in the change from water into wine, impressive as that is; and nor is the mir-acle in the fact that the later wine is better than the earlier wine, good as that is. It is important to remember that we are not talking here about metaphor-ical wine or metaphysical wine or symbolic wine or spiritual wine, and we most certainly are not talking about grape juice. This is good, vintage stuff, and plenty of it for everybody—but even it is not the miracle. What, then, is the miracle? The miracle is found in the transformation not of the wine but of the future. Notice the words with which the miracle is defined: "You have saved the best for now"; or, in other words, "The best is yet to come; the future is better than the past; your best days are ahead of you." That is the miracle—of better things to come—of which Jesus is the first and most important sign. Where is Jesus? Yes, he is in the manger; yes, he is at the wedding; but—and this is the big point that John wants us to fully comprehend—Jesus is out there ahead of us. He paves the way before us, he claims the future for us, he hallows—makes holy—what is to come, just when we are either tired of the present or resentful of the past, or fearful and anxious about the future.

As a footnote, I ask you, "What is Jesus' most important work in the world?" What is the thing that he is called upon chiefly to do, and does? I suggest that it is not healing the sick, or punishing the wicked, or performing miracles, or giving ethical guidance—important as all of those things are. His most important work in the world is to rid us of our fear, both of this world and of the world to come. Jesus' great mission in the world is to rid you of your anxieties about life, about living, about death, about dying. That is his work for believers, and how often do we hear from his own lips another set of three words? "Be not afraid." These are the words that describe his passage through the Gospels. He comes into the world, he inhabits places like mangers and weddings, crosses and tombs, in order to tell us, "Be not afraid." He tells us that where he is and where he goes we need not fear to follow, for by his real presence in life and in death, and in life beyond death; by his presence in the past, in the present, and in the future, he has made all of those places fear-free zones. Be not afraid. The best is yet to be. That is the secret of the miracle at Cana, when the most anxiety-ridden moment possible is resolved by a promise of courage and boldness, and of joy in the future. No wonder that, when the disciples perceived what was going on, they believed in him.

So, what does he do? He gives us the future, he makes it our own, he invites us into it. He doesn't just send us out there on our own; he simultaneously goes with us and stands out there to greet us. He gives us fresh courage as we start out all over again on paths both familiar and foreign. He goes before us, as he said. "Fear not, I am with thee, even unto the end of the age." "Emmanuel, God with us." "Be not afraid; in the world ye shall have tribulation, but be of good courage: I have overcome the world." All of these words of Jesus, littered throughout the Gospels, are beacon lights in the darkness, pointing upward and beyond, and they shine in the darkness and the darkness has not overcome them. The record of the New Testament in every Gospel and in every Epistle, and in every word and narrative, is filled with the account of courage and strength taken by the fearful, the anxiety ridden, and the weak because of the real presence of Jesus in and beyond adversity. That is why, at the beginning of a new week, a new decade, a new century, and a new millennium, you and I, fearful and anxiety ridden as we are, must hear this good news for the Epiphany.

What the wise men discovered, and what Jesus himself revealed, is the power of his real presence in the places where often we would least expect to find him. We celebrate his real presence in that most unlikely place of birth, the manger. We celebrate his real presence in that most unlikely of social settings, a wedding. We celebrate his real presence in that most painful of places, the cross. We celebrate his real presence in that darkest of places, the grave. We celebrate his real presence in those most unusual creatures of bread and of wine; and we celebrate his real presence in the past, the present, and the future. There is no place we need fear to go that the real and transforming presence of Jesus has not already been, and is not already at. *That* is the real presence! You can depend upon it.

Christmas has come and now, yesterday, on the twelfth day, has gone, and it is time to pack up the mangers, pull down the greens, and get back to "normal." Those are the normal, natural instincts of people like ourselves, on the whole, who prefer reality to miracles. The Epiphany miracle, however, which lasts well beyond the season of its name, is that Jesus' real presence is our reality. That is his astonishing claim, and ours. He has come into the world to find us as, and where, we are. Therefore, like those wise people from the East, let us too look for him as, and where, he is; for where he is, we will wish to be.

Plenty Good Room

Text: . . . Many will come from east and west and sit at table with Abraham, Isaac, and Jacob in the kingdom of heaven. . . .
—MATTHEW 8:11

You will have noted that we have had two lessons about healing this morning—two wonder-working stories, if you will; two miracle stories, two medical stories. In the first lesson, from the second Book of Kings, we heard the story of Naaman, the man who nearly wasn't healed because he didn't believe in the power of the possible. He declined to believe that what he could do was sufficient, he declined to believe what was readily available to him as a simple home remedy, a basic cure, and he declined to believe that anything so simple, so available, and so free could possibly be the real thing for the healing of his leprosy; and so he stormed off in a rage. He had heard of the prophet in Israel, he had made a great journey from a foreign land to be healed, and, simply put, he was insulted, he was dissed when, after he sent his servants inside to announce to the great physician that he was there, the servants came out with a message from the doctor telling him to go dip himself seven times in the River Jordan, and that that was all he had to do.

It was as if you or I had spent a fortune in very expensive referrals to some high-priced clinician on the top floor of the Massachusetts General Hospital and the doctor sent out a nurse practitioner to tell us to take a dip in the Charles River and go home, and call him in the morning. First our dignity would be insulted and we would think to ourselves that we had come to see the doctor, not an intern, not a medical student, not a nurse, and not a nurse practitioner; and then our confidence would be assaulted, because if the cure was this simple, this cheap, and not expensive, painful, or exotic, it could not be worth the doing of it. This is what Naaman means when he says, "Are not Abana and Pharpar"—wonderful words—"the rivers of Damascus, better than all the waters of Israel?" In other words, "I could have stayed at home and done this, for all of this trouble."

The day is saved by his servants, who, probably tired of their master's complaining and kvetching time and time again, say to him these very useful words: "If the prophet had commanded you to do some great thing, would you not have done it? How much rather, then, when he says to you, 'Wash, and be clean'?" Deciding to act upon the counsel of his servants, Naaman did the possible, if you will: he dipped himself seven times in the River Jordan, and he was made clean, with his leprosy vanished and his skin taking on the texture of a baby's.

This important man of significance nearly lost his opportunity to be saved because he did not trust the act that was possible for him to do—which is a footnote that I often use to Harvard students at commencement time. This church is filled with seniors whose first efforts will be to save the world, to find a cure for cancer, a cure for inflation, a cure for the common cold. They will document and patent it all, they think, and they will do it before their fifth reunion; and then when they find that they can't do it all they give up and by and large do nothing, or they go to law school. Rather than setting their hands to the possible, they seek the impossible, and they neglect the opportunity that is right before them. The lesson, at its most obvious, is clear: God does not set before us impossible tasks. He may set difficult tasks, or tasks that we would rather not do or that test and challenge and confront us, but the old aphorism is true: "God enables what God requires," and sometimes what God requires is surprisingly simple and obvious—love your neighbor as you love yourself; do unto others as you would have them do unto you—not complex, for the problems are usually with ourselves.

Enough of that for now. In the second lesson we encounter the second healing story. Here we have another worldly man, another non-Jew, who requires help. This time, however, it is not for himself that he seeks help but for his servant. The hero of this lesson is the Roman centurion Cornelius, and we know that he is an important man because, like many important men, he tells us just how important he is: "For I am a man under authority, with soldiers under me; and I say to one, 'Go,' and he goes, and to another, 'Come,' and he comes, and to my slave, 'Do this,' and he does it." Here is a man who understands not only the theory of power but the authority and the exercise of power: he doesn't shrink from power, he's not ashamed of it, he's not embarrassed by it, he doesn't boast about it; he simply knows what it is and how to use it. He was the best sort of Roman functionary, yet this man of power and influence, this man accustomed to running the show, could not command his servant to be healed, could not snap his fingers and have his servant, who lay at home paralyzed and in great torment, rise up and walk. He had reached the limit of his power, and, more important, he knew that he had reached it.

So, Cornelius seeks out Jesus. In the verses just preceding our lesson today, if you want to check the context, Jesus has already gone around healing people of leprosy and other diseases and has acquired quite a reputation, so Cornelius did not have to go to the Yellow Pages to find out who was available as a miracle worker, for he knew about Jesus, and when Jesus entered into his town he sought him out. In the words of the New Testament he "beseeches" Jesus, a word that is quite the opposite of command: he asks, he entreats, he solicits, he begs, he does what it takes to get Jesus' attention—and these are not too strong words here. Then something quite remarkable happens: Jesus says, "Okay, fine, I'll come to your house, I'll heal your servant," without any great theological dialogue at all; but Cornelius says, "No, no, I am not worthy to have you come under my roof, but only say the word, and my servant will be healed." For Cornelius it couldn't be simpler: "Just say the word, right where you are, and I know that my servant will be healed. You don't have to come into the house, you don't have to touch him, you don't have to ask him any questions, you don't have to examine him, you don't even have to see him. You are so great and so good, only say the word now, and I know that this servant of mine at home on his bed of pain will be healed." That stuns Jesus.

Jesus is not easily or often surprised, but here he is stunned and impressed, and we know that he is because he says to those who are with him, "Truly, I say to you, not even in Israel have I found such faith." Of course he didn't find such faith in Israel; they were always testing and prodding him, asking him by what authority he did this, or who was worthy to receive that healing, or what was the theological precondition of all of this—all of these grids, all of these questions, all of these interrogatories, and here is this Gentile centurion who says, "All you have to do is stand where you are and say the word, and my man will be right as rain." Jesus was impressed.

How do we know this? By what means would Cornelius have this understanding? Perhaps he was so desperate that he was ready to believe anybody at any time? Clearly he was not as picky or as prickly as Naaman; he didn't have to think twice about what needed to be done.

In the words of our text, Jesus says, "Truly, I say to you, not even in Israel have I found such faith," and in expanding upon that remarkable conundrum—that in the land of the faith such faith could not be found—he says, "I tell you, many will come from east and west and sit at table with Abraham, Isaac, and Jacob in the kingdom of heaven, while the sons of the kingdom will be thrown into the outer darkness; there men will weep and gnash their teeth." What an extraordinary statement! Here this Jew says to this Gentile, "You, and many others like you, will sit with the great patriarchs of Israel enjoying God's favor and presence, while those who believe that they have a right to sit in God's presence, that they have a permanent reservation on the seat, will be cast into the outer darkness, where there will be crying and gnashing of teeth." Then, almost as an incidental detail to the story, Jesus says to the centurion, "Go; be it done for you as you have believed"; and the servant was healed at that very moment.

Now, Naaman and Cornelius are marvelous examples of healing miracles, medical tales, wonder works where the sick are made well and God is glorified. To some, even to many, and perhaps even to some of you, that is sufficient, for God makes the impossible possible, and that is why God is God. For that reason alone we should believe, we should be quiet, we should be grateful, and we should go home. There is something else at work here, however, that is useful for us to consider at this time of year when we celebrate the feast of the Epiphany, the Manifestation of Christ to the Gentiles, the public display of the identity of God in the world. This is no private little manger event, this no secret private parochial God; here at Epiphany we celebrate God writ large, made live, abroad and stalking the earth. Epiphany is the Manifestation of Christ to the Gentiles—which is the formal title of the Epiphany season—to the non-Jewish world, and hence to the whole world. Both Naaman and Cornelius are Gentiles, both healings are made possible by the intercessions and interests of Gentiles, and all of the major figures except for Elisha and Jesus are Gentiles. Remember, it is Naaman's servants who push him toward the river and his healing—perhaps even pushing him in, hoping he would stay in, and it is Cornelius, that Roman under authority, who beseeches Jesus to heal his own servant, sight unseen.

Perhaps we might say, in language popular a generation ago in theological circles, that these are "tales of liberation." Easy to say, for surely both Naaman and the healed servant were liberated from their diseases and healed from their afflictions. I wish to use *liberation* in a much larger context, however, and will argue that it is God who is being liberated from the parochial captivity of those who regard him exclusively as their own, of those who think it unimaginable that God would have any activity, interest, or care for anybody outside their—or our—gilded circle. God, by these two tales, is freed to be God not just of the Jews, whom he never forsakes, but of everybody, everywhere, under every other possible claim. God is freed to be God. The message that God means to communicate to the world through Jesus Christ at Epiphany is that God has compassion, concern, and connection with and for the whole world, and not just for our particular tiny familiar corner of it. The Manifestation of Christ to the Gentiles means literally that God so loved the world that he did not confine himself to a tiny portion of it. Indeed: "Many will come from east and west and sit at table with Abraham, Isaac, and Jacob in the kingdom of heaven"; or, as the spiritual, so gloriously sung by the choir this morning, puts it:

> *Plenty good room! Plenty good room!*
> *Plenty good room in my Father's kingdom;*
> *Plenty good room! Plenty good room!*
> *So choose your seat and sit down.*

It is important to realize that neither of these two healings is subject to conventional theological testing. Naaman is not asked whether he believes in the God of Israel, and the servant of Cornelius is not asked if he believes in Jesus Christ as his personal Lord and Savior. While it is the faith, unspecified and unconfessed, of others that brought them there, they, these two healed men, are the objects of a benevolent God who heals them because they belong to him, they are a part of his creation, his kingdom. God heals them because God made them and loves them, and God claims them as his own. To the Jew or to us they may appear to be the "foreigner," the "other," the "stranger," but to God they are his own, even as we are his own.

Why is that so hard, so impossible, so difficult to believe and to accept? Why is it that the most committed Christians find this notion of an inclusive God so difficult to take seriously? Why is it that those who believe the least among us at least believe that God is capacious enough to take it and us all in? Have you ever thought of that conundrum?

Last week I was in Florida to give a book talk to a large and attentive audience on Tuesday evening in the Coral Gables Church. At the question period, as I have found to be the case over and over again in my travels across the country during the last two or three years, the very first question went something like this: "If in this world Hinduism is true, Islam is true, Judaism is true, then how can Christianity be true? Isn't Christianity the only way, and hence the best way?" You can fill in the appropriate biblical verses cited to support that point of view.

This was not meant, as it frequently is, as a hostile question; the woman who asked it was genuinely perplexed. As I discovered later, she had been brought up in a warm evangelical faith, and even though she had lived all of her life in rural, parochial, Protestant poverty in the Deep South, she knew that she was better off than most of the people on the globe because while she didn't have much, she had Jesus and they hadn't, and that meant that, as the old spiritual said, "She had a title to a mansion on high." Now that her consciousness had been expanded and the world was a much smaller and more cosmopolitan place than she could have possibly imagined, connected by the telephone, the telegraph, the telegram, the Internet, C-SPAN—all of the things that bring the world into our households in an instant—she wondered what God really had in mind for those millions and millions of people who quite happily are not Christians, and are not even Protestants. I replied, at first obliquely, by reminding her of J. B. Phillips's small book of many years ago, *Your God Is Too Small,* in which he says, in essence, "If you think your God is only *your* God, and hence the *only* God, then your God is too small."

Today's healing stories are tales of a large God, a capacious God, an enormous God whose love encompasses not just those who believe in him in just the same way that we do, but all of his creatures and all of his creation, whose love is expressed in languages, in ways, and in customs that they best can understand. It would be a careless and a callous God indeed who would create the world and want the credit for the whole system, and then leave out of his compassion and consideration vast quantities of his own creation. That strains credulity, and pushes the envelope. We who bear the name of Christ must never shrink from proclaiming and celebrating what he means to us as a manifestation of God in the world, but we must also never be so arrogant or ignorant as to suggest that we are the only and exclusive means by which God is at work healing and redeeming his creation. This is a particularly American sin, since there are some among us who actually believe that we are God's best and final laboratory in the world, and that the best argument for Christianity in the world is us. I pray God that that is not so, and you had better pray God too, that that is not so.

This past summer, as I found myself in Hawaii, I recalled in horror that we were the ones, particularly from New England, who took Mother Hubbard dresses to the Hawaiian Islands and dressed the natives up in them, stole land from them, and left them with our neurotic version of the gospel, thinking that a subservient Christian was better than a healthy and prosperous heathen. There were many native Hawaiians at the wedding of which I was a part, and one said, "I wouldn't tell people that you're from New England." I asked, "Why? I'm so proud of being from New England." He replied, "They regard New Englanders as the source of all of their troubles"; and we were, and are.

Remember also that ours is the country whose Southern slaveholding Christians believed that they were doing God's will by whipping and branding their human property into submission for the salvation of their souls, while their bodies, their children, their wives, husbands, fathers and mothers were sold off as real estate and chattel, all in the name of the gospel. We cannot hide from it, we cannot duck from it; it will plague us to the end of time. A God small enough to be reconciled to that kind of moral schizophrenia is a God too small for this creation, a God too small for the gospel, and a God too small for me; and he ought to be too small for you too.

It is hard for me to believe that were Dr. Martin Luther King Jr. alive today he would be seventy years old; and even harder to believe that Duke Ellington would be one hundred years old: these anniversaries are overwhelming. We should note, though, that on this seventieth anniversary of the birth of Dr. King, the chief characteristic that we ought to call to mind from his example and ministry is his large-hearted image of a God who was big enough and gracious enough to forestall justifiable vengeance upon professing white American Christians who behaved so badly, a God of compelling and forgiving love by which we all, oppressor and oppressed, would be bound together and sit down together not only in heaven but right here on earth. That was the substance of his dream—that God would envision and enable our vision of our neighbors and ourselves as enlarged: "plenty good room" both here and now for us all.

My mother told me of her grandmother, Minerva Spratley Williams, a devout Christian, who had lived in the closing days of slavery in Virginia. She was once asked by her daughter, my mother's mother, if she thought that white people would be in heaven—an interesting question. Apparently Great-Grandmother replied with something to the effect that she hoped not, but that if they were, she hoped that she would not have much to do with them. Not for her was our anthem, "Plenty Good Room": there should be separate rooms to pay for the terrible oppression of her people at the hands of white people.

If there is any reason at all to remember Dr. King, it is to remember that he did not invoke what this country truly deserved—divine retribution, a vengeance from on high—but rather a generous, hospitable God in whose kingdom in heaven there was "plenty good room," and that so too on earth there ought to be as well. Dr. King caused us to look into the deep pit of our own self-destruction, he forced us to take a good look at it, then he helped us to step back; and for that we should be grateful.

A large God, then, one who is not restricted to our parochial, peripheral vision, should make us both glad and modest: glad that we are a part of God's economy, that we figure in God's plan, that God cared enough to send the very best, Jesus Christ, and glad that in Jesus we have seen "the brightest and best of the sons of the morning," and have a human example as to what that plan is; and modest because we cannot presume to speak for God, or to speak for those to whom God speaks in ways different from the ways in which he speaks to us. Modesty means assuming that God knows more about the business of human salvation than we do, which is a very hard lesson for us to understand; but understand it we must.

Who do you suppose goes to heaven? Who do you suppose is up there? What do you suppose are the demographics of the great white city in the sky? Only Republicans? Only "real" Americans? Only Protestants? Only straight people? Only white people? There are people who actually do believe that that is so, but that, of course, is a description of hell and not of heaven.

Remember the famous guided tour of heaven, where God takes a new-comer around? In one room there are a lot of people dancing and drink-ing. "Who are they?" asks the visitor. "Oh, those are the Southern Baptists, making up for lost time." In another room there is loud, noisy conversation, rackety-rack, clackety-clack: "Who are they?" is the question. "Those are the Quakers, also making up for lost time." In yet another room there is a group of people just beginning to have a good time. "Those are the Presbyterians," says God. "They are learning how to have fun." As they turn the corner, at the end of the corridor there is a room in which a lot of people are looking very serious. "We must be very quiet here," God says. "We mustn't disturb them, for these are the Catholics, and they think that they are the only ones up here."

In these days of ecumenical sensitivities, in this month of prayer for Christian unity, we recognize how silly and, we hope, how dated such a story now is; and we should be stimulated to realize that the God who can comprehend in one breath Protestants and Catholics, Christians and Jews, also does the same for *all* of the believers of the world, and has already done so. This should not make us think any less of our own revelation, but rather it should make us both modest and glad that the God who created the world and everybody in it has "plenty good room" for us all; and if God can love them, so too can and must we, for God's sake and our own.

Unfinished Business

**Text: Then I saw a new heaven and a new earth; for the first heaven
and the first earth had passed away, and the sea was no more.**

—REVELATION 21:1

Those of you who know anything at all about the Revelation of St. John
the Divine know that this is one of the greatest visions of things to come. It
is found in the middle of that great and mysterious book at the end of the
Bible, a book written by John on the island of Patmos in the Aegean Sea, a
book that some would suggest was written "under the influence." I leave
you to fill in the answer to "Under the influence of what?" There is something quite strange and even unbiblical about this picture. John paints a
glowing image of the new heaven and the new earth, in which the dwelling
place of God is now with us. God dwells with us, we with God, and the
great estrangement and separation, the great divorce that happened in the
first book of the Bible, the Book of Genesis—when we were graduated
from Eden, as it were—has now been brought back together and the great
divorce is over. In this reunion between God and God's people there will be
no more tears, no more sighing, no more sorrow, no more death, and pain
will be a thing of the past: "The former things are passed away . . . and he
that sat upon the throne said, 'Behold, I make all things new . . . I am the
Alpha and the Omega, the beginning and the end.'"

John, we are told, not only wrote down his vision while under the influence, but wrote it in a time of terrible persecution, frustration, and violence
against the church of God, at a time when what he saw could not be further

from what was really happening. It is fantastical writing, and that is the purpose of visions—to take us from where we are to where we would and should be, and to do so in an instant, in the twinkling of an eye. Visions are a splendid form of woolgathering, for without having to go anywhere we can be translated from the here and now to the there and then. I know you understand perfectly what I mean, for some of you are on such a journey even as I speak. God gives us the capacity to remove ourselves from where we are to where we ought to be, or would like to be, without the trouble of buying a ticket or even of moving. Remember those visionary and poignant words of Robert Kennedy? "Some see the things that are, and ask, 'Why?' I see the things that are not, and ask, 'Why not?'"

Yet, there was another purpose to visions and to visionaries, for they remind us of what is not, or at least not yet. To hear, as we do today and on other similar occasions, about the "new heaven and the new earth," and all things being made new because the former things have passed away, serves to remind us that this is not yet the case. When last I looked, the old heaven and the old earth were still very much with us, perhaps too much so, and there is more rather than less of them all around us. The "former things" are not very far removed from us: death, dying, sorrow, sighing, pain, trouble, and tears have not been banished from our experience; and somewhere in this church at this very moment some one of you can testify to one, if not more, of those sad realities. It does no good to pretend that they are not here or that we are not affected by them, and to articulate the great vision is to remind ourselves of how far away from it we are, and how far away it is from ourselves.

A living parable of this truth, which stands in opposition to John's great vision, is that wonderfully uncompleted space in New York City that bears his name, the great Cathedral Church of St. John the Divine, known to its friends as "St. John the Unfinished." It is as it stands the largest Gothic cathedral in the world, it stands in the greatest city in the world, it is dedicated to St. John the Divine, and, like St. John's vision, St. John's Cathedral remains unfinished, incomplete, a work in progress. Entering upon its second century, and in this third millennium, it remains a parable of unfinished business.

The Bible, I will argue, is also a work of unfinished business. Think of it. Things get off to a splendid start in the Book of Genesis, but then the work of the garden is never finished. The help leaves before it is completed. Moses also gets off to a terrific start, but while he was allowed to see the Promised Land from afar, which was the object of his life's work, he was not allowed to enter into it. So near, and yet so far. The prophets—all of them, major and minor—were men of enormous vision, but what fueled them in life was not achievement but frustration; and our Lord himself can be described not only as "the Great I Am," but as "the Great Incomplete." He came to bring in the kingdom of heaven; there is no other way to read the gospels of Jesus Christ: "Thy kingdom come, thy will be done, on earth as it is in heaven. . . ." That was his agenda, and by the standard of that agenda he failed. His work was incomplete. He left behind unfinished business, and we are still waiting for it to be done; he died before he could complete any of it. Think of that when you think of Christianity as a fixed and finished enterprise. Then there is St. Paul, without whom there would be no New Testament at all. St. Paul is always talking about what is to be while living in the frustration of what is not yet. His correspondence is an endless tape of unfinished business, works in progress, things waiting to be done or things waiting to be undone. Then the whole work of sixty-six books concludes with St. John the Divine, and a vision that simply reminds us of how far we have yet to go before that new heaven and that new earth are accomplished.

A decade ago this coming summer, I had the sad honor of attending to the last days of my old friend John Marquand, still of blessed memory to many of us here. John was the soul of fastidious attention to detail, and one might even say that his was a particularly compulsive personality. He was fascinated by his own details, and even more by the details of others. He was, all at once, Allston Burr Senior Tutor of Dudley House, secretary of the Faculty of Arts and Sciences, secretary to the Faculty Council, and secretary of the Administrative Board of Harvard and Radcliffe Colleges. No man was better suited to dotting life's i's and crossing life's t's than was he. John was one of the most literate men of his generation, and he was possessed of an enormous, insatiable curiosity that he fueled at every opportunity. When we spoke of death, his death, as we did more and more as it drew nearer and nearer, he was torn between a huge curiosity about what was to come—whom he would meet on the other side, who would be there and where they would be—and the sense of leaving so many loose ends on this side, so much unfinished business. He was not eager to die. Who is? He was, however, as in all things, interested; and like Winston Churchill and the members of the London Psychical Society of the late 1890s, he promised, if possible, to let me know if he discovered anything. I haven't yet heard, but I live in keen anticipation. More and more, as the end drew near, he said that he hated unfinished business, but that death, he supposed, made the incomplete complete.

You can fathom where I am going with all of this today, when we commemorate the life and the service of Martin Luther King Jr., whose birthday we celebrate officially tomorrow. Like the lives of all martyrs, Martin Luther King's life is a monument to unfinished business, and that is the nature of martyrdom: a life that is offered up and taken away before it has done all that it was meant to do. His life is a monument to unfinished business, but the monument is not to his unfinished business, but rather to ours. His "incomplete" was completed by death. His unfinished business is that which now remains for us to do.

Candor requires me to say that for many people the remembrance of Martin Luther King Jr. is a painful exercise, for not only is there a sense of tragedy to a life taken so violently and prematurely from us, but there is also the remembrance of the savagery of the struggle, the hard-won concessions for social justice, and, now, the sense that the moral momentum of that moment for transformation has long passed. We have neither guilt nor hope: black people can argue that we have won too little that endures, and white people can argue that the "debt has been paid," and that it's time to get on with it. In all of this, Martin King remains a distant, shadowy figure, familiar and yet far removed from the present reality of our world. When we invoke his name, as we will do in thousands of churches, halls, and schoolrooms tomorrow, we are made painfully aware of all of his and of all of our own unfinished and unperfected business, and I am reminded of this in the urban humor of black stand-up comedians. Recently, one of them said this: "As a black man or woman, try to get a cab in any urban downtown area to take you to any address on "Martin Luther King Jr. Boulevard." If the driver is white he will likely pass you by; if he is black, and you get to where you are going, alas, you will find it to be in the most dilapidated neighborhood in town." The very memorial to the man extolled by the violence of his death and the urgency of his cause reminds us of all of this great unfinished business.

Now, for some people, and perhaps even for some of you, all this talk of unfinished business is discouraging; and for those of you who believe in the orthodoxy of progress, it is downright heretical. Others might well be angry and frustrated. Do you remember, in one of the most vivid and poignant of the stories in the New Testament, the frustration of the disciples whom Jesus encountered one morning on the beach after they had been out fishing all night and had nothing to show for their effort? Jesus himself was no fisherman; he was merely a preaching carpenter, but with no lack of confidence in his own wisdom in an area about which he knew nothing, he told them to try again. Can you imagine it? The anger, the frustration of the disciples, receiving advice from this dry-shod nonfisherman on the shore, telling them to go out and try again? In frustration tinged with anger, they replied, "We have toiled all the night and taken nothing." Then they grudgingly added, "But if you say so, we will try again." They did, and of course they took in a bumper crop.

It is always good to have a good ending like that, especially if the story is about you and inspired by you, and useful to you. The front part of the parable, however, makes much more sense than the happy ending. "We have toiled all the night and taken nothing": we have worked all the day and have nothing to show for it; we have labored all the years, all the decades, all the centuries, and again, we have little to show for it. That we recognize as true, for that is the world and the nature of unfinished business—work that is interrupted, work that is imperfect and incomplete. Perhaps, if you think about it, it is only God who has the satisfaction of completing anything, who actually has the satisfaction of seeing the beginning, the middle, and the ending of something useful and beautiful. Perhaps it is only God who finishes what he starts. That is the beautiful symmetry of the creation story: he did it all in six days, completed it, saw that it was good, and rested on the seventh. It doesn't get much better than that. Perhaps it is only God who can do that, and the rest of us must live in an incomplete, unfinished, and imperfect world among the loose ends, until our time comes. Perhaps that's what it means to be fully and finally human.

Last Friday evening I participated in a wonderfully unique moment in the manufacturing of Harvard history. It was the first ceremonial recognition ever, to our knowledge, of students here in Harvard College who, as candidates for March degrees, will not be here to take part in the formal ceremonies in June. Now, it is true that some of these students had "walked," as we call it, in last June's ceremonies. I think that that is a dubious practice, about which I am on public record as being in violent opposition, for it strikes me that "walking" with no diploma is a bit of misguided social promotion that makes a mockery of the academic sacrament, something like having a fake wedding, or a funeral without a proper corpse. I,

however, am outvoted on that point as on so many, and we go on with the
charade.

This ceremony on Friday night, however, was something else. True,
there were no diplomas there either, and it lacked the pomp and circumstance of a June commencement, but it was in some sense an exercise in
faith that the exams and paperwork would be completed and the March
degrees would duly be conferred. It was a ceremonial recognition of immi-
nent departure, with good words from the dean, the provost, and myself,
along with words from three candidates and some friends. It was lovely, and
intimate—if a bit ambiguous—and we were just sending the candidates off
on their way toward their happy prospects. In the common notes of conversation heard over and over again, however, among the thirty or forty
people assembled in the Lamont Forum Room, was a mild tinge of regret
that there was so much unfinished business, so many loose ends untied, so
many things that one wished that one had done that one won't have a
chance to do any longer, or, at least, not as a student in Harvard College.
There was a bittersweet sense that the end had come but that incomplete
and unfinished business remained.

Fortunately, life is more open-ended than college, and the time we are
given, be it long or short, is time in which to begin and to carry on what
others will finish. Life itself is unfinished business. Only God has the chance
to complete what he has begun; and so in some real sense it is selfish to pity
the fact that Martin Luther King Jr. did not finish all that he had set out to
do, and that he has left it to us to carry on. It is as if we have the right to
expect to inherit the completed fabric of somebody else's labor, and how
rude and crude of them to go before the job is done, and to leave it to us to
fill in the blanks. Where, though, is it written that we have the right to
inherit that which is complete and full and totally done? Certainly not in
Holy Writ, as I have just tried to demonstrate, and certainly not in the
annals of human experience, as you know if you have any familiarity at all
with history. In the movies and on television everything is tidied up with a
neat ending: the wicked are captured and punished, the virtuous are
rewarded, and the decks are cleared for the next episode, in which the same
things are begun, endured, and completed all over again. That is why it is
called "fantasy," and that is why we view it as entertainment: because it is so
far removed from reality. That is not the way of the world. "We have toiled
all the night and taken nothing": *that* is the way of the world.

Perhaps the saddest aspect of Dr. King's legacy of unfinished business is that we have managed to lock him and it in the confines of our painful discussions about race. If you want to stop a conversation in this republic, introduce the subject of race. Even enlightened folk such as yourselves will soon find it edgy, nonresolvable, difficult, and bringing out feelings that you would rather not have on display. So, we avoid it, and if that is the only place in which we will find Martin Luther King Jr., then we will avoid him as well. True, Dr. Du Bois said at the start of the twentieth century that the problem of America in that century would be race and the problem of the color line, and he has been proven right, dismal prophet that he was. King, I suggest, was about more than race. Race was the subject, but it was also the sign of both the promise and the failure of America to live out the glorious hope upon which it was founded, the biblical city set on a hill—the city, the culture, the country, the nation—of which we shall sing in the final hymn. Dr. King argued that as long as black people were denied their full participation in the American dream, the American dream would always be the American dilemma, and it has proven to be the case. He was right and he remains right. There can never be moral peace without moral justice. There never will be a peaceful moment in this republic until we have made peace with our racial animosities and have turned the dilemma into the dream. Those who suggest otherwise are simply, to borrow a phrase, "whistling 'Dixie.'" Ours will always be, I fear, an uneasy country, frivolous and anxious at the same time.

King understood all of this, which was his genius and his problem, and he understood it not as a lawyer, not as a social reformer, and not as a social scientist, but as a Christian. He was a believer in John's impossible vision and in Jesus' unfinished work, and it is that unfinished business that is meant to discomfort us and make us nervous until we are prepared to take up our part in it. We fail the whole enterprise if we fail to remember that it was his identity as a Christian—first and last as a believer in Jesus Christ, and as a lover of his gospel—that defined Martin Luther King Jr. If we fail to remember that, and simply buy into the civil rights movement as an exercise of social reform and legal amendment, not only will we have missed the authentic work, but we will also have missed the authentic dream, and we will be all the more deprived. It was not to the American dream that King called us, but to the Christian hope, by which Jews and Muslims, agnostics and atheists and everybody else, would share fully in the promise of this land. Without the Christian hope there would be no American promise. King understood that, and that is what he preached.

So, what difference does all of this make? What difference does it make that we now have this holiday set aside in January? What difference does it make that there will be hundreds and thousands of pageants and plays and programs and speeches and services today and tomorrow? What difference can you and I make in living for Christ in pursuit of John's vision, even as did Martin Luther King Jr.? What on earth can we possibly do? How can we live well with our painfully unfinished business?

The great theologian Howard Thurman had an answer to this. Howard Thurman ministered in Marsh Chapel at Boston University across the river during the years when King was a graduate student in the Boston University School of Theology, and he said then, and has said since in subsequent of his writings, "A person speaks to his time with his life. It is all that he has, all that is given to him, and therefore it is all that he can give." Having said that in his sermon on the New Freedom, he cites this anonymous poem:

> You say the little efforts that I make
> Will do no good.
> They never will prevail
> To tip the hovering scale where
> Justice keeps in balance.
> I do not think I ever thought they would,
> But I am prejudiced beyond debate
> In favor of my right
> To choose which side shall feel
> The stubborn ounces of my weight.

In the unfinished business of this life, the imperfect work to which we are all called, and the work that Dr. King never had fully completed, the question is how we will exercise our right to choose "which side shall feel the stubborn ounces of [our] weight."

We do not live to win. We do not live even to finish. We live to persevere and to endure. Nothing more than this is necessary, but nothing less than this will do until that new heaven and that new earth come, the former things have passed away, the sea is no more, and the vision has become the reality.

It's About the Father:
The Prodigal Son

Text: A certain man had two sons. . . .

—LUKE 15:11

The eleventh verse of the fifteenth chapter of the gospel according to St. Luke states, "A certain man had two sons. . . .," and if a picture is worth a thousand words, then a story is worth a dozen sermons. That is why Jesus spoke more often in stories—or parables, or word pictures—than he did in sermons or in long formal discourses, and that is also why I have chosen to look at some of Jesus' most famous parables as the basis for my sermons over the next six weeks that we share in Lent. Most of you are not very good on the fine points of doctrine and theological distinctions, and those of you who are usually miss the point. A parable, however, treats us all in the same way: it invites us in rather than setting up hurdles, it turns us around, and it sends us right on out again; that is what a parable is all about. During these Lenten Sundays, I invite you into these stories of Jesus, and we begin today with the parable that history and tradition have long called the parable of the prodigal son.

Note that I say that "history," or "tradition," has given this story this title, because nowhere does Jesus use the phrase. There is a very good reason for that, for the story is not about the son or about the sons but rather it is about the *father*. How do we know this? Because the text begins with the utmost simplicity and clarity, "A certain man"—the subject of the sentence—"had two sons. . . ."

It pleases me that some people notice my sermon titles on the pillars outside, or in the *Globe* or the *Term Book,* or wherever else they may see them, and regarding my title for today, one person said to me, "You give it all away! You say 'It's About the Father: The Prodigal Son,' and there it is. Why would anyone have to come hear about it?" I replied that one should never overestimate the intelligence of a congregation. It is no secret, this story about the prodigal son; it is not a secret or a mystery story; we don't have to be detectives trying to unravel it. I will tell you right at the start what it is all about and why the story is told and what it has to do with you: "A certain man had two sons . . ."

Now, these sons can be so easily diverting and take up such a disproportionate amount of time that most of us think that the story is about them. Jim Forbes, my colleague at the Riverside Church in New York City, once told of a preacher who gave a sixteen-week—think of it! sixteen weeks!—sermon series on "The Prodigal Son," and at the end of it a woman who greeted him at the door of the church said, "I am so sorry that that poor boy ever ran away from home." We know what she meant.

The two sons get all the attention; they suck up all of the air of the narrative—but we are wiser; we know what it is all about. Part 1, if we think of this as a three-part play, gives us the prodigal, who, like so many of us, wants it all, and now. He does one memorable thing, and says another. What he does is described in the wonderful language of the King James Version of the Bible: "He wasted his substance in riotous living." Hear the cadence? Hear how beautifully it scans? "He-*was*-ted-his-*sub*-stance-in-*ri*-o-tous-*liv*-ing." It doesn't say, "The son got messed up and threw it all away." No, it says, "He wasted his substance in riotous living," and we all have a clear idea of what he did. Then, when he realizes his true state—when he "comes to himself," as the text puts it—he says the other memorable line, perhaps one of the most glorious lines in the New Testament: "I will arise and go to my father." I have come to my senses. . . . So much for the prodigal son.

Fashionable revisionist readings tell us that our sympathies should be with the generally unsympathetic elder brother. He, after all, is the one who is dutiful and stays home, and does the job. He looks after the estate, he guides the servants, he sees to the fields and the books, he looks after his aging, and perhaps difficult, father, and he responds with normal annoyance. I know that many of you are sympathetic to the elder son: you are saying to yourselves, "Come on, now, let's be fair, the elder son *did* stay home and look after things as a dutiful son. He was always there to be relied upon, he paid the taxes, he did his brother's work while the younger left home to lead a profligate life of debauchery and wasted all his money. He has a right to complain, to kvetch." Yet when the elder son responds with annoyance at the favor shown his younger brother, he gets not a fatted calf but a sermon and a lecture: certainly a raw deal.

Now, this could be just another Semitic tale about sibling rivalry: Cain and Abel, Esau and Jacob, and these two boys—the stuff of a bad miniseries, or another example of biblical dysfunctional family values—but it is not. It is about the *father,* and not about the sons. It is not about two sons who shared the same father; it is, as Jesus put it, about a certain *man,* a *father,* who had two sons with whom he shared his love. The sons, both of them, illustrate the very character of their father, which is unconditional love—not "I will love you if you do this, I will love you if you don't do that," but "Because of who you are and because of who I am, I must love you." The father loves his sons: "I may not like you, I may not seek your company, I may not enjoy you, but we are bound unconditionally and inextricably." He may not approve of their ways, but he loves them; and he loves them so much that he accepts them just as they are—which takes some doing, for if the truth be told, neither son is particularly agreeable.

The prodigal is willful, foolish, profligate, self-centered, self-pitying, and indulgent. He comes home only when he has nowhere else to go. The elder brother is petty, spiteful, jealous, self-righteous, and rather lacking in imagination. *I* think we should pity the poor *father,* who has to live with this conspicuous vice and the even more conspicuous virtue: perhaps *he* should have run away and left the place to the two of them to fight it out.

He didn't, though, because the story is about him, and we know he won't run away, because we won't get Jesus' message if there is no father in the story. We know of his character, his nature, because of what his sons say and do. The prodigal tells us of the character of his father when he says at his lowest point, in the midst of his degradation, at the point below which it was impossible for even him to sink, "I will arise and go to my father." He didn't expect the fatted calf, but he knew enough to know that his father by his very nature, by his very character, would not, could not, disavow him, and that although he deserved little more than did the hired hands on his father's farm, his father would be there to receive him. He knew, this boy knew, that his father's nature was love; and his knowledge was rewarded and returned. The story tells us that the father, when he saw his son on the horizon, *ran* to greet him, ran to get him, to receive him and bring him home. Perverse and foolish, this boy had strayed, but his father ran to get him.

So too did the older brother know this, and it is on the basis of the father's love and justice that he complains—for you complain only to someone in whose justice you have confidence. Both sons presume upon what they know to be there and what they know to be theirs: the unconditional love of the father for his own.

I hope you are getting this. Is it coming through? Are you following this, understanding it? This is the heart of the gospel and of Jesus' message: no one is too far gone, too low, too abased, too bad to be removed from the unconditional love of the Father, not even the baddest of the bad; and no one is too good, too dutiful, too full of rectitude, for that love. It is the nature of the Father to love those to whom he has given life. The prodigal confesses his sin: "I have sinned and am not worthy to be called your son." The Calvinists here will notice that the prodigal son acknowledges his sins, but it is not the confession that triggers the love but the father's love that triggers the confession. Don't forget that! It is the confidence in the love of the father that allows the child to ask forgiveness for his sins, his crimes.

Surely we should preach about judgment, discipline, punishment, responsibility, and all of those parental things, those difficult Puritan virtues. There is enough of that preaching in the Bible to go around, however, and then some. Here, Jesus' emphasis is upon none of those but upon the Father, whose love is there for us to claim even when we choose to ignore it or to feel ignored by it. That is why the theologian Helmut Thielecke some years ago renamed the story, no longer calling it "The Prodigal Son," but "The Waiting Father." The Father who waits for you and me to come to our senses and to go home, come home, arise and go to our Father.

At the beginning of another Lent it is the loving, waiting Father to whom our hearts now turn: among us there are perhaps more prigs than prodigals, more younger sons, older sons, younger sisters, older sisters, more elder brothers who feel neglected by the Father than prodigals who run away from him; but no matter which of these sons is our patron saint, the same loving Father waits for us to return, longs for us to see beyond our own limited vision, invites us out of our self-indulgence and/or our self-pity, and says, "Come home, come home to me, rest your anxieties in my love. . . . come unto me, all ye that labor and are heavy-laden, and I will give you rest." That is what the Father says to his children.

Today, my friends, my puzzled, bewildered friends and fellow pilgrims, at the beginning of Lent and as you stumble your way through, not being sure where you are going or if you should be going, you have an opportunity to come home to the loving and the waiting Father; you have a God-given opportunity for repentance and renewal. Lent is not simply the season to contemplate your sins; it is the season to do something about them as well, and to accept the standing offer that God has for you. The Father loves and waits; he wishes no one to be destroyed or estranged. In our fickleness and in our unsteady ways he is the one constant figure, and the constancy of God's love makes it possible for us to want to come home. Home, it is said, is where when you arrive they have to let you in. That too is the character of God's love, which it is now our duty and our joy to celebrate and to claim.

What You Hear Is What You Get:
Lazarus and Dives

Text: They have Moses and the prophets: let them hear them.

—LUKE 16:29

My text is the twenty-ninth verse of St. Luke's Gospel, the words that Abraham utters to Dives about his brothers.

This is the second in my Lenten series of sermons, "Parables for Lent." When I came to thinking about sermons during a breezy August day last summer in Plymouth, I thought that I would like to focus on parables at some time, and what better time is there than Lent? Not the easiest and most pastel parables, but the harder kind that make you think. Last Sunday we started with a slow and graceful parable, "The Prodigal Son," or, as I suggested—with a nod to Helmut Thielecke—it should really be called, "The Loving Father," for who could forget that the story is not about the prodigal son but rather about his poor father? Next week I will preach on the parable of the talents, and today we look at Lazarus and Dives, and this is one of those parables where a little more obscurity would be a good thing. At the close of the lesson this morning a peculiar silence, a pregnant silence, filled the church, the silence that falls when you have heard more than you wanted to hear: you got it, you understood it, and it was more than is comfortable to understand. That is because of the theme of the rich man, poor man. If ever a parable could do with a little protective coloration, a little filtration or sunscreen, this is it.

There can be only one outcome in the comparison of the rich man who sups gloriously and lives well in this life, and the poor man who begs the crumbs from his table and is covered with sores that dogs lick. It does not take a theological degree to figure out that there is to be a reversal of fortune; that's the clear and uncomfortable part: the rich who are up come down, and the poor who are down go up. Why is this uncomfortable? It is uncomfortable because most of us aspire to be the rich man. We see nothing wrong with dressing well, eating well, and having the means to do so. In much of American Christianity, alas, virtue is in fact equated with wealth, and wealth is the reward of virtue. Remember that notorious radio preacher The Reverend Ike? I loved The Reverend Ike! He used to say in his gospel of prosperity that the "best thing you can do for the poor is not be one of them." A few weeks ago while in Pasadena—there are no poor in Pasadena; it is illegal to be poor in Pasadena—I heard a popular woman tel-evangelist say simply and clearly that "God wants you to be wealthy." Now *there's* a gospel, that is good news. "Aha! You need it all": that comes through the screen.

If God does want you to be wealthy, though, and the wealthy end up as the rich man in this parable, then God must have a perverse sense of humor. No one aspires to poverty; no one wishes to be in a perpetual state of dependence, living off the kindness of strangers. Yet if we understand this parable aright, the very poor whom we neglect and despise in this life, the indolent, the shiftless, the irresponsible, will be rewarded in the next, and at our expense; and if you think that welfare is expensive in this world, just wait until the next. The economic and social gulf that divided us on earth will become that fixed chasm, that place impossible to bridge in the next life, and the poor who could help the rich will not be able to do so.

The economic implications of this parable, for a country that thrives on riches and ambition, are, and ought to be, terrifying. Did you see in the papers this week the pictures of the powerful congressional Republicans at the luxurious Breakers Hotel in Florida with their very wealthy friends and contributors, schmoozing away? When Senator Lott was asked if this was not unseemly, he replied briskly, "It's the American way," and he's right; there are no flies on Senator Lott: it is the American way. That is why this parable will not feature in many Washington prayer-breakfast homilies, or in any of the places where gather those who cherish their earthly rewards and ambitions; and you know that this is true.

In the hands of a good Marxist, if there are any left, this parable would be a screed against wealth and in favor of the coming social revolution, but it is more than a mere socialist tract, although there is enough to make any secular capitalist nervous. This parable is not about wealth and poverty, or even about power and weakness: in the first instance it is about humility and arrogance.

The poor man died and was carried to Abraham's bosom, taken there as a reward not for his poverty but for his humility and his virtue. To the casual and unthoughtful observer, the poverty of the man, his sores, his abject condition, may well have disguised the fact that despite those circumstances he was faithful, he kept as best he could the law and the prophets—the only way into Abraham's bosom. His poverty was not a punishment for his sins; his poverty obscured his humility, his virtue, his reversal of fortune, and he who was ignored was after death openly rewarded in heaven.

The rich man was punished not because he was rich but because his riches got in the way of his piety:

Rich man Dives, he lived so well,
Don't you see?
Rich man Dives, he lived so well,
Don't you see?
Rich man Dives, he lived so well,
When he died he found a home in Hell. . . .

"Rich man Dives lived so well, don't you see!"

We are impressed with the rich man because of his riches, and we are diverted by the outward show, failing to see the content of his character. When he ends up in endless torment in hell, we discover what we could not see before—that his arrogance concealed his unfaithfulness: he neglected his moral duty on earth, and now he must pay. *That* is the reversal of fortune.

In the Middle Ages this parable was a very effective inducement to charity and philanthropy. The rich were told that only the prayers of the poor could help them into heaven, and that therefore on earth they should perform conspicuous good works so that the poor would commend them to God. Thus the rich built almshouses and hospitals, orphanages, schools, and churches as both atonement for what their ancestor Dives had not done, and as investment in the future life. An almshouse was erected just outside Winchester in England, and many years ago on my first visit I was taken to St. Cross, a home for twelve indigent men, twelve poor, pious men, who in return for provision of bread and ale were required to pray daily for the souls of their benefactors.

Closer to home, here in America both John D. Rockefeller and Andrew Carnegie were told by their pastors that their wealth would kill them if they did not make provision for the poor and do good works. Do you really think that Mr. Rockefeller was such a nice man that he gave his money away? Do you think that Mr. Carnegie scattered libraries all over the landscape simply because he liked to read? No! They were scared into generosity! Out of the parable of Lazarus and Dives has come nearly all of Christian philanthropy.

The situations are cast and unchangeable; that is what is meant at verse twenty-six: "And besides all this, between us and you a great chasm has been fixed, in order that those who would pass from here to you may not be able, and none may cross from there to us."

That is the end of the story of Dives and Lazarus, but it is neither the end of the parable nor of this sermon, for now it gets interesting. Dives no longer tries to bargain for himself; now he wants help from his five brothers, who still live in their father's house and presumably share in the wealth that Dives once enjoyed. He wants Abraham to send him to warn the brothers to get their act together lest they end up like him, but Abraham says, in effect, "No more deals, you're done. That's it, forget it."

Where have we heard an echo of this story before? About fathers and sons? We've heard a version of it in action at Christmastime, when in Dickens's *A Christmas Carol,* three messengers are sent to Ebenezer Scrooge to warn him of the consequences of his lifestyle, to tell him to change his wicked ways so he can go out and buy his big turkey, and by implication to help him to repent—which, in true Dickensian style, he does. Here Dickens is a more appealing evangelist than Abraham, who refuses to warn the brothers and regards them as beyond salvation. Dives thinks that they would be impressed with a messenger from the dead, as Scrooge eventually was, but Abraham says, "If they do not hear Moses and the prophets, neither will they be convinced if someone should rise from the dead."

"They have Moses and the prophets: let them hear them."

One of the great commentators on the parables says that this one should be called the parable of the six brothers, rather than the parable of Lazarus and Dives: Dives, who has learned his lesson too late; and his five brothers, who, while heedless and careless by their brother's own admission, still have a chance if only they would "hear" and not simply "listen to" Moses and the prophets.

This, then, is a parable about hearing the good news and acting upon it before it is too late. It is too late for Dives, and nothing can help him now, but it is not too late for the brothers, who have always had what they needed to be saved from the fate of their brother. They have Moses and the prophets: let them hear them. This is not a rebuke; it is an invitation.

Jesus often gives the law and the prophets a hard time, reinterpreting them or even superseding them, but in this parable he affirms the substance of the Jewish faith as all that is necessary to salvation. What is it? We heard it in the first lesson:

Hear, O Israel: The Lord our God is one Lord; and you shall love the Lord your God with all your heart, and with all your soul, and with all your might. And these words which I command you this day shall be upon your heart; and you shall teach them diligently to your children, and shall talk of them when you sit in your house, and when you walk by the way, and when you lie down, and when you rise.

In other words, Moses and the prophets represent all of the moral law, with its obligations to God and to neighbor. Those who forget this law forfeit their right to God's blessing. Those who neglect their neighbor, who fail in acts of piety and charity, not only have neglected their neighbor, but have neglected and offended God.

This is not new news. It has been around from the beginning: every Jew hears it every time he prays—"Hear, O Israel. . . ."—and if you are unimpressed by this rehearsal of God's law, then there is nothing in this life that will impress you, not even a messenger from the dead. To be heedless of this is to be irresponsible, and to meet the same fate as Dives.

The story is a cautionary tale: it is not yet too late for you and for me. It may be for the five brothers, but it need not be for the rest of us, for after all the story is told to and for us. So, what is the "bottom line"? Get your act together *now!* Listen to the gospel and hear it; then act upon it in whatever ways you can. Here it is in clear color: God does not expect you to do the impossible, but God does expect you to do both what you can and what you must.

What God wants of us is not secret, not a philosophical or metaphysical mystery; it is as clear as Moses and the prophets can make it. When Jesus is asked to put it in a nutshell he obliges, so that the likes of you and of me can remember it and not have to wait for a messenger from the dead to come to us. This is what Moses and the prophets and Jesus would have us hear:

> You shall love the Lord your God with all of your heart, soul, strength, and mind. And your neighbor as yourself. On these two commandments hang all the law and the prophets.

That is what Jesus says, and this is what he means. In other words, all virtue, all kindness, all charity, all ethics, all obedience, all philanthropy, all duty, all love, and all joy hang on hearing these two commandments and responding to them, this summary of the law. To hear these—that is, not simply to listen to them but to hear them so that you aim to live by them— is life itself, a virtue for both rich and poor. Not to hear them is death, for then you are cut off from God as surely as you are cut off from your neighbor, in a great unbridgeable chasm.

These, then, are words of life; and if you hear them, if you really *hear* them, that is what you will get, both now and forever.

When the Gospel Is Unfair: The Parable of the Talents

Text: I tell you, that to every one who has will more be given; but from him who has not, even what he has will be taken away.

—Luke 19:26

Those of you who have been with us over these Sundays in Lent know that I have taken up the parables of Jesus, the title of which series might well have been "When Jesus Tells a Story." Last Sunday I spoke about Lazarus and Dives; today I will speak about the least popular of the parables: the parable of the talents, or the parable of the pounds, depending upon which gospel version you are reading. Today's text tells it all: "I tell you, that to every one who has will more be given; but from him who has not, even what he has will be taken away."

When Jesus tells a story he knows how to get our attention, which, after all, is the first point in telling a story—getting people to listen, and to pay attention—and today's text is an attention getter! In this parable, by the terrible and terrifying punch line that is our text, our attention is grabbed, and this is another one of those places where a little more obscurity would help. Now, some will say that Jesus didn't say those words, that a man in the story said them, or that the quotation is a Harvard Divinity School exercise, and will want to know who *is* telling the story. We want Robert Funk and his Jesus Seminar to explain it all to us: Was it made up? Was someone cross with Jesus? Alas, even the Jesus Seminar cannot remove this from the text:

both the account in Matthew and the version we read today in Luke tell essentially the same story and conclude it in the same way, with this manifestly unfair confiscation and intimidation. This is redistribution of wealth at its best.

When I was considering a title for this sermon in the cool August breezes in Plymouth, I thought that I would call it "When the Gospel Seems Unfair." That had a nice ring to it, but on closer consideration I changed it because the gospel doesn't merely *seem* unfair in this parable; it *is* unfair. If we are looking for offense, or if you are looking for an excuse for not listening, here it is for the taking. This is it.

Let us cut to the chase—or, in this manifestly economic parable, to the bottom line: what gets our attention is the fate of the third man and his poor investment strategy.

On Wall Street, I am told, the most precious commodity is *information;* it is *not* money! Ask Professor Hayes if I am wrong—he is here this morning— but I am told that your money is only as good as your information. So, what did the other investors "know" that our poor hapless third man not know? Well, if the most important thing in the market is information, then the worst thing must be poor, or wrong, information. We don't know what the other investors knew or didn't know; we do know what our investor thought that he knew. How do we know? He tells us, by way of explanation and excuse: "For I was afraid of you because you are a severe man; you take up what you did not lay down, and reap what you did not sow." Perhaps it is not a matter of poor information, for the Master does not deny this description of himself; perhaps it is a matter of acting badly on good information—knowing what you need to know, knowing that it is accurate, and taking the wrong action, coming to the wrong conclusion.

Remember the French Maginot line? Experience had taught the French the route of the German invasion, and they knew that the Germans were likely to invade again, straight across the border. So, the French built the best forts and the best barricades that money could buy in order to defend the line, and what happened? The trouble, of course, was that the Germans went *around* the line and attacked from the sides and from the back. Accurate information presupposes intelligent use of it.

Our hapless investor, the third man, knew what he needed to know— that his master was hard and shrewd and had great expectations—and so, for fear of losing what he had been given, he hid it, he "laid it away in a napkin," which today would be like putting it in a coffee can and burying it in the garden, or hiding it under the mattress, or stuffing it in a sock and hiding it in your sock drawer; the meaning is the same: he hid it. For him it was not, "Nothing ventured, nothing gained"; it was, rather, "Nothing ventured, nothing lost."

He discovered to his peril, however, and we to our discomfort, that it was lost and that what he had was lost also. The master is what he said he was, a man of great expectations, with those who ventured much for him being rewarded and those who risked nothing at all losing everything.

Now, read as a parable about capitalism, this is a reassuring story to those who put their money in trust and their trust in money. Is this a story about trust funds or investment strategy? Of course it isn't! In the first instance it is about accountability, about doing the best that we can by one who has placed trust and confidence in us. It is a stewardship parable with responsibility, invectives, and rewards; and yet how boring, how tedious, and how predictable if that is all that it is. Luke's account calls this the parable of the pounds, and the financial element is clear; Matthew calls it the parable of the talents, and there we have a little room with which to play, because while a talent is indeed a denomination of money, it has also come to mean other qualities and endowments. It is one thing to say, "He has a lot of pounds on him," and quite another to say, "He is talented"; and so when we say with the very same words, "She is talented," we mean that she has gifts that are not only financial. Talent in this sense can also be a synonym for grace. To say that Yo-Yo Ma is talented is to say, for example, not only that our fellow worshiper has a gift, but that he has used it, indeed increased it, and by so doing has made many others rich by it.

That helps, I hope, but that's not all. We have to come back and ask, "What was it that the others had and our investor had not?" What is referred to, when in the stark words of the text we read ". . . that to every one who has will more be given; but from him who has not, even what he has will be taken away"? What is the "it" here? If it is money, then this is the worst form of confiscatory, punitive capitalism, where indeed the rich get richer and the poor get poorer. I don't think that we are talking about money, however. No, I think we are talking about something else; I think that this is a parable not about investment but about something much more important, a parable about imagination, of seeing what isn't there and multiplying it. That is what the other two investors had that the first one lacked. They saw not only what they had, but what they might further have if they acted prudently and creatively—if, indeed, they dared to take a risk. The third man, our friend, saw only what he had, and he was afraid to lose that. He therefore keeps what he is given; he does not risk either it or himself. Growth is not possible for him or for the investment, and in his caution he loses not only what he was given but what he has, not thinking to put the money in the bank in order to acquire interest while the master is away.

His "sin" is that he cannot see further than the security of the moment, and he trusts neither himself nor the master, and thus by fear, or by caution—which sometimes can mean the same thing—he is driven to inaction. As Harvey Cox once said, "Not to decide is to decide." Here, not to act is to act, but in an unimaginative, uncreative, ungraceful way, and he is thus not fit to be trusted because he does not trust in himself. Think of it: those who have imagination, who are gifted to see and to risk beyond the security and fears of the moment, often gain the benefits of their vision. They are seers and visionaries—not just shrewd investors, but valiant dreamers moved by insight as well as by sight. They see things that are not, and act upon them, and thus bring them into being.

A few weeks ago, perhaps like some of you, I watched the production *Mandela and de Klerk,* with Sidney Poitier and Michael Caine in the principal parts. I thought it a brilliant production, and I now expect President Mandela to sound like Sidney Poitier; but, cutting across the plains of expectation, I found that the star of the operation was Frederik Willem de Klerk—not because he was good or virtuous or astute but because he acted upon not only what was, but what was to be: he took the risk of moving beyond the predictable and the safe. Oh, he was pushed, of course, and maneuvered and manipulated, and if he could have found a way out without making any changes he probably would have; but when all is said and done he took the risk, he used his imagination, and he advanced a process and probably helped to save a nation: he used his talents and made them work for him as best as he could.

Why does Jesus tell this story, this parable about the talents, if it is not a lesson in economics or in moral courage? He tells it, I believe, to remind us that courage and moral imagination—as Dr. Robert Coles calls it—not just faithfulness, are the key ingredients in the claiming of God's kingdom. You can't just be good, or just think well about goodness, or think well about thinking well about goodness; you have to risk doing good, you have to take risk. As Diogenes Allen says, "The only way forward is forward." You have to imagine what it is like to serve and love a living savior, and then act upon it, and act in the absence of assurances and available information while knowing that you will be held accountable.

Matthew's version of this parable makes the point that each one of us is given talents to invest according to his ability. That is a good and useful point. God has wasted nothing on us: all that we have is useful. Remember that. We may not have the same skills or opportunities or graces as our neighbors, but we have what we need to do what we must. *We have what we need to do what we must.* To fail to do what we can because we cannot do as much as our neighbors is not modesty, it is cowardice; it is lack of trust, and it is irresponsible. What good would our latent powers be if we didn't use them? What good will our spiritual reticence do if we fail to do what we can? Where will that leave us? What will we have to munch on over lunch?

Instead of fretting over the "unfairness" of the gospel, or complaining about the nature of the one who tells such demanding and sharp-edged, terrible parables, perhaps we ought to reflect at lunch today over what we have been given. What talent? What skill? What treasure? What opportunity have I, and how ought I to put it to maximum use? Perhaps I can make a decision; perhaps we are not given to greatness at Harvard because everyone here is waiting for that one moment of greatness, and nothing gets done. Perhaps the business of this afternoon is to do only one small thing, but maybe it is that one small thing done well and regularly that is just what is needed by someone in some place at some time.

No one is without talent. The world is simply divided into two groups: those who know what their talents are and use them, and those who do not. Now may well be the time, today may well be the day, when you begin to look not at your losses but at your graces, and decide for the sake of the Master how best to use them.

If you want a cliché with which to remember the terrible parable of the talents, it is simply this: "If you don't use it, you will surely lose it."

How to Change Your Life: Communion

Text: She has done a beautiful thing for me.

—MATTHEW 26:10

On Palm Sunday, things move very quickly. Very quickly we move through the rehearsal of the triumphal entry into the city of Jerusalem, where, with our ancestors of old, we wave our palms, shout "Hosanna!" and gladly welcome the Christ. Quickly we move from there to now, having read the Passion, having stood once again at the foot of the cross, having questioned and examined and experienced the motives of that incredible cast of characters. On Palm Sunday, more than on any other Sunday of the year, we are reminded that the essential Christian narrative, the story by which we are formed, the oldest, the first, and the central story, is that which we have just read—not the stories of Christmas, or of Epiphany, or of Advent, or of the miracles; not the healing stories, nor the Sermon on the Mount, nor the parables; but the story of the Passion. This is the story that the faithful told to one another, this is the story that is at the heart of the gospel, and if you cannot take this story, then there is no good news for you. You cannot choose; this *is* the story, and everything else comes from it. Once a year we rehearse in the most dramatic and effective way that we know possible the whole narrative of the Passion. This is the heart of the Christian faith, this the essence of the good news; and you cannot fast-forward to the end, for there is no end without this story.

Things may move quickly on Palm Sunday, but the story of the Passion is so enormous, so big, so vivid, that it may almost be too much to absorb all at once; and so the sermon on Palm Sunday, while it is about the whole Passion, needs some smaller story by which to take in the larger—a little magnifying glass, if you will, through which to look at the big picture. Let me indulge in a music analogy. Listening to the story unfold on Palm Sunday is like listening to one of Bach's great passions, the St. Matthew or the St. John, which go on for two or three hours in an enormous array of musical forces, with orchestra, choruses, and soloists all gathered together in a work so magnificent, so overwhelming, so overpowering that it is impossible to take it all in. Bach knew that, and that is why he provided among his large passions the simple chorales interspersed as hymns throughout the larger tapestry of music. Those simple hymns, those chorale tunes, the greatest of which we will sing at the end of this service, provided toeholds for the people, places to grasp on to to sustain themselves when the enormity of the big picture was almost too much to bear. That is what the sermon on Palm Sunday is meant to do, especially when it follows the Passion narrative: it is meant to provide a toehold, a small-scale work set within yet apart from the larger, magnificent narrative.

So, our toehold today—our chorale, so to speak; our hymn in the middle of this enormous cantata—concerns that wonderful scene before the Passion narrative in Matthew's Gospel where Jesus is on his way to his final destination in Jerusalem but makes a stop on the way, a detour at the home of Simon, the leper, at Bethany. The story is contained in the twenty-sixth chapter of the Gospel of Matthew. Jesus stops at Simon's house, and, as he so often does, he enters into the social intercourse of the place: he dines there, and in the middle of supper a strange thing happens. A woman comes up to him with an alabaster jar of very expensive ointment, and pours it out, all of it, on his head. The disciples, we are told, are aghast at her gesture, and offended by her effrontery. She probably should not have even been in the room, for it was not the done thing for women to be present when the master and his male friends were chatting: the women were elsewhere, or at least they should have been. This, then, was a woman out of place and, as far as the apostles were concerned, in the wrong place at the wrong time.

She is accused of waste—of "misplaced priorities," we might say in the antiseptic language of today—and the disciples, we read, give her a very hard time. Jesus, however, rebukes them and accepts her gesture, accepting her extravagance as his own. She alone, he notes to them, understands what is about to happen. She understands that he is about to die, and she has anointed him for the grave; and her anointing is of the same order as was the wise man's gift of myrrh at the manger. In the midst of life, here is a sign of death and burial; and out of this extraordinary scene, this interruption of the routine, Jesus confers upon this woman both a fame and a future. "Truly I say to you," he says, "wherever this gospel is preached in the whole world, what she has done will be told in memory of her." We do not know her name, we know nothing of her antecedents, and we can only speculate upon what she might have looked like, but hers is the most enduring of all fame: "Wherever the gospel is preached she is to be remembered, and her deed told in memory of her."

Think of this. Just a very few days later, Jesus will ask that whenever his friends gather when he is gone, and eat the bread and drink of the cup, they do so in memory of him. He is to be remembered in the celebrations around the table, and she is to be remembered wherever the gospel is preached. So, on this Palm Sunday, the Sunday of the Passion, the Sunday where at the heart of the gospel is preached the Passion of Christ, we remember her. She is in our midst. We meet here today in memory of her.

What is it, on balance, that is to be remembered about her, from that strange encounter at Bethany on the way to our Lord's Passion and death? I think it's very simple, and I'll make it even simpler than it is: I will give you three points.

First, we remember that "giving" is what she did. She gave the most expensive, the most extravagant thing she had, and she was improvident, imprudent, and impetuous. She probably couldn't afford it, and that is what true giving is: the giving away of what we cannot afford, parting with what we would rather keep, spending elsewhere what could be saved for ourselves or, as the banks put it, used for some provident purpose. Yet, what we are asked by Jesus to remember about this woman is that she gave; that in that imprudent, improvident, impetuous way, she gave. Hers is an invitation to ordinary, unimaginative people like ourselves to live, and therefore to give, extravagantly. I know it goes against the grain, for we are naturally stingy, all honorary Yankees, all spiritually tight. Just look at yourselves, or if that's too much, look at your neighbor; you know what it's like. Not only do we say of ourselves that we can't afford it, but we say of others, when they make extravagant gestures, "I bet they can't afford it!" Giving, however, is what she did. As Billy Ray Cyrus likes to sing—and I expect that's the first time he's been cited from this pulpit—"All gave some, and some gave all." Jesus wants us to remember this woman because she gave all. Giving is what she did.

Second, "receiving" is what he did, and that too is a compelling part of this story. He accepted her gift, and thus he accepted her. A gift is a symbol of the giver, a gift is a part of the giver, a gift is the giver. It is not that what we are is what we give, but that in giving we give what we are; and to accept a gift, as we all know, is to accept the giver. The girl accepts the ring because she accepts the giver of the ring, and when she rejects the ring she rejects the giver of the ring. That is why in old etiquette books for young girls they were warned about what gifts they could and could not accept from boys, for in accepting the gift she would accept the giver, and all that went with the giver; and it was as much an act of intimacy to receive as it was to give. The disciples understood this, which is why they objected; for when Jesus accepts the gift of his anointing from this unsuitable person, a woman out of place, they realize that he is accepting not simply her anointing but her herself, and that therefore the rules are changing, and things will never be quite the same again. It was generous of her to give—do not underestimate that—but it was radical of him to accept. She did the giving; he did the receiving, and by that exchange is the third point made.

By her giving and his receiving they shared a fellowship, an intimacy—a communion, if you will. That is what they did: they had communion, which is a sharing, a giving, a receiving, and not simply a liturgy but a liturgy that has as its central ingredient a giving and receiving of gifts, and the changes that result from that exchange. Near the end of the wedding service in the Prayer Book, when we are about to pronounce the couple husband and wife, we say that by the giving and receiving of rings and the joining of hands they have become something else, and somebody else's, and nothing is ever the same again. That is what communion is, in this context, and make no mistake: it was communion in that room at Bethany just as much as it was communion in the Upper Room on Thursday night. Remember that.

So, what has all this got to do with us? Well, if we want to change our lives, and that has been our emphasis together over these past forty days; if we want to see what life is like with faith as opposed to without faith; if we want to make a difference in the lives that we have brought to this house this morning; if we want the exercises of this Lent to lead us to the experience of a new and different life—then let us try the formula of this little gospel story on for size:

1. *Learn to be extravagant givers.* What have you to offer that you cannot afford to give away, that is the very thing with which you must choose to part. Is it your love that you are sequestering for the right and perfect person? Is it your hand that you're not willing to extend just yet? Is it your heart that you're not willing to open? Is it your mind that you're not willing to share or to change? What will you part with that you feel you cannot afford to give? That is the very thing that you must give. What extravagance will you risk to transform your life? What foolish, generous, gracious, uncharacteristic thing will you terminally tight, spiritually contained people give? Your lives will never change until you are prepared to learn how to give generously. Money is the easy thing—not for most of us—but it really is the easy thing, and we'll talk about that later. It's not money we're talking about here, but something far more fundamental. Think about the most precious part of you, and that is what you must be prepared to lavishly give away.

2. *Knowing the risk of giving, now try the even greater risk of receiving.* Learn to be a generous receiver. Somebody wants to love you; think of that. Somebody somewhere out there is desperate to love you. Let him. Let down the barriers, open the doors, remove the inhibitions, let him in. Somebody less worthy of you wants you to accept him or her. Try it. Open your hand to receive what someone else is prepared to give to you. The old spiritual fathers used to say that we *get* so little from God because we are prepared to *accept* so little from God. Open your hands that you may be prepared to receive what is out there for you. Open your hands, and open your hearts to the abundance that is waiting to fill them both. Now, to be a generous receiver is to be vulnerable. How often have we extended our hand to somebody and that person wasn't prepared to take it? There is nothing worse than an extended hand not received. Once burned by that we never do it again, or so we think; and we will never experience the joy of receiving unless we are prepared to receive what is prepared for us. Open yourselves up to the gift that

somebody is preparing to give to you even as I speak; and, most important, open yourselves up to receive the gift that God gives to you in Jesus.

3. *Finally, in giving and in receiving we share.* We share with one another, and we share with God, and so in order to make a difference in your life, in order to change your life, you must make communion not your ritual sacrifice but the path you hope to follow in life, not alone but with others, in fellowship with God and with one another. The interesting scene of that intimacy in Bethany is that the woman presumably did not know Jesus, and nor did he know her. It was a communion of strangers, and it is that that we are bidden to remember forever.

In Holy Week we are meant to share in the Passion of Jesus that we might share in his resurrection. He gives us himself generously, lavishly, in love, and we are meant to fully and freely accept that love and to share it in fellowship and communion with everybody else. To give love, to receive love, to share love is what it is all about, and that little scene at Bethany reminds us of the whole Passion, the whole gospel.

Generous givers and receivers of the extravagant good news of Christ, that love is what we share with the whole church and the whole world as we "enter with joy upon the meditation of those mighty acts whereby thou hast given unto us life and immortality."

For this we now give extravagant thanks to God the Father, through our Lord Jesus Christ. Amen.

Starting Over

Text: Therefore if any man be in Christ, he is a new creature: old things are passed away; behold, all things are become new.

—2 CORINTHIANS 5:17

St. Paul is the evangelist of Easter. He has nothing whatsoever to say about Christmas or Advent; he begins and ends with Easter. Easter is the gospel as far as St. Paul is concerned, and without St. Paul there would be no gospel for us; and so on Easter day I take as my text a sentence from Paul's second letter to the Corinthians, from the seventeenth verse in the fifth chapter: "Therefore if any man be in Christ, he is a new creature: old things are passed away; behold, all things are become new."

"All things are become new." Oh, if that were only so! If that were only true—that all things would become new, and that we would become new people, different from the people we were when we entered this church. Oh, that we could become new, that we could start all over again—wipe the slate clean, get rid of everything on the hard drive, and start all over again. All of us want a second chance, a new opportunity, a new lease on life: we want to start over and to change our lives because we have made such messes of the ones we have. Everybody in here is the *s* in *mess:* you know it and I know it, and if you doubt it, just ask somebody who knows you. I hear this all the time from the people who come to see me. "If only I could do that again," they say; or, "If only I could take that back"; or, even more poignantly, "Knowing what I now know, if only I could start over . . ." I couldn't put it better than Robert Donald Spector did in one of those little squibs that appear in italics in the *New York Times* on Mondays. This one appeared on January 7 of this year, and this is what it said:

INFERIORITY COMPLEX

If I had Solomon's wisdom,
Possessed all the power of Atlas,
And moved with Mercury's swiftness,
I'd find a way to mess things up,
Because I'd still be me.

Starting over. Beginning again. Our students are coming back from their holidays tomorrow, hoping against hope to start all over again, to make a better start than the one they made in January, or the one they made in September. Starting over. Beginning again. We all want to do it.

On Tuesday night I had to give a talk at Northfield–Mount Hermon School in the back of beyond in the part of Massachusetts nearly into New Hampshire. The whole student body had been compelled to turn out to hear me, and I told them that I knew they had better things to do with their time, because I certainly had better things to do with my time, but there we were, stuck with one another. It went well, I am happy to report. Needless to say, I spoke and they listened and we finished more or less together, as I hope we will this morning. The best part on these occasions, I find, is always the question-and-answer period, because I can go on for hours, and what they're really interested in is what they ask in the question time. One boy stood up in the large hall and asked me what inspires me. I suspect that he expected that the answer would be "God," or "Harvard," or something like that, but I surprised myself, and perhaps him, by saying on impulse, without thinking for a second, that what inspires me is the beginning of each new day.

When I wake up each morning and pinch myself to see if I am still alive, I rejoice that I have been given a chance to start over. When I get up in the middle of the night, as I do from time to time, and stumble on my way to a private mission and hurt my toe, I don't swear; I say, "Thank God! I am still alive; I can feel this!" It means too that I probably have a chance to start over, because at the end of the day, when I put my head down and go to sleep, everything has not always gone the way I have wanted it to go. Things have been left undone, bad things have been said, good things have been left unsaid, and lots of things have been left in abeyance. It happens every day; and every night one takes that burden to bed. In the morning all is possibility, all is opportunity, all is good and all is God. Starting over is what it is all about, and for that I thank God. That is what inspires me.

Now, I know you are all smart enough, clever enough, sophisticated enough, I hope, and self-interested enough, certainly, to see where this train of thought is taking us on Easter morning. Ours is a religion of the dawn. Creation begins in the morning. The women come to the tomb in the morning. The morning is when it happens. Lose the morning and you have lost the day. resurrection is an event of the morning, and when Jesus is raised from the dead it is always morning, always daytime, always the new day, the fresh page on the calendar, the new exercise book, the new moment on the horizon. Whatever was yesterday is past and done; and not only is the day new, but we are renewed by it. The theme of Easter is that you and I are become something new. We are given a second chance to get it right—a second bite of the apple, if you will. The new life is the continuous theme of the Bible. Over and over and over again the Bible is the story of one chance after another, one renewal after another, one extension after another, one new opportunity after another, until it comes to its climax in the story of the resurrection morning. This is St. Paul's point in our text and throughout every word he has written in the New Testament. "If any man be in Christ," then by definition that person "is a new creature. Old things are passed away; behold, all things are become new."

What does he mean by that? He means that the resurrection is God's invitation to us to start over; and what a blessed surprise, what a glorious relief that is! Who of us here is content with things as they are? Who of us is content with ourselves as we are? Who among us does not long to be more loving, more generous, more tenderhearted, more passionate, more creative, more thoughtful, more imaginative, more useful? Who of us would not love to have the courage to act upon our convictions as opposed to upon our fears? Who of us would not wish that we could afford to be good, to be nice. Think of most of the quarrels of which you know or of which you are a part. Think of the irritating differences among us. Most of them stem from our inability to trust our own fundamental instincts for goodness—not those of our neighbors or our colleagues or our friends. We don't trust our instincts to be good; and it is not distrust of neighbor that we feel, but distrust of self, for we don't want anyone to take advantage of us. I see it in myself every day. "If I concede this point to one of my col-leagues," goes my reasoning, "then he will walk all over me: I will open the door and my colleagues will drive a train through it. If I let down my ego, my guard, my professional defenses, my professional dignity, then not only will I lose face, but I will become a first-class wimp. So, I will huff and I will puff, and I will continue as I always have, protecting my turf against all and whomsoever, asserting my rights, nursing my grievances, guarding my flank, hitting out before I am hit, doing unto others before I am done unto."

Now, you may think that I am being too hard on myself, charming and able as I am, but I am not talking about myself alone! I am talking about you as well, and if these things are not true of you, then certainly they are true of the person sitting in the pew next to you. Just look at that person and you will see what I mean. Aren't you tired of all that? I am. Don't you want to change? I do. Don't you want to start over? Desperately, I do. Don't you want to change your life so that you are not a continuing parody of yourself? Easter is that opportunity for change. Easter is the invitation to change. That is why, I suspect, you are here today. You know all of this. You don't need to be told. It helps you if you are told, but you don't need it. You have come from God-knows-where to this church because you are in des-perate search of a chance to start over; and your reasoning—dare I suspect it—is something like this: if God can raise Jesus Christ from the dead, in the most astonishing reality the world can claim, then maybe, just maybe, per-haps something new and good can happen to me. "I don't ask, just yet," we reason, "to be raised from the dead, but I do ask that things be different at one o'clock than they were at ten o'clock. Is that too much to ask, O God? I'm here; Easter is my second chance."

A contemporary Christian writer in England has noted, "There is little good in filling churches with people who go out exactly the same as they came in." It's a waste of your time, not to mention mine, and not to men-tion God's, if you leave this church exactly as you were when you arrived. Something has to happen to you to make a difference in your lives, and you can't wait to die for it to happen. When St. Paul asserts that anybody who really understands and follows Christ is a new creation, he means that because of Christ we see things differently and we respond to things differ-ently. Things are not different but we see them differently, and thus we are different.

How, we might ask, does this work? Well, let us remind ourselves of just who it is who tells this resurrection story, and on whom the first impact of its meaning occurred. Remember, when the resurrection of Jesus occurs, and it is recorded in Scripture, nothing happens in the world. Nothing happens. Jesus is raised from the dead and a few women and a few Jews know it, but nothing happens. The sun does not stop, the rivers do not reverse course, the wicked do not cease from troubling, and the weary still do not have any rest. The resurrection, as far as the world is concerned, is a great anticlimax. Violence still stalks the land; people still lie, cheat, and die; good continues to be the apparent hostage of evil; and the devil is as industrious and creative and profitable as ever. On the first Easter day and on the day after the first Easter day, nothing happened in the world. All things continued as ever of old: peace did not break out; kissing was not done in the streets.

So, what changed? That is the wrong question. The question is, rather, Who changed? From what to what? The heart and the burden of the New Testament is not that the world changed, but that ordinary men and women, the most ordinary of whom were those men and women who followed Jesus, and huddled at the foot of his cross, fled at his death, and were astonished when they discovered that he was alive again—that these ordinary, bewildered, befuddled human beings, our ancestors, were changed from the ordinary to the extraordinary. They did not change the world but they themselves were changed, and thus was their attitude toward the world and all that was in it changed. They were no longer terrified of their shadows, frightened, or fearful of death. They were no longer in awe of people who had power and terror over them. Read about those apostles in the New Testament; read about what happens to them, about how they lived their lives, how they faced the world, how they astonished everyone who had known them before the resurrection. Can these be the same people who never understood one of Jesus' parables, who were always late, who were never at the right place at the right time, who denied him, who shivered at the foot of the cross, who ran into the darkness, and who didn't even believe the good news when they first heard it? Could it be these same people who were now turning the world upside down?

What happens to the women on Easter morning? Think about it. They had gone on a mission of mourning and mercy to attend to the body of Jesus, to anoint the body and to repair the damage done by the spears and nails on Friday, to wrap him up and give him a proper Jewish burial, since he had simply been dumped in the tomb on the eve of the Sabbath. They had gone to do the work that we now pay undertakers to do. What happens to them that morning? They become the first apostles—you heard me right, because an apostle is a witness to the living, resurrected Christ. These women became the bearers of the good news, which means that they become the first evangelists. When Jesus was born, remember, it was the angels who were given the happy task of announcing the good news, but when Jesus is resurrected, the angels are replaced by the women. If ever there was an argument for the ordination of women, that is it. That's good news—for them, and for us.

Think of the men—weak, feckless, misunderstanding, and never getting it right. What happens to them? Slower than the women, inevitably, nevertheless they finally understand; and from a group of second-raters they become the evangelists, the apostles, the courageous martyrs, the men who, in the words of their New Testament critics, "turned the world upside down," and whose sacred blood has consecrated the earth.

Did you watch on television the vigil, on Holy Thursday and Good Friday, in the Colosseum in Rome, where the Christian martyrs had been done to death? No one remembers the name of a single Roman grandee of the day, and yet these ordinary Christian martyrs live forever because they became new creations with the resurrection of Jesus. They surprised themselves, I suspect. They had no idea they were capable. Haven't you ever done something that absolutely shocked you because you didn't realize you had it in you to do? They surprised themselves, and they surprised the world. As Paul Tillich once proclaimed from this very pulpit, "Nothing is more surprising than the rise of the new within ourselves."

Every time I get a new idea I'm shocked, for I have so few of them and I like the ones I have. When a new idea comes along I can't believe it, it just overwhelms me; and I suspect that I am not alone in this. The discovery of something new within ourselves is empowering, a pleasing surprise, and when we discover something that we didn't know before, or something that we didn't know that we knew, we are all the more surprised and amazed. Everybody in this church can testify to such moments; and these are the moments of resurrection and new creation that both surprise and empower, to which St. Paul referred in our text. I suspect that nobody on earth was more surprised than the disciples themselves by the new power and strength they had acquired as a result of their conviction that Jesus was alive and living for them. These were people who could not organize a one-car funeral! Then, suddenly, they become the empowering agents of a whole new creation. They experience the truth of the old hymn: "Because he lives I too shall live. . . ." Because he has conquered the future, there is nothing in the past or in the present or in the future that can intimidate or inhibit me.

How, however—and I can see you thinking it now—can all of this be, in light of the sad and sorry state of the world in which we find ourselves? It's all right to cite ancient biblical history, and St. Paul, and all of that, but we live in the twenty-first century in Cambridge, or Belmont, or Dorchester, or Watertown, in the real world, in a time of enormously troubling proportions. Think of the trouble in the Middle East, with the Jews and the Palestinians at one another's throats and with no useful help or counsel from us—more's the pity. How can we speak of newness and starting over, with the gaping wounds of scandal among our fellow Christians in the Roman Catholic archdiocese of Boston, and throughout the country? How can we speak of anything renewing and renewed under the psychic wound of 9/11? I read my papers, for better or for worse, as well as you do, but I think I read my history better than most of you, and my reading of history, as a Christian, tells me that in the world there is nothing new: it's the same old, same old. There is always war, and rumors of war, and there will always be war, and rumors of war. There are always conflicts and troubles and treachery, and there always will be such. Nothing in the gospel promises us paradise on earth. If there were paradise on earth we wouldn't need paradise, so there is no paradise on earth, even in the United States; and to confuse the American way of life with the kingdom of heaven is to make a fatal error.

Jesus himself says, "In the world ye shall have tribulation." Get used to it! Get over it! Get on with it! He also says, "Be of good cheer; I have overcome the world." What does he mean? He doesn't mean that he has caused the problems of the world to cease—certainly not. He means, "I am not, nor will I ever again be, intimidated or inhibited or defined by the tribulations of the world. I will not be defined by my problems, I will not be defined by my neuroses, I refuse to be victimized or to be described as a victim or to be classed among victims. My vision will not be limited by the headlines; I will both live and die by a standard that defies the standards of this world. Where the world tells me to hate I will love, cost what it may; where the world tells me to stand pat I will move on, to wherever I am to go; where the world tells me to be prudent, fearful, and cautious, I will be brave and foolish and courageous, no matter what. Where the world tells me that my destiny is shaped and determined by the past, I will claim that God is my future and that I shall yet become what God means for me to become. Christ means for me to start over again, and to keep starting over and over and over again until by his grace I get it right." Your mother was right: "If at first you don't succeed, try, try again." That is the gospel, the good news.

Today the world mourns with Her Majesty The Queen the death of her mother, Queen Elizabeth, The Queen Mother. What a great life, what great innings, at one hundred and one going on one hundred and two: what a great old gal! What was her secret? One of her ladies-in-waiting is reported to have said that in addition to a healthy appetite for the best gin available, the Queen Mother never looked backward but always looked forward. Think of it: this woman, who had lived the entire twentieth century, never looked back but always ahead.

Now, here is a moment I've been waiting for for a very long time. As many of you know, I met the Queen Mother last summer, and had drinks with her in Royal Lodge after church in Windsor Great Park. We had six minutes of conversation; I timed it. We had been in church and we spoke of the sermon as people do after church, as doubtless you will today. Her Majesty said to me, "Wasn't the sermon wonderful?" Well, actually, it wasn't. As a matter of fact it was quite terrible, but I did what anyone would do under those circumstances: I lied. I said, "Indeed it was, Ma'am," and then she said, with eyes glistening and fixed right on me, "I do like a bit of good news on Sunday, don't you?"

Who doesn't like a bit of good news on Sunday, especially on Easter Sunday? Isn't that why you are here today? Isn't that why you have made the effort to be in the right place at the right time, doing the right thing? Here is the good news of Easter, and I'll give it to you in three short, easy things to remember over lunch. I've said them before, but they are no less true today than when I said them before:

1. Easter is not just about Jesus; it is about you. He has already claimed his new life; now is your chance to claim yours.

2. Easter is not just about death; it is about life, and not just life after death—that's the easy part—but real life before death, right now. You do not have to die to live.

3. Easter is not just about the past, way back then and long ago; it is all about the future. Literally, I say to you, your best days are ahead of you. "Old things are passed away; behold, all things are become new."

What you do with this good news is up to you. You can listen to it, you can overhear it, you can read about it, or you can claim it and make it your own. You can make it your own for this life, this moment, right now, without worrying about yesterday or speculating about tomorrow. You can seize the moment this day, this very hour, and you can start over. You can claim your second chance, your second birth, your new lease on life, your second bite of the apple, for it is entirely up to you. The proof of the resurrection is not simply in your hands, it is literally in your life; and this is not only good advice but it is good news, and that is why they call it the gospel. If you want to make the resurrection yours both now and at the hour of your death, get on with it now, for Christ's sake and your own.

As the Easter gospel demands, "Awake thou that sleepest, and arise from the dead, and Christ will give thee life." Start living it. Start claiming it. Start making it your own today, for the first time, and you will be the only proof of the resurrection that this tired old world will ever need. If anybody here is in Christ, you are a new creation. "Old things are passed away; behold. . . ." *You* are doing a new thing. Amen.

Easter Christians?

Text: If then you have been raised with Christ. . . .

—COLOSSIANS 3:1

My text is the first verse of the third chapter of St. Paul's letter to the Colossians: "If then you have been raised with Christ—" and you remember how the rest of it goes: "If then you have been raised with Christ, seek the things that are above, where Christ is, seated at the right hand of God." It is an Easter invitation to new thinking.

Would you describe yourself as an Easter Christian? You can answer that quietly, seriously, candidly, but if I have any sense of the kind of Christians you think yourselves to be or would like to be, there is a kind of annoyance in the notion of your being called an "Easter Christian." Some of you might resist answering yes to the question, and with very good reason, for if you were brought up in the kind of church in which I was brought up, many years ago, the title "Easter Christian" was not a compliment. It was the harangue that the pastor gave on Easter Sunday to all those people he had not seen since the last Easter Sunday. It was a form of passive-aggressive hospitality: "How very nice to see all of you Easter Christians." I had a pastor who would wish us a "merry Christmas," a "happy Fourth of July," and a "blessed Thanksgiving." It was amazing that people came back every year to be insulted and called Easter Christians.

You would answer, I am sure, "No, we are not Easter Christians, because here we are today, and those Easter Christians"—who were seated where you are now—"have all gone elsewhere, doubtless to Upstairs at the

Pudding, or to the Harvest, or to wherever Easter Christians gather on every day but Easter." So, I can understand why you might resist the term. I want you to understand, however, that it is a term of high praise, a term of deep endearment, a term of profound affection that you and I should wear proudly, because I will argue that there is no other kind of Christian than an Easter Christian, and genuine Easter Christians understand that Easter Sunday is only the beginning. Easter Christians are the people who look for the power and the joy of the resurrection every day, and particularly every Sunday. If you are an Easter Christian I hope you will say so, and I hope you will allow your presence here today, on the fourth Sunday of Easter, to testify to your Easter Christianity. Without Easter there would be no Christianity, and hence there would be no Easter Christians.

So, we're all Easter Christians, and the character and the nature of what that means can be found in the two lessons that we have heard this morning. I wonder if you were struck, as I always am when I read the Easter account of the Gospel of Mark, which we had read for us this morning, in chapter sixteen. A footnote, for those who are footnote minded, is that the Gospel of Mark is the oldest Gospel, the first circulating Gospel among the four that we have, and in its spare and lean prose it sets the standard for the other three. The church has always cherished the Gospel of Mark, as it has the earliest accounts of the most formative parts of its experience in the Gospel form, so we have to take Mark seriously when he sets out to tell us the events of Easter morning, Easter afternoon, and Easter evening, and the rest of the Easter experience. Perhaps you noticed that, in the Gospel narrative, after we have departed the garden, it begins: "Now when he rose early on the first day of the week, he appeared to Mary Magdalene, from whom he had cast out seven demons. She went out and told those who had been with him, as they mourned and wept, but when they heard that he was alive and had been seen by her, they would not believe it."

In the space of three more verses there are three more accounts of astonishing unbelief, disbelief, misperception, doubt, no perception, in the course of the encounter with the risen Christ. It is no accident, St. Mark avows to us, to know that the greatest news available to us—that of the risen Christ—is accompanied by the most profound and natural and expected of human emotions: doubt and disbelief. It is almost as if it were too good to be true. Our usual rule is that if it is too good to be true it is not good enough, and doubtless untrue.

This gives us a little insight into the personality and character of the moment as we are encountering it in Mark 16. It tells us, for example, that they "mourned and wept." We know from the account in another Gospel how sad the apostles are on the eve of the Sabbath as they make their way to Emmaus. They are nursing their wounds, they are sticking their tongues into the aching tooth, and they know they are alive because it hurts. The pain is real, the death is real, the sense of loss is real, and there are moments—and I'm sure you've had them—when there is a kind of security, a power even, in one's sadness, one's sorrow, one's affliction. We cultivate this—not all the time, but there are times when it is good to feel bad, and that is the wrong time for someone to come up to us—spouse, friend, roommate, even pastor—and say, "Cheer up! It will all turn out for the best! Cheer up! You've no reason to be down in the dumps. Look on the bright side. Have a nice day." We all know what we want to do to people who say that to us at the wrong moment; and that wrong moment is when we are nursing our pain and our sorrow, and our grief is the one reality on to which we can hold when it does indeed feel good to feel bad.

"Leave me alone. Do not confound me with facts that will discommode me in my sadness. I am quite content that Jesus is dead. That I can understand. That is what he is supposed to be. Do not tell me that he is risen, and that you, Mary, of all people, saw him with your own eyes. I want you out of here; just vanish from our sight." We recognize that feeling, but it is just that combination of doubt and disbelief with which St. Mark constructs the power of the gospel—the good news—of the risen Lord. We are meant to understand that a characteristic of an Easter Christian is not simply careless, indifferent acceptance of whatever truth happens to come along. No! One of the characteristics of Easter Christians is a sense of doubt and disbelief at the impossible probability of goodness. Doubt is the pathway down which one travels to the household of faith.

We know this, but it is amplified in more power than we might otherwise imagine in this brief encounter at the end of Mark's Gospel, between the imperishable good news of the resurrection of Jesus and the grudging doubt of those who most wanted to believe in him. We must understand that this is not some accidental editorial confusion, but that there is purpose in juxtaposing the impossible good news with the persistence of a nagging doubt. They are meant to go together. They are meant to remind us that the good news is neither cheap nor easy nor readily accessible, and not generally to be found behind a cheap and easy slogan. There has to be some tension between the desire to believe and the reality of our circumstances. So, St. Mark wants us to see this chemistry of faith and doubt working together for good.

It was Louis Untermeyer who, in a poem that was popular when I was in college, gave form to this notion of what he called a "buoyant doubt:"

Ever insurgent let me be,
Make me more daring than devout;
From sleek contentment set me free,
And fill me with a buoyant doubt.

"Sleek contentment" is that one thing that the gospel is not meant to give us. "Sleek contentment" is not one of the characteristics of Easter Christians. It is that "buoyant doubt" that we find here in the gospel that leads us to the possibility, and ultimately to the reality, of an Easter faith for Easter Christians.

That's the first thing I want to extract from the two lessons that we have this morning—the notion that doubt is an ally of faith, and that without those disbelieving first Christians there would be no room for the gospel for Easter Christians. Their good news comes upon them not like an explosion, not all at once, but much more like the gradual dawning, the gradual unfolding, of a truth in which they are allowed to grow in order to see. It strikes me that the notion of a once-and-for-all, abracadabra-kazam kind of Easter experience is contrary to the Easter experience as described in the gospel. It is a growing process, a perception, a discovering, evolving encounter that produces Easter Christians, and that is what this gospel is all about.

The second thing that one might want to take note of from reading Mark's Gospel, and the Acts of the Apostles, which are concerned with the appearances of Jesus and his resurrection, is that Jesus does his most active evangelizing in those forty days after his resurrection. It ought to be a sign to us that the action is not on Easter morning. Very little of any significance to most people happens on Easter morning. The tomb is empty, certainly. The stone is rolled away, certainly. The angels are sitting there chatting with various and sundry, certainly, but Jesus, and the work that he does, is far away from the garden. He goes before them, as he says, and he goes before them into the forty days after Easter, popping up all over the place.

Just think about it. Once you thought you had dealt with him, put him away, and could get on with reliving your life, getting back to those interrupted nets and tax gatherings and all the things that you had put down for Jesus, there he is, trudging along the road with the apostles to Emmaus, watching them as they fish, giving them instruction, having breakfast with them on the beach, appearing in the Upper Room. Jesus is like the Scarlet Pimpernel—he is everywhere—and just when you think he has done it, he does it yet again. What are we to make of this? That Jesus is simply ubiquitous? Well, he is that; but there is something else at work here that I think that the post-resurrection appearances are meant to make clear to us. They are not only proofs of the resurrection of Jesus, though they are that; they are also proofs of the persistent love of Jesus. He keeps appearing so that we will have one more opportunity to perceive and receive him. It is not a once-and-for-all opportunity: "Now you see him; now you don't." Not at all: the gospel actually begins in the evening of Easter. The good news is that Jesus is not willing to stop until he has done everything in his power to make himself real to us. If it takes an appearance at supper, he'll do it. If it takes breakfast on the beach, he'll do it. If it takes helping us at our fishing, he'll do it. He will appear in the most unlikely and unexpected of places—not to prove that he can, but to prove that he cares. Hence, these post-resurrection appearances of Jesus, where he appears first to one, and then to two, and then to three, and then to the eleven, and then to dozens and to hundreds, are signs of what the hymn calls "the love that will not let us go."

We have often heard about and talked about and read about the perseverance of the saints, and what that means is the struggle for belief and faithfulness that the saints maintain every day of their lives, just putting one foot in front of the other. This Easter phenomenon, however, and, most important, the post-Easter phenomena, are an expression of the persistence of Jesus to come after us—willing to follow us, to find us, to pursue us, to continue the dialogue of Easter morning so that we might become Easter Christians. That strikes me as a pretty powerful testimony, not to the astonishing facts of Easter, but to the astonishing persistence of Christ after us.

Now, once he gets our attention and we are persuaded that this resurrection is not just for him but for us as well, strange, extraordinary, and marvelous things begin to happen. He says in Mark, for example, as we heard this morning:

He who believes and is baptized will be saved; but he who does not believe will be condemned.

There will be signs that will accompany our belief in the resurrection. Easter Christians will be known by certain signs. What does Mark say they are?

In my name they will cast our demons, they will speak in new tongues; they will pick up serpents, and if they drink any deadly thing, it will not hurt them; they will lay their hands on the sick, and they will recover.

One of our ushers, one of my students, is writing a term essay, perhaps even as we speak, about snake-handling Christians in the deep American South, Christians who take this particular set of verses in this chapter in Mark very literally indeed. They drink poison and play with poisonous snakes in order to demonstrate that they are Easter Christians. That's a rather extreme form of Easter Christianity, and I can't wait to see what my student has to say about all of this tomorrow by five o'clock in the afternoon. I know, however, that most of you would find that a rather severe test of your Easter Christianity—drinking poisonous drink, handling snakes, speaking in tongues, raising the dead.

Well, for you there is an easier way of demonstrating what it means to be an Easter Christian, and you can find it in the second lesson, in the letter of Paul to the Colossians. In it, Paul says, "If then you have been raised with Christ . . ." you too will show certain signs, certain things that people will be able to see in you and you in others; and, as with a secret Masonic handshake, you will be able to identify yourself and be identified as an Easter Christian. It doesn't involve snake handling or drinking poisonous substances, but perhaps something far more dangerous than both of those— that is, embracing the reality of change in your own life. It means taking on the attributes of an Easter Christian and putting aside the old life to which you are now, in Christ, dead.

Some of you know of the account a while ago—in the *New York Times,* I think it was—of a homeless person standing outside Goldman Sachs in Wall Street with a tin cup, uttering the mantra "Change! Change! Change!" and the bright young stockbroker rushing out of Goldman Sachs saying, "I'm trying! I'm trying! I'm trying!" Change is the recipe of Easter Christianity, and Paul makes it very clear what is expected: "Set your minds on things that are above, not on things that are on earth. For you have died, and your life is hid with Christ in God. When Christ who is our life appears, then you also will appear with him in glory."

You don't, however, have to wait for glory to manifest the signs of an Easter Christian, and these are what they are, as he says in the third chapter, the fifth verse: "Put to death, therefore, what is earthly in you: fornication"—unthoughtful and promiscuous sex; put it aside—"impurity, passion, evil desire, and covetousness, which is idolatry. On account of these the wrath of God is coming. . . . In these you once walked . . . but now put them all away. . . ." Instead of handling snakes and drinking poisonous substances, you are invited, as Easter Christians, now to put away "anger, wrath, malice, slander, and foul talk from your mouth." You're not supposed to lie to one another; you are supposed to have put aside the old nature with all of those practices and put on the new nature, which is being renewed every day.

Those are the things to be given up. What are the things to be taken on? "Compassion, kindness, lowliness, meekness, and patience, forbearing one another . . . forgiving each other. . . ." "This is too clear to be true," I can see some of you thinking right now. "This is too clear, and therefore too easy to do; there must be something wrong with it. Give me a serpent or two, give me a drink of kerosene; I'll try that, but don't ask me to stop lying, don't ask me to stop blaming, don't ask me to clean my mind of foul thoughts or to clean up my speech." If you aspire to be an Easter Christian, however, that is what you will do, and because you can do it is no reason not to do it. The great trick in our intellectual world is to think of something that we want to do and then imagine it to be so impossible as not to be able to do it, which relieves us of the responsibility of trying to do it.

Every one of us can be an Easter Christian, for every one of us can put on those things for which we long and for which our new life calls, and which will make a difference in the next hour in the way we live our lives. Easter is the claim of something new upon us after Easter Day. On Easter Day you expect to hear all these things and maybe even to think about them a little bit over lunch, but the test of an Easter faith is thinking about Easter things and doing Easter things and becoming an Easter thing after Easter Day has come and gone. It is the invitation to something new yearning to be born within your tired old body, your tired old soul, your tired old mind, your tired old imagination. In there, there is something waiting to come out: compassion, lowliness, loveliness, kindness, mercy, forgiveness; these are in us, waiting to be resurrected to new life, waiting to be summoned forth that we may walk in newness of life, that we might be the Easter Christians we are called to be.

Phillips Brooks has said, "The great Easter truth is not that we are to live newly after death, but that we are to be new here and now by the power of the resurrection." The proof of the power of the resurrection is the change working in us now, the empowerment that enables us to accept the charge that God has given us, the empowerment to accept our new identity as Easter Christians. "If then you have been raised with Christ . . ." set your mind on the things that are above and not on the things that are below.

Arguments That Fail

Text: Now when they heard of the resurrection of the dead, some mocked; but others said, "We will hear you again about this."
—ACTS 17:32

This is a sermon about arguments that fail, and it began in a most interesting—and for me, at least, appealing—place. On the Tuesday after Easter I found myself in one of my favorite places in all the world—not in London, not even in Cambridge, but in my barber's chair in my hometown of Plymouth, getting my post-Easter haircut. That barber shop is a very special, almost consecrated, place for me, for in it I got my first haircut now more than fifty-five years ago, and in it my father and his father before him were each made presentable. We sit in the same chair, and there is a wonderful sense of continuity, stability, and order: kingdoms may come and go, nations rise and fall, but "Fast Eddie's" barber shop has stood firmly on the Plymouth green for longer than I can remember. It is a grounded place where all pretensions and distinctions are set aside. The barber, of course, is not the same fellow but the third incarnation of the proprietor of that shop; and "Fast Eddie" is moderator of a lively and far-ranging discourse that covers all of the subjects that sensible people want to discuss, distilling jokes—many of which I cannot, alas, use here—and offering political wisdom and insight. He likes to provoke debate, and so on Easter Tuesday in the presence of my fellow townsmen, Eddie said to me, "Well, I suppose you had a big crowd up there in Cambridge on Easter?" "I certainly did," I replied, taking some pleasure in the fact. "I suppose you argued them into the resurrection again?" he continued, as he began working with the clippers perilously close to my ears. "I never argue with my congregation," I said, "especially on Easter." "Good thing," piped up somebody from a chair down the way, "they wouldn't believe you anyway." "I don't argue on Easter," I said, "I proclaim!" "That's because they can't talk back to you, like in here," said my barber; and he was, as always, right.

That little colloquy reminded me of Reinhold Niebuhr, the great theologian of a generation ago, and of his observation that on Easter he always preferred to go to a liturgical church where there was the celebration of the Eucharist with great solemnity and pomp and the sermon was very short, because then he didn't have to listen to some preacher argue or explain his way through the resurrection. I understand that, I think, and I try to practice it with some degree of moderation on Easter day. No one, as we know, has ever been argued into faith, though many people have been argued out of it.

All of this leads us to this remarkable account of a fairly unsuccessful argument in the Acts of the Apostles, where St. Paul engages with the Greeks in his great argument at Athens. We usually think of Acts 17 as Paul's great sermon on Mars Hill—or the Areopagus, as it was called in Athens—but this is more than a mere homily or sermon; it is Paul's attempt to evangelize and to do so on the terms of those with whom he is evangelizing, and in many ways it is a commendable and credible argument that he is about to undertake. Now, if we had read earlier in Acts 17, we would have discovered that as Paul walked along the streets of Athens he was disgusted, annoyed, and ticked off with the number of pagan monuments and idols and altars that he saw, overwhelmed by the sense of pagan deities, and that he said so in the synagogues where he preached and in the communities of the gentile Christians to whom he talked.

We also must remember that this discourse in which he is engaged is not with Jewish Christians or gentile Christians but with those whom Kirkegaard once described as the "cultured despisers." We have to remind ourselves that to the Athenians their gods were not pagans but Paul was the pagan, the Jews were the pagans, and the Christian believers were the ones who believed in strange and extraordinary things and who had false gods and false doctrines. So it is in this setting that we come upon Paul, a Christian Jew with Greek learning and Roman citizenship who, while wandering along the streets, decides that he's going to take on these people. We find him preaching wherever he can: in every square, on every street corner, in every open space there is Paul, arguing with the sophisticated and wise citizens of the city. He finally comes to that most remarkable place—the Harvard Square of Athens, if you will—in which all of the debaters and arguers and proclaimers are gathered together: they are curious to hear what Paul has to say, and he is eager to share it with them.

Athens, we are told by the writer of Acts, was full of arguers and debaters, of people who loved to speculate and to philosophize, and in the verses just before our text we discover that one of these Greeks, attracted to Paul's discourse, says, "What would this babbler say?"—or, as one translator put it, "What is this babbler, this charlatan, trying to say?" Others said, "He seems to be trying to sell us foreign gods; he seems to be trying to argue us into some other form of religion," and it is at this point that Paul begins to speak to them of the resurrection.

Rather than being turned off, as most of us are when the Hare Krishnas approach us on the street or the Jehovah's Witnesses come to our front door, the Athenians were intrigued, curious enough to hear more of what this babbler had to say. "Now all the Athenians and the resident foreigners had time for nothing except talking or hearing about the latest novelty." That is what Acts says of them. They were ready for Paul, and he was ready for them, and it should have been an ideal encounter.

Any of us who are students of rhetoric or debate or argument or preaching have always been directed to Acts 17 as the structure, at least at the beginning, of a brilliantly subtle argument. It is wonderfully constructed, and I commend Acts 17 to you when you go home this afternoon, or some other time, to just look at it from a purely structural point of view, for it is very subtle: Paul is not altogether forthcoming. We know that he was annoyed and angered by the profusion of pagan idols, for he had earlier said as much to the Jews and the gentile Christians. To the Greeks, however, he begins by saying, "I see that you are a very religious people, a devout people. And how do I know that? I have seen the many evidences of your devotion on every street corner, along the highways and the byways, all the things that attest to your devotion, your sanctity." It's a wonderful device. He doesn't say, "You're all wrong, you're a bunch of frauds wandering around in the wilderness of ignorance and sin." He says, "You're good people, you worship goodness. I see evidence of this everywhere I go."

I have just come back from a week on the road. My last day, on Friday, was in Atlanta, Georgia, and on every street corner in Atlanta there is a church. If you walk up and down that great Peachtree Street there's a Presbyterian church, there's a Methodist church, there's an Episcopal church, there's a

Southern Baptist church, there's a whole host of churches—great, splendid, big places that put our little house here to shame. So at the end of the day, on Friday night, when I had to give my talk in Trinity Presbyterian Church, I began by saying, "I perceive that you are a very religious people here in Atlanta, for I have seen on every street corner. . . ." For those who knew, it worked, and the rest of them sat back and said, "Yes, we are a deeply devout community." So Paul begins in this wonderfully inviting way; then he begins to move to his peroration, where he says, "And I have been drawn particularly to one altar which you have erected, and on it is this inscription: 'To an Unknown God.'" Now, within the Greek culture that is an ultimate sign of devotion, for anyone can worship gods they know, but to worship one who is unknown—that is ultimate loyalty and mystery wrapped into one. We know what this is like somewhat, with this extraordinary case in Washington where we have to disinter one of the "unknowns" in Arlington Cemetery because science in this particular case has caught up with our sense of mystery and awe. Anyone who has ever visited Arlington is moved by the sight of all those stones and the names on them, but the highest moment, the highest point of reverence in that great national Valhalla, is the Tomb of the Unknown Soldier, known only to God. Same is the case in Westminster Abbey, with the Tomb of the Unknown Soldier, who was killed in the First World War. So that is a place of holiness and reverence, and Paul focuses on this object of Athenian piety, having brought them along, and here he springs the trap: "What therefore you worship as unknown, this I proclaim to you." The King James Version of the Bible puts it much more bluntly and is probably closer to the original audacious meaning: "Whom therefore ye ignorantly worship, him declare I unto you." A marvelous kind of confrontational moment.

Paul comes to his climax and closing, where he describes the nature, the character of this God, and we know where he is going. This unknown God, for Paul, is the God who created the heavens and the earth; the God of love and justice and mercy and peace; the God who was known by Abraham, Isaac, and Jacob; the God who led Moses out of Egypt into the Promised Land. This is the God worshiped and served by the prophets, this is the God who has made himself known in his son Jesus Christ, and this is the God who, in order to indicate his love for the world, raises Jesus Christ from the dead. "This is he of whom you have not heard but of whom I now speak to you." Now, to you and to me, who have heard this over and over again— this listing of God's qualities—we know the end of the story, most of us were here on Easter. We've heard it all before; this is not new news. "Interesting arguments," you might think, "a nice rehearsal of the facts, perhaps even compelling, yes, I'll buy that, that's okay," but if you've never heard it before and it is contrary to everything you've understood, it would make sense only up to the point where the coup de grâce is exercised: the resurrection of the dead. This is the sign of God's ultimate love. It is not simply the sign of power, though it is that, for it is the power to reverse nature and confront death, we know that; but it is ultimately an act of love. We may not understand it, but we know enough to take it seriously.

The Greeks, however, are another matter. They are used to fine and subtle arguments, they have invented the art of philosophical discourse, they have no particular regard for preacherly effects, and so they hear the argument up to this point, and, as our text says, at the mention of the resurrection some of them begin to scoff. This is too much for the thin back of the argument: this resurrection is literally the rhetorical straw that broke the theological camel's back, and so they begin to laugh, to snicker, and they think, "Well, it was pretty good up to that point, but that is where it actually falls apart." Even Paul, with all of his passion, his rhetorical and philosophical skill, could not turn an experience into an argument. Others, while not persuaded, were at least intrigued, and hence our text: "Now when they heard of the resurrection of the dead, some mocked; but others said, 'We will hear you again about this.'" In other words, "The debate will continue; we have to process what you say." Perhaps it could even mean, "We are curious to see how an apparently intelligent man such as yourself can believe in such a crazy proposition as this resurrection thing. We'll take this up again."

Have you not had this experience? You tell someone, "I'm a Christian," and they say, "That's lovely, you feed the hungry and clothe the poor and you do good works," and you say, "I believe in Jesus," and they say, "He's a lovely man, he did good things, he fed people and turned water into wine," and you say, "And he died." Then they say, "Great tragedy that he did, great tragedy, poor fellow, he was just ahead of his time." "He rose from the dead," you say; and the conversation stops. We can go all the way up to there, but we can't go any further. They say, "We'll talk about this later; have a happy day," and off they go. That's what's happening here in Acts 17, and the great debate ends with something of an anticlimax: "So Paul went out from among them. But some men joined him and believed, among them Dionysius the Areopagite, and a woman named Damaris, and others with them" (Acts 17:33–34).

Now, Paul and Peter were used to having thousands of people responding to the gospel, and the Acts of the Apostles is an account of their triumphant tour of proclaiming the gospel against all adversities, but at this first moment it is not a great success. It is like giving a tremendous altar call and nobody comes forward, or very few people come forward. If you get a man named Dionysius to come forward, I think that's pretty good, however, and I've always wondered about this man named Dionysius and this woman Damaris. Who was Damaris? Was she a woman of ill repute, or a distinguished matron of Athens? We don't know, and there are no adjectives to describe these people, which leads us to infer that it was a motley, modest, not overwhelming response to Paul's great argument.

The stakes were high, the argument sound, the yield very small indeed. Paul won points but not many hearts and minds on Mars Hill, and perhaps when he left the site of his argument with his few converts he was rehearsing in his mind better arguments that might have carried the day: "Perhaps I should have said this instead of that, perhaps I should have used this argument instead of that, here's an illustration that I could have used had I remembered it." I, for example, always come up with my best retorts after the encounter has concluded. As he or she is passing down the steps, having given me a rather snappy remark at the door of this church, I see them going and I think, "I should have said this; this is what I shall say next time I see them." We are always better in reruns, when we slay 'em dead with the power of our one-liners and our ironic put-downs after the fact, after the arguments have failed.

Most of us know the sad experience of arguments that fail: the premise was sound, the logic impeccable, the diction superb, and all that was wrong was that the other person was so thick-headed as to be unpersuaded by our brilliant analysis. In the Faculty of Arts and Sciences I have made brilliant observations for more than twenty-five years, and devised artful arguments in any number of causes, nearly all of which have gone down in flames before the obduracy of my colleagues. The printed faculty minutes with my name in them read like Acts 17; I *know* how Paul must have felt, and so do you.

Now, if this was where either the gospel or this sermon ended there would be little left to say, but there are still a few things that must be said. Practical minded as we are, we must now ask ourselves what we can learn from this remarkable encounter on Mars Hill. Is there any useful word from the Lord here for us? Well, obviously I wouldn't be standing up here if I didn't think that there was.

So, there are three things that I propose we consider and ponder. First, to the point of the argument here in Acts 17: that Easter does not depend upon an effective argument but upon a convincing experience. Paul in his later letters dismisses the skills of the debaters and rhetoricians and argues, if you will, that we are to know Jesus and the power of his resurrection by the experience of newness of life in our own lives. When we discover the opposite of emptiness, then we will need neither argument nor explanation, for experience will have taught us all that we need to know. "Consider how you have lived," asks the prophet Haggai in the first lesson: "You have sown much, and harvested little; you eat, but you never have enough; you drink, but you never have your fill; you clothe yourselves, but no one is warm; and he who earns wages earns wages to put them into a bag with holes" (Haggai 1:5–6). Nothing that you do is ever quite right, adequate, or sufficient. When you consider your life and find what it is that is missing, only then will you have room for the risen Christ, and you will need no argument, for you will have the experience of victory. Easter does not depend upon an effective argument but upon a convincing experience.

The second thing that we might learn from Paul's experience on Mars Hill is that more often than not our arguments fail rather than win. When was the last time you scored a thumping victory in an argument and still kept your friend? When was the last time all of your points came together in a telling crescendo and you walked away the undisputed winner of the debate? Sometimes we simply have to concede and live with the fact that our best case will not necessarily prevail. Two freshman roommates in the third week of the term, arguing about the existence of God in Holworthy Hall—thank goodness the existence of God doesn't depend upon the existence of God in Holworthy Hall—you all know what that is like. You're right, but you can't win; you've got the argument, the circumstance, the facts, the passion, but you can't put it together, and this does not mean that as a result you change your convictions, but it may mean that as a result we change our arguments. More often than not our arguments fail rather than win.

Finally, and this removes us from the immediate domain of our text: perhaps some arguments are worth losing, at least for the time being. Winning is not necessarily everything. Who of us has not been in a situation where we were about to apply the coup de grâce in an argument with a spouse or partner, colleague or friend—to deliver the ultimate retort that would be the nuclear weapon in our conversation—and suddenly knew that if we triggered it we would demolish all that is in sight? Who has not been in that situation and come to an almost instantaneous realization that verbal victory is not worth the price? In the television series, and now film, *A Year in Provence,* Peter Mayle, the Englishman, has suffered much at the hands of his French antagonistic neighbors when all he wants is simply to be accepted. He decides to learn the native game of bowls and determines to defeat the local bully, who is the champion—to humiliate him by being better than he is at his own game—and so we lead up to the climactic match. It is clear that the Englishman has learned a thing or two when at the penultimate moment an adviser says to him, "If you really want to win here, perhaps it might be wise to lose," and so he does, and in so doing wins that which he most truly wants, which is acceptance. It's a win-win proposition, to use the title of a brilliant sermon delivered here on Easter morning. Perhaps some arguments are worth losing.

History is filled with those whose arguments failed, causing them to be counted among the losers of their own day, about whom we now know better.

John Quincy Adams, graduate of this College, lost every debate on the floor of the House of Representatives against the monstrous evils of slavery. His marvelous role in the Amisted adventure notwithstanding, he was by the standards of his day a loser; no argument could prevail against the ruling culture, yet we know now, as he knew then, that he was right.

What can one possibly say in that connection, comparing John Quincy Adams, let us say, with John C. Calhoun—I'm sorry for those of you from the Carolinas. We don't always win when we are right, and sometimes it is best to be on the losing side.

Not all good arguments win most of the time, and not all bad arguments are easily vanquished in their own time. The resurrection, to those first apostles, seemed but an idle tale, and they did not believe it until the argument was superseded by an experience of the risen Christ and their own poor lives were renovated by the reality of new life and new living. The arguments may not always work, but our work is to live the life of the one who lives in us and who transcends all arguments. Indeed, the greatest argument for the validity of the Christian life is the life of a Christian: we *are* the arguments for the resurrection; we *are* the living proofs for the existence of God.

"They will know we are Christians by our love. . . ." goes the old song, and the best argument is the living evidence of conviction. Arguments fail, experience never; and for that we thank the living God.

Growing Up

Text: Rather, speaking the truth in love, we are to grow up in every way into him who is the head, into Christ. . . .

— EPHESIANS 4:15

My text this morning concerns the act of growing up: when we stop growing, we start dying; it is as simple as that. Growth is essential to life, and when growth stops, so do we.

This is the point St. Paul is trying to make to the Ephesians in our second lesson this morning, and perhaps it is written more clearly in the Good News Bible:

> . . . so we shall all come together to that oneness in our faith and in our knowledge of the Son of God; we shall become mature people, reaching to the very height of Christ's full stature. Then we shall no longer be children, carried by the waves and blown about by every shifting wind of the teaching of deceitful men, who lead others into error by the tricks they invent. Instead, by speaking the truth in a spirit of love, we must grow up in every way to Christ, who is the head. (Ephesians 4:13–15)

Paul wants us to understand that our faith is dynamic—that is, that it is a development, a movement, a process that takes us from where we are, familiar and comfortable as that may be, to where we are meant to be. Growing up means growing into the full measure of Christ, as Paul puts it—seeking his height, attaining his stature. It is not growing any which way, or growing as we please, or growing as nature permits: it is growth into the particular stature of Christ, who provides the standard, the measuring rod by which we judge our growth.

If your household was like mine there was a spot—in my house it was the pantry door—where, as a child growing up, the regular recording of my height took place. On my birthday every year my father would take the ruler and put it on top of my head, and on the pantry door frame mark how high I stood. It was a ritual, one to which I looked forward, and over the years as a little boy I could see by the door frame how high I was growing. I wasn't growing in general, however; I was growing in relationship to the stature of the door frame, and I think that in my naïveté I felt that I would actually reach it—the top of the door frame—and my poor father would have to get on a ladder to measure the full stature that I had attained! All of us in the Christian faith have Christ as the measure by which we trace our growth, and if you look at the mark on the door this year and it is at the same place as it was last year, you will see that something has happened, and not something good. If you stop growing, you die.

This may seem simple to say, simple to read, and even simple to hear, but it certainly does not comport with the average experience of the average Christian, with whom this church is more than averagely filled. Most of us think that faith is holding on to those few principles and ideas we first believed a long time ago. Faith for so many of us is grasping what was graspable once upon a time, and we hold on to it and clutch it with a death grip until death itself claims us. The risk of growth—that is, of grasping something bigger—involves letting go of something that we have held on to, and that is very difficult for most of us. To be faithful insofar as we can be, in our understanding, is to hold on to those few convictions that we can remember, and never let them grow. Change is not our thing.

Think of it. Most of us do not come here to this church to be changed, but to be confirmed; and if you thought that you would not be confirmed here, in the convictions that you brought through this front door, you would go somewhere else. That is the Protestant principle. "Freedom of choice" it is called, and you would exercise it. Those of you who like my sermons, or who say that you do, or the sermons of any agreeable preacher here or anywhere else, like them by and large not because they are likely to change by one iota any of your precious convictions, but because they confirm you in the opinions you brought with you from home, or from birth, or from the

"Coop." So, when you say, "That was a good sermon," most of you mean, "That was a sermon that I would preach, if I wished to. That is a sermon that confirms everything that I already believe or feel. A good sermon is one that I would give." I understand that, and even accept it, to a point. That is how I define, in my courses, an "A" examination; I say that an "A" examination is the examination that *I* would write. *That* is the standard of excellence!

Now, that may be acceptable in academia, but it is very risky in a faith that is defined as a dynamic transaction and transformation. Faith ought not to be what we last remember, the thing that we dare not let go of, the thing that allows us to resist all change, challenge, and confrontation, although all too often it is, and we know very well that it is. That is why religious people, by and large, are so fundamentally conservative. Think about it. We are afraid of change. To change one's mind is thought of as a sign of insta-bility and insecurity; to change one's mind is a dangerous thing because the whole center of the universe becomes unstuck. Yet change is the essence of growth, growth is essential to maturity, and maturity is essential to a dynamic faith.

We have to change our notion of maturity. I remember that when I became fifty-five I received two dreadful pieces of unsolicited mail. First was my membership, unasked for, in the AARP, and second was a copy of their rather depressing magazine, called *Modern Maturity*. The image of both of those is sedentary, secure, stable, and grounded, with all passions spent and an eternal life in the Republican Party. I was not yet ready for that and nor am I now; and nor does the gospel, as I understand its reading today in particular, define maturity as a place of stasis. Maturity is the place of dynamic transformation into the full stature of Christ.

Let me illustrate. A few years ago, when I was working on *The Good Book: Reading the Bible with Mind and Heart,* I was fascinated to read about the southern clergy's attitudes toward slavery and its compatibility with the Christian faith. One Christian, a Southern Baptist, writing in 1869, not long after the war had ended and not in his favor, had to come to terms with the defeat of the South, with slavery, and with his Christian faith. All three of these phenomena now had to be addressed, and this is what he said:

> Now I would certainly be opposed to the restoration of slavery in this country, but I have undergone no change on the righteousness of slavery, nor can I change until convinced that our Bible is not the book of God.

That was one man's opinion, and I think we might call that the conservative position on the subject. Nearly a century later, in 1956, another Southern Baptist, writing in the *Southern Baptist Expositor,* the *New York Times* of the Southern Baptist Convention, and calling himself a "sixty-three-year-old white man, a Baptist, and a Southerner," said:

> Throughout the first sixty years of my life, I never questioned but that Peter's confession that "God is no respecter of persons" (Acts 10:34) referred exclusively to the differences among white Christian persons. Neither did I question that segregation was Christian, and that it referred to the separation of white and Negro people. Three years ago (1953) these views were completely transformed. I became convinced that God makes no distinctions among people whatever their race, and that segregation is exclusively by God in the final judgment. I exchanged the former views, which I had absorbed from my environment, for the latter views which I learned from the New Testament. I came to understand the meaning of Paul's pleas, "Be not conformed to this world: but be ye transformed by the renewing of your mind, that ye may prove what is that good, and acceptable, and perfect, will of God." (Romans 12:2)

So writes our observer, in 1956. Between the first and second opinion, separated by nearly a century and a culture resistant to change, is to be found growth, the principle of dynamic maturity, the Christian ideal of transformation by the renewal of one's mind. Had not the American South changed its views on race in our lifetime it would be dead today; and I make that statement not as a prophet, but as a historian. Growth is essential to life: no growth means no life, and certain death.

What, then, does it mean to "grow up" in the faith? To some it might mean developing in the tradition that they have received and have always known. Growing up, in this sense, provides a sense of stability, order, and security; and one can say, as Popeye the Sailor Man once said, "I yam what I yam." That is also somewhat the appeal of our first lesson, from Proverbs: "Train up a child in the way he should go; and when he is old, he will not depart from it." There is no better pedagogy of child rearing than that verse from Proverbs.

I always think of that verse when I think of my old friend Charles Francis Adams, of the Class of 1932. Yes, he was a "real" Adams, and one look at Charlie would tell you so, for he had the high forehead and thin lips of all the male descendants of John Adams and John Quincy Adams, in a family that all look like statues of themselves; and Charlie had all of their moral rectitude as well. I once asked him what it was like to bear such a distinguished and conspicuous inheritance, and he replied in the words of his late father, also a Charles Francis Adams, who had been Calvin Coolidge's Secretary of the Navy: "Being an Adams is a full-time job." Charlie became the way he was because each of his predecessors, back to the first John, believed in Proverbs 22: "Train up a child in the way he should go, and when he is old, he will not depart from it."

On Mothers' Day we know that it is not just the fathers who do that training, and that it is rarely they who do it, for most of us grew up at our mothers' knees: for better or for worse it was our mothers who set the patterns of our growth. Surely there are the "Mr. Moms" of this world, and there is now every permutation of motherhood and parenthood and fatherhood known to our twenty-first-century culture, but the burden—fair or unfair—of imprinting upon a child the syllabus of growth more often than not falls to mothers. What is that old canard that has been trotted out on the second Sunday in May for nearly a century? "God could not be everywhere, and so he invented mothers."

Fond as I am, however, of remembering what my mother said, did, and taught—and I owe her everything—I remember that the most important thing she taught me was to grow away from her, and into Christ. Growing up was a process not simply of remembering but of becoming; and to become what one is meant to be in Jesus Christ is the only true sign of growth, and the only true form of maturity that we can hope to attain.

Some of you know that my father was a farmer, and while I know I shouldn't be speaking of fathers today, we won't be together on Father's Day and there is a point to be made here about growth. My father was a farmer who grew cranberries, and he knew from a lifetime of experience that growth was not a random or a casual thing, or something you could leave to Mother Nature or Father Time. He knew that growth required a great deal of work, imagination, and perseverance. He was constantly fighting weeds that grew with great force, vigor, and abandon, and were always stronger than the vines he was trying to grow. He knew that growth was itself not a virtue, for in the untended garden the bad weeds grew just as well as, if not better than, the good plants. Have you ever thought of the comparison between growing orchids on the one hand, and trying to kill dandelions on the other? The weeds in my father's fields would have to be pulled up by the roots early enough that they would not compromise the good but weaker growth, and all was not safe until the good seeds had grown into the harvest—that is, until they had become what they were meant to be from the beginning: flowers into bloom and fruits and vegetables into things we could eat and admire, as the human soul grows into the maturity of the full measure of Christ.

My father understood, as all real farmers understand, that growth is the result of struggle; and that is the point that Paul is trying to make in Ephesians. In order to grow in Christ, he tells us; in order to grow into mature Christians and not simply to stay as we were when we arrived at the door of the church this morning, for instance, we have to struggle with the weeds—that is, with the opinions, with the false sense of complacency and security, and with those who would pull us in this direction or push us in that. This is how he puts it: "We shall become mature people, reaching to the very height of Christ's full stature. Then we shall no longer be children, carried by the waves and blown about by every shifting wind of the teaching of deceitful men, who lead others into error by the tricks they invent." (Ephesians 4:13–14)

Paul is referring here to the competing doctrines and theories that try to charm and seduce, and usually do succeed in seducing people by clever artifice and easy nostrums into choosing a path that confirms their prejudices rather than a path that confronts their fears. The choice is available to us: would we rather rest in comfort with our prejudices—those with which we have grown up, which have nourished and preserved us up to this moment— or would we rather risk confronting our fears and being transformed beyond them? Paul says that maturity is not a place of the *status quo* or of stasis, but a place of—dare I use the word?—adventure! Are all of us so far past the claims of adventure that we'd rather stay where we are than go where we might? Have all passions been spent, so that there is nothing left but to grasp with ferocity that little tiny flimsy bit of stuff that we call our faith and conviction? Would we be willing to open our hands and minds and see what is out there, what adventure invites us into real spiritual growth? Maturity, contrary to the image of *Modern Maturity,* and contrary to the image of cozy retirement, is not standing still but pressing on until we reach the full stature of Christ.

Yesterday I took part in the funeral of an old friend in Maine, and then afterward I paid a short call on an even older friend who is now, more or less, at age ninety-eight, confined to her home. When I was in college she was precious and dear to me, the organist of the church where I first worshipped as a student at Bates, and we had kept up over many, many years and formed a deep and abiding friendship. I hadn't seen her in at least five years, however, and so I thought I would pay a call. I had heard that she was in pretty good shape, all things considered at ninety-eight, so I visited the house I hadn't entered in more than thirty-five years and there she and it were, nearly as I had remembered them from my college days. We greeted one another warmly, and she said, "You can see that I have shrunk, or maybe you have grown . . . ?" Then we did what old friends do, which is that we began to talk. With a familiar twinkle in her eye, she said, "Oh, it is hard getting old; they don't tell you about it, but it is very hard getting old. The effort, though, keeps me going." I spoke fondly and warmly of the past, as is my nature, while she spoke urgently of the present. There was trouble in the parish church, it seemed, and she wanted it sorted out as fast as it could possibly be done. She moved slowly on a cane throughout the familiar rooms of that house, but her mind and her spirit were as alert as I remembered them from forty years previously. She had not *grown* old: she was growing, and she was old—and there is a big difference between the two. Secure in her faith, she was coping with the troubles of age and time, but she had neither given up nor given in. I told her I would soon be sixty, and she laughed and said, "You'll see!"—which was strangely reassuring. I left her house lighter than when I had entered it.

We often think of St. Paul as fully formed, secure, and the picture of soul stability: Mr. Know-It-All, Mr. Unmoved, Mr. Unmovable, Mr. Unmoving. We confuse him, alas, with Martin Luther. Yet, not just here in Ephesians but throughout all of Paul's writings in the New Testament, he is—and I hope you will remember this phrase about St. Paul—more dynamic than dogmatic. He is constantly growing, stretching, pushing, changing, moving, open to the spirit, allowing himself not to be conformed to this world but transformed by the renewing—in the present tense—of his mind. Paul thus is the apostle of growth and of dynamic faith, and that is why he speaks with particular clarity to those of us in an academic community, a community of young and easily influenced people.

Once upon a time, people came to Harvard for the purpose of being transformed through an invitation to change that was gladly accepted. We were a form of sausage factory, pouring students in at one end in the fresh-

man year, and turning them out at the other end in the senior year as a rec-
ognizable and transformed brand type. Sad as that conformity may have
been, today I worry that the harvest of diversity by which we all profit
tends to mean that people come here—faculty and students alike—defensively. That is to say, they come here with an attitude that says, "I am *not*
going to allow Harvard to change me one whit or one iota. I will continue
to be that good solid stolid unimaginative kid from Dubuque; I will stay
the feisty girl from the Bronx; I will be the ethnic Jew or militant black or
interesting Hispanic that I was when I arrived. I will be what I was; and I
defy Harvard and thirty-five thousand dollars a year to change me in any
way." So, everybody conserves an identity like a rare species in a museum,
defying the law of cultural gravity that says that by our very presence here
we will become something and somebody else, and that we are meant to,
and that that is good. If you students here today are still clinging to the
same opinions you had in the fall term of your freshman year, you are wast-
ing your money and our time. There are other places you can go to be con-
served under glass, to be admired for all time: this is a place where you
ought to engage in the business of transformation willingly and gladly.

I see it even more acutely in religion. How? Generation after generation
I hear faithful undergraduates saying, "Let's hold on fast and tight for dear
life to what we knew to be true when we arrived, and let us go only to
where those convictions are confirmed and reinforced. Let not anything
come near us that might produce any kind of chemical reaction."

Some will argue, perhaps even some of you, that this shows strength of
conviction, the power of our faith against the dangerous winds of change and
temptation, against Harvard cultural or religious social conformism; and that it
is no bad thing to hold fast to that which is good. We here in The Memorial
Church are not exactly examples of a hotbed of innovation on either side of
the choir screen, and that is why you come and why I stay. I understand that.
The downside of this, however, is that our faith, if we are not careful, can
become resistant to the very dynamic forces that form it. It can be a retardant
to the growth of the spirit, a retardant to the spiritual maturity that forces us to
grow toward the light. Our defensive living keeps as much out as it keeps in.

I wonder about those gated communities where people erect electronic
fences and other security devices around their posh suburban homes and
think that they are keeping the burglars out, when the fact of the matter is that
they are keeping themselves prisoners of their own false senses of security. A

faith cannot be like that, nor can a church be like that; and such a faith of confirmed prejudices and conformist security denies the possibility of the transformation to which St. Paul and the gospel invite us. Both St. Paul and the gospel say, "For Christ's sake, and your own, will you please grow up! Will you please seek to attain the full measure of the stature of Christ. Will you look at the measuring stick on your closet or pantry door, and will you try to exceed where you were last year, so that you might *grow up!*"

Remember that naughty line of Alice Roosevelt Longworth, when she was informed that President Calvin Coolidge had died? She said, "How can you tell?" Do you want that said about you? "So-and-So is dead." "How can you tell?" Or worse, "So-and-So is dead." "Oh, I've always known that!" Of course you don't want that. Cardinal Newman, himself a profile in change and transformation, and one of the heroes whom I have grown to love and appreciate in my mature years, once said, "Growth is the only evidence of life." Paul would agree with him.

Do any of you here—and you'd have to be of a certain age, but there are some of you—remember the marvelous horticultural critic on channel 2, Thalassa Cruso? She was the Julia Child of plants, and what Julia did with soufflés Thalassa did with houseplants. She was a ferocious, energetic English lady gardener, and once, many years ago, she gave a demonstration in the Junior Common Room at Lowell House. The invitation to all undergraduates was to "Bring me your tired, sagging, weary old houseplants. . . ." There are no worse collections of houseplants in the world than those kept by undergraduates, for they can't bear to part with a single plant and they haven't time to care for them, and so they keep the overgrown leafy, leggy, mite-ridden things in the windows, hoping to bring a little sense of the greenhouse effect into their rooms. So, Thalassa invited them to bring their specimens to the Common Room, and she would tell them what was wrong with them, how to fix them up, and what to do with them. The room was filled with dreadful plants, and she had on her smock and carried her secateurs and her scissors, and she went round the room; and she'd take a plant and say, "Dead!" and pull it out, and the undergraduates would cry, "No, no, no! My mother gave that to me when I was a junior . . ." Other plants she would decapitate, others she would repot, and of others she would say, "There's no hope for this, throw it away." Then, every once in a while, with the worst-looking thing, she would take her shears and cut it at a certain point and say, "Aha! There's life here, it will grow; transplant it. Put it in a dish of water, and call me on Monday."

Growth is the only evidence of life. If you don't grow, you are dead on your feet, and all that remains is for us to bury you.

As we have the end of this term and of this year clearly in sight—just three more Sundays and it's all over—and as we celebrate the achievement and promise of the young and remember with joy the endurance and experience of the old, I urge you now to grow up—that is, to grow into the full stature of Christ. I do not promise that it will happen overnight, I do not promise that it will happen tomorrow, and I do not promise that it will happen without struggle, but I do promise that it is the only alternative to the living death in which some of you find yourselves right now. I urge you to grow up. Do not be content with what you now think you know or feel to be absolutely the last word. Do not turn your face into a fossilized bit of private truth, for if you do, both it and you will turn into petrified stone. The life will have gone out of your face and out of you, and you will be preserved for all time; and what fun is there in being preserved for all time as a petrified pillar that has gone nowhere and is nowhere and is going nowhere? Grow into a deeper transforming knowledge of Christ's purpose for you and your life; and the only way you can do that is to open your hands, your heart, your mind, and your life. Never be satisfied with your own *status quo,* spiritual or otherwise. When you refuse to open yourself up to possibilities, you die. Growth is the only infallible evidence of the life of faith, and that has to do, as Emerson once said, not with what lies behind us or with what lies before us, but with what lies within us.

Yesterday, at the funeral in Maine, I heard the minister tell an old story during the course of his eulogy. In the nineteenth century, a famous preacher in England approached the most famous British stage actor of the day, George McReady, and said in some frustration to the great thespian, "How is it, sir, that you speak only fiction to people, and thousands come to hear you, and I speak the truth of the gospel of Jesus Christ, and can barely fill the church?" I've often asked myself that very same question. McReady is said to have replied, "The difference, sir, is this: I speak my fiction as truth, and you speak your truth as fiction."

In this my last sermon to you of the term and academic year, I have spoken as best I can the truth that will transform you and set you free, and it can be summarized very briefly: for Christ's sake, and for yours, *grow up!*

Remembrance and Imagination

Text: . . . think on these things.

—PHILIPPIANS 4:8

What are "these things" to which St. Paul commends our attention in our text for today? "All that is true, all that is noble, all that is just and pure, all that is lovable and gracious, whatever is excellent and admirable; fill all your thoughts with these things," he says.

My sermon this morning is something of a commencement address, filled with splendid and impossible advice and easily dismissed as "what one would say" on occasions such as this. Dean Sperry, my predecessor as Plummer Professor, once found himself standing on the platform at Williams College, watching the long procession draw near. While waiting, he glanced down at the program in his hand, and found to his complete surprise that he was listed as the commencement speaker. When asked later what he did and how he did it, he replied, "I said the usual things that one says on such occasions, and I said them three times."

The things that I will say this morning are among the "usual things" that one says—to graduating seniors especially—but because this is the last time that many of you are likely to hear them, at least in this place, and at least from me, for St. Paul's sake, for my sake, and, most of all, for your sake, I invite you to listen, and to "think on these things."

Recently I have been rereading J. B. Phillips's translation of the New Testament, and as usual I find his version more engaging even than the King James Version. The King James Version says, ". . . think on these things," but Phillips renders it, "Fill all your thoughts with these things," which is a very different way of putting it.

In the abstract, the "noble thoughts," as we might call them, seem cool and aloof, and removed from our everyday experience. There are at least two ways by which the temptation to abstraction can be avoided, both of which were familiar to St. Paul, and each of which worked for him and for the Philippians; and I suggest that they will work for you here and now. The first of these acts, to translate these noble thoughts from abstraction to life, is the act of remembrance; and the second is the act of imagination. On this Communion Sunday, this Festival of Pentecost, we are engaged in acts both of remembrance and of imagination. Let me try to translate them into the substance of our text.

St. Paul always invites his listeners to acts of remembrance, constantly reminding people to remember. "Remember what it was like before you knew Christ. Remember what it was like before I came to you. Remember what it was like when you were young in the faith, or frightened, or intimidated, or new." Even more, throughout all of his writings St. Paul invites people to remember their moments of victory, of achievement, of success, of pleasure, of satisfaction. He invites us to remember those precious moments in our lives. Remember what the Lord has done for you, remember what you have done for the Lord, remember what others have done for you, and remember what you have done for others. Memory is the great key to this enterprise.

One of the last rites for seniors in Harvard College is to remember, and many of you have been doing much remembering these last few days. In fact, for most of you seniors in Harvard College, the past is much clearer than the future, perhaps even clearer than the present. No tree, no gate, no pathway is without its capacity to evoke a memory, to make us remember. Sometimes you remember the bad stuff, an unpleasant encounter or two, bad work done in class or lab, moments when you behaved badly or were badly treated. To this very day I remember things that I wish I hadn't said to a college roommate now forty years ago, but by and large the memories that we invoke are good, and the act of remembering is very good indeed. There are moments of love, even of nobility, moments of joy and graciousness, moments where justice and truth and virtue were experienced if only momentarily. We are to remember these moments because in them we find evidence of God's presence and activity in our lives. To remember is to be reminded, even in our loneliness, that we have never been alone, abandoned, or forgotten. It is the essence of religion to remember, for it is in recollection that we find out—that is, remember, or put back together again—how God has dealt with us; and in doing so we remember how on a rare occasion or two we too have acted nobly, honorably, with purity of thought and heart, performed excellently, responded graciously; and just as it will surprise you to discover how good God has been to you, it will also surprise you to discover those moments in your own young lives when you have exhibited these very qualities upon which you are now called to think.

At the risk of stroking sufficiently large egos, let me say that you are probably better than you think you are. Better still, put it this way: at least one person somewhere remembers some act of noble kindness you have performed and have perhaps forgotten, it being too small for you to remember. Somebody, however, does; somebody knows how good you are, how kind you have been, how thoughtful you have been, and you know how good somebody else is. So when St. Paul says, ". . . think on these things," I believe he means that we are to think not simply in abstraction, but in the frail flesh of our own human experience.

Acts of remembrance are keys to acts of imagination, and they are important too. If you can remember, you can imagine. If you can look backward with the rediscovery of things once lost but now recalled, surely you can look ahead with some imagination as to what might be. Paul's little list here in Philippians is not for the past alone but is a recipe for the future. These are the qualities upon which we both think, and then act, our way into the future.

Let me illustrate what I mean by this. At about this time of the year, seniors in college are frequently asked, "What are you going to do next year? What are your plans?" It has become something of a rude question; it makes them nervous, and it makes us sound like all of their mothers put together, and at this point that is not a good thing. However, I have given up being sensitive on this point. Of course nobody knows what his or her own future is, even if there is a job at McKinsey or a fellowship at Cambridge or an admission to graduate school: you still do not know what the future holds. The reverse is also true: those of you who have no plans beyond lunch today must remember—to quote a famous book—that there *is* a plan for you with your name on it, and it will find you when you and it are ready. So, all I have to say to you, you overindulgent anxious seniors, is relax, every one of you! As St. Paul has said in our lesson, "Be anxious for nothing"; that is, you can't control everything, so be anxious for nothing.

The real question to you is not whether you have a job or a plan, but whether you have an imagination. Can you think of anything beyond the moment? What do you imagine life will hold for you? What do you want life to hold for you? Anybody can see what is there. Anybody can go where a map will take him. Seeing what isn't there, however, traveling without a map, is what makes life interesting, and that is what the imagination is all about, and it is the use of the imagination that sets the spirit free. It is the use of the imagination that allows the Holy Spirit—which we celebrate today—to be set free in each and every one of us, giving us the appearance at times of being drunk and out of control and without a plan, and yet it is that very spirit-filled imagination that sets us free.

Perhaps some of you saw the *Globe*'s feature last week in which a number of us were asked what we would be doing in life if we weren't doing what we are doing. Many of my friends, perhaps even some of you, were shocked by my reply. Never in my wildest imagination, and I have a very wild and fertile imagination, had I imagined that I would have spent the past thirty-one years here among you. That was neither a plausible plan nor even a reasonable fantasy. No! I had imagined something better for myself than this. I imagined myself first as curator of American Decorative Arts and then eventually as director of the Museum of Fine Arts here in Boston. The man on the telephone asked, "Did you imagine yourself starting out as director?" I said, "Oh no, but I'd be director by now, I assure you." I wanted to be Jonathan Fairbanks and Perry Rathbone wrapped up in one.

To some of you this might seem an instance of a bad plan, a thwarted ambition, an unrealistic expectation, a dangerous fantasy, but I do not offer it as any of the above. I offer it as an example of the claims of the imagination upon the future, and the fact that the future had a claim upon me. They were not one and the same; it was an amazing coincidence that "my" plan was trumped by "the" plan, and it only goes to show that there is a plan, whether or not you know it. In that plan, as Paul would say, we are meant to imagine, indeed to construct, a world in which all that is true, all that is noble, all that is just and pure, all that is lovable and gracious, whatever is excellent and admirable, may flourish . . . at least in us. You must be able to imagine a world, and your place in it, where this may be so.

Remembering your past, imagining your future—these are good acts for your last rites.

How, however, will we get from here to there? A few verses later in our text, St. Paul gives the answer when he utters the now famous lines: "I can do all things through Christ who strengthens me" (Philippians 4:13). The road to the future, passing through imagination and remembrance, is the road by which Christ leads us from today to the day after tomorrow. Those are words of empowerment; those are words of enablement. They make all things possible through Christ, who strengthens us.

You may have noticed that we have some very visible and audible young visitors in these front pews this morning, and I have a word to you parents and godparents on behalf of these children: unless they are even smarter than you think they are, they will not remember much of what happens today, and even less of what I have to say. Their memory will depend upon you; you will remind them of what happened, but you must be able to imagine for them today what their future will be. There is a plan for each and every one of them, with each one's name on it, and your job, parents, is not to get in the way but to let God have his way with these children—God, who, with Christ, will enable them to do everything and anything through Christ, who strengthens them. Your children must have the benefit of your spiritual imagination now in order that the future into which we will shortly welcome them will be one in which they rejoice.

These words remind us that we are not on our own, and that as we are we can do nothing. St. Paul was not deficient in the ego department. Remember Churchill's famous remark on Clement Atlee? "He is a modest man because he has much about which to be modest." Paul is more Churchill than Atlee, but even he recognizes that on his own he is nothing, and with Christ, who strengthens him, all things are possible—or imaginable.

Here's a fact you may find hard to take, but I find it instructive. Think of this: Christ did not change Paul's world. Think of that. Christ did not change one thing in Paul's world. The Romans still ran the show; the Jews and the Greeks were still difficult; life was still nasty, brutish, and short; death was certain and often painful. None of those facts was changed or mitigated. What Christ changed was Paul's imagination, and by doing that he empowered him, enabled him, to live as a changed man in an unchanged world. That would not have been possible for Paul on his own, but only with the power of Christ in him, the power of the Holy Spirit, whose gift we celebrate today, allowing him to remember, to imagine, and finally, to persevere, carrying as realities the impossibility of these things about which he asks us to think: "All that is true, all that is noble, all that is just and pure, all that is lovable and gracious, whatever is excellent and admirable"—in a sordid, shabby world, dumbed down and tuned out, we are meant to—"fill all [our] thoughts with these things"—these noble thoughts.

I will give you my definition of what a Christian is. To be a Christian is to be a changed man or a changed woman in an unchanged world. Anyone can be a Christian in a Christian world, but, in case you haven't noticed it, this is not a Christian world. This is a pagan world, a fallen world, a secular world, a sordid world, a shabby world, and it happens to be the only world that you and I have. That's it. To be a Christian in it is to be changed in the middle of that which is unchanged. Despite all of the anticipated exhortations of our commencement ratios here and elsewhere, few of the candidates for degrees will do very much to change very much in this tired old world. Better people than you have tried and failed, and who are you to think that you won't? What you are meant to do is to remember and imagine God's changes in you, and in the little seemingly inconsequential universe in which you are center, sun, moon, and stars. The power to see that power at work in you is perhaps the greatest power on earth; it has already done wonders in you: it has brought you hither to this very point. Just remember that, and then imagine what is ahead.

Now, young friends, St. Paul ends this chapter with words that I wish to appropriate for you, as your pastor, your teacher, and your friend, on this last Sunday in which we will be together in this College church. It is Paul who is speaking here, but I ask you to imagine the words belonging to me as well. Here is what he says, at verse nine: "The lessons I taught you, the tradition I have passed on, all that you heard me say or saw me do, put into practice; and the God of peace will be with you."

Things You Should Know About: Endurance

Text: And will not God vindicate his elect, who cry to him day and night?

—Luke 18:7a

The seventh verse of the eighteenth chapter of Luke is a great question, to which you might want to know the answer: "And will not God vindicate his elect"—that's you—"who cry to him day and night?" This is the third in a series of sermons I have preached on things you ought to know about before you leave, before it's too late. Two weeks ago I preached about ambition, and you all have plenty of that. Last Sunday I preached about frustration, and you all know what that is. Today I preach about endurance, and if you have got this far you know what that is as well. Ambition, frustration, endurance . . .

Most of you, I suspect, think that you know what endurance is: you think that it is the same thing as survival. "I have endured—survived—four years of Harvard College; I have endured—survived—my roommates of the spring term. Same difference," you think. "It's all about semantics, and I'm so close to the end I don't have to worry about semantics anymore, and what difference does it make anyway?" Well, yes, there is a difference. *Survival* is such a passive word, and it means a lot to those who have survived, especially to those who neither expected nor deserved to survive. I don't knock the experience, but if I may be permitted just one more word game before we get on to the text, let me say this: survival is to endurance what existence is to living. One is necessary for the other to take place, but there is a quantity and a quality of difference between the two. Those who confuse the one with the other are deceived; those who settle for mere survival when they should endure, and who settle for mere existence over life, are deprived; and those who settle for less are both deceived and deprived. In this final service of this term, this year, and of your academic career, it is my job to see that you are neither deceived nor deprived and that you will understand ambition and frustration and endurance.

Now, what about this text, which in some accounts of the New Testament is called the parable of the importunate widow? Let us begin by confessing that it is an annoying text. Why? Because here is a parable with only two characters and both of them are disagreeable and unattractive. First there is the widow, who does nothing but complain, complain, complain, kvetch, kvetch, kvetch, and while we admire her persistence, we do not like her. She persists in presenting her claim to the judge, not willing to take no for an answer, and those who persist in hanging around in this way are not generally likable. Then there is the judge: arrogant, prideful, overbearing, "who neither feared God nor regarded man." Aloof, protected by the power of his office, used to seeing it all and hearing it all, he comes across as case hardened and indifferent. He is no prize, and Jesus himself calls him "unrighteous."

What are we to make of these two "nonheroes," as it were? The short answer is that the widow by her pleading wears the judge out: she prevails because she doesn't give up, she persists, she perseveres, she endures even when she has nothing.

Now, this widow may be a fairly unattractive profile in endurance, and we might prefer someone more heroic: David against Goliath, perhaps; or Daniel in the lions' den; Esther before Hamaan; Jesus on the cross; Paul and Peter at their martyrdom—all of them worthy candidates for degrees in 1996. She pales beside all of these great and heroic figures because she is so *ordinary;* and that is perhaps why we should pay attention to her: because contrary to popular rumor, and despite much of the hype that will be ventilated this week about all of you candidates for degrees, all of you had better prepare for the ordinary that is what we call life, into which you will be expelled on Thursday. You will grow up, look for a job, raise a family, wash the clothes, grow fat, hope for love, grow old, and then die. You doubt it?

Look around you; you cannot escape it: first look at us, then at the dead, then at the alumni—in that order.

There was a major Internet conference here this week, and President Rudenstine invited Bill Gates to come back anytime to collect a degree, to build a new university, or to do whatever he wants to do. Surely there may be the next Bill Gates among you, or other people who will do great and good things, but it is a wicked conceit that suggests that the only calling available to you is greatness. What a thundering horde of "greatness" is unleashed upon the world just about this time every year, and yet the world continues to stumble along in its routine mediocrity, now bordering on mendacity: maybe we should suspend all college graduations for a year and see what happens. Instead of seducing you with notions of greatness and of your place at the head of the line, perhaps we ought to summon you all to ordinariness, even to adequacy, for that, it seems, is where care and attention are needed. What we need are fewer leaders and more worthy followers to help the leaders. In other words, we need people who are not waiting for their crescent moment in which to excel and to do a heroic act: rather, what we need are people who regard their daily life—the routine, the ordinary, the mundane—as the place in which they mean to do ordinary things extraordinarily well. What does it take to do that? Imagination? Power? The right opportunity? Those golden connections and networks so assiduously cultivated and marinated here in the corridors of power?

Perhaps what it takes is a massive dose of undeserved luck or serendipity if you are secular; providence if you are pious. Remember the formula of Horatio Alger? "Good but poor boy does duty, finds that the lost dollar bill he returns belongs to the boss's daughter; boss so grateful that he promotes Horatio; Horatio earns enough to marry the boss's daughter, inherit the firm, and live happily ever after in a style which in his poverty he could not even imagine." Some of you are here on Horatio Alger fellowships, hoping that it is all true, but it, of course, is the stuff of fairy tales; and perhaps it will not surprise you to learn that Horatio Alger was a graduate of the Divinity School, a Unitarian minister on Cape Cod, and died penniless.

Luck, providence, preparation . . . Remember the old canard "Opportunity comes to him who is prepared"? Perhaps all of the above are necessary, but what is really necessary is something that will get you through when everything that is supposed to work doesn't; something that will get you through when all else fails. That is what we call "endurance," or, translated into the vernacular, "staying power." What do you do when you can do nothing and have nothing with which to do it, and nothing works? You endure. That is what most of us, most of the time, are called upon to do. For most of us our artful devices won't do, won't work, won't satisfy: they come close, but no cigar. Are we to conquer? Acquiesce? No, neither of those are useful options, and we are called upon to endure.

In my old public junior high school, where we saluted the flag, recited the Pledge of Allegiance, and read a passage from the Bible—I know, I am dating myself—we also sang the school song, by Maltie Babcock Davenport, which said it all:

> Be strong! We are not here to play, to dream, to drift;
> We have hard work to do, and loads to lift;
> Shun not the struggle! Face it! 'Tis God's gift:
> Be strong! Be strong!

Easy to say, you say, and it is, and all it would be is a slogan, one of those Rotary Club, Outward Bound, Prince Philip, William Bennett kinds of things, except that—and this is a big exception—for our importunate widow of the text, endurance is the key to her ultimate success: she endures, she persists. Why?

She persists because she is both driven and sustained by a belief, a conviction in something beyond the damning circumstances of her own reality. She believes in a justice that she cannot see. She persists, and thus endures her situation, because she knows that there is more to her and to her life than her present circumstances. She endures injustice because she knows that there is justice. She endures in her suffering because she knows that there is more to life than suffering. She is not defined by her circumstances, a weak and helpless widow who was done wrong, although that may be who she appears to be. That is not who she is, for she believes that what has been denied her is also available to her; it is the reality of that absent good that helps her to endure the reality of her present evil. So, do not be defined by your circumstances, but define them: that is what it means to endure. Do not be the victim of your imagination, but allow it to liberate you. The widow was not defined by her circumstances: she perseveres, she *insists* upon being vindicated.

During this season of the year I spend a lot of time at commencements. Last week I was at my own college, at Bates; this afternoon and tomorrow I go to Wellesley; Thursday it is yours; on Friday there is another. On all of these occasions I worry that we are selling you, you only too willing buyers, a bill of goods. Instead of preparing you for "success," we should be preparing you to cope with failure when things don't turn out right— whether it is your marriage, your job, your children, or your nation. We should all along have been inculcating in you not "modalities of thought"— that ridiculously pompous confection of the Core Curriculum that is utter nonsense—but capacities for endurance. Instead of breeding eagles we should have been breeding camels who will make it across the desert because they have what they require on the inside and will not quit. Camels have staying power; camels are what we want!

The unrighteous judge gave in to the widow's pleas not because he was just or gracious, but because she wore him down. He deserves little moral credit, and that is a pity, because more of you aspire to be judges than to be importunate widows. Jesus uses the judge to vindicate the widow's hopeless hope. What if the judge had been indifferent and didn't care? If the widow persisted in her plea to one who was not inclined to help her, what then can be said of those who are invited to place their confidence in a judge who is justice itself, whose very nature it is to care for those who need caring?

This, in case you haven't recognized it, is a commercial for God. Put your confidence in something that works. It is God who will keep you when all else has failed you; and it is to God to whom you will turn when you have exhausted all of the alternatives. It is God on whom you will call when you get that fateful diagnosis; it is God on whom you will call when the bottom drops out; and it is God on whom you will call when you pass through those seasons of doubt and despair, when life itself seems not worth the living and you cannot remember the last victory; and it is God on whom you will call with your very last breath.

So, do not give up or give out; do not lose heart. Your roommates may mess up, your colleagues may be impossible. It is the ambition of all of us in life to be that one person who can overcome life's frustrations; and to grow up is to realize that that is not possible. We need strength for the journey, for the long haul, so that we may endure and not be done in, so that we may be sustained by the things we cannot see and which are more real that those things that we can.

Why does Jesus tell us this parable? Remember how Luke 18 begins? "And he told them a parable to the effect that they ought always to pray and not lose heart." How does he end it? With these words: "And will not God vindicate his elect, who cry to him day and night?"

Endurance is what you must have when you cannot have anything else. Endurance, my dear, young, bewildered friends, is what you must have; and what must sustain you in those circumstances is the firm conviction, however awkwardly expressed, that there is a reality beyond what appears to be your reality. For believers, that reality is God, who not only does not abandon you when the going gets rough, but who keeps you going in the rough going; and it is sad that it is often only at the moment of our darkest doubt that we call upon God. There will be many, many dark moments: do not lost heart; do not be discouraged.

The secret of endurance is to place your fragile self in the conviction of God. No one else will tell you this in this next week before your commencement, so listen carefully: "And will not God vindicate his elect"—that's you—"who cry to him day and night?" You can bet your life he will: he already has!

AND DON'T MISS PETER J. GOMES'S
OTHER BESTSELLING BOOKS

More than 200,000 copies sold

Now available in paperback

Coming in 2004, Peter J. Gomes will conclude his "trilogy of the good" with *The Good News: From Bible to Gospel*

An inspiring collection of wisdom from the man *Time* magazine hailed as one of the seven best preachers in America.

Alternately bracing and soothing, these short pieces are a wonderful way to begin or end each day.

— David Gergen,
U.S. News & World Report